D0788937

Alejo Carpentier: The Pilgrim at Home

ALSO BY ROBERTO GONZÁLEZ ECHEVARRÍA

Calderón ante la crítica: historia
y antología (co-authored with Manuel Durán)
Relecturas: estudios de
literatura cubana

Alejo Carpentier:
The Pilgrim at Home

Roberto González Echevarría

Cornell University Press   ITHACA AND LONDON

HOUSTON PUBLIC LIBRARY

R0140642135
HUM

This book has been published with the aid of a grant from the Hull Memorial
Publication Fund of Cornell University.

Copyright © 1977 by Cornell University

All rights reserved. Except for brief quotations in a review, this book, or parts
thereof, must not be reproduced in any form without permission in writing
from the publisher. For information address Cornell University Press, 124
Roberts Place, Ithaca, New York 14850.

First published 1977 by Cornell University Press.
Published in the United Kingdom by Cornell University Press Ltd.,
2-4 Brook Street, London W1Y 1AA.

Material from "Manhunt" by Alejo Carpentier, translated by Harriet de
Onís, from *Noonday* 2, copyright © 1959 by The Noonday Press, Inc., is
reprinted with the permission of Farrar, Straus & Giroux, Inc.

International Standard Book Number 0-8014-1029-0
Library of Congress Catalog Card Number 76-28013
Printed in the United States of America by York Composition Co., Inc.
*Librarians: Library of Congress cataloging information appears on the last
page of the book.*

Para Isabel

Contents

Note on Translations

Unless otherwise specified, all translations are the author's. The titles of works that have not been published in translation have been kept in the original.

Preface

This book took shape at Cornell University, in the midst of an intense exchange about critical theory with colleagues in the Department of Romance Studies and on the editorial board of *Diacritics*. Part of the book owes much to my discussions with my colleague and friend Ciriaco Morón Arroyo, whose knowledge of Ortega y Gasset and of European thought in general gave me many a lead. Conversations with my longtime friend and colleague at both Yale and Cornell, Giuseppe Mazzotta, taught me a great deal and guided me in my forays into medieval literature. Philip E. Lewis and Josué V. Harari performed the fraternal task of reading the entire manuscript. I have learned from their suggestions and corrections more than this book could possibly show, and I cannot thank them enough for their kindness. I have also profited from my friendship with a select brotherhood of *carpenterianos*: Eduardo G. González, Modesto G. Sánchez, Sharon Magnarelli, Ramón García Castro, Alan Cheuse, and Klaus Müller-Bergh.

I was given invaluable assistance by Marta Garciarena de Betancourt, Technical Adviser at the Biblioteca Nacional de Venezuela, Caracas. Araceli García-Carranza and Roberto Fernández Retamar lent much-needed bibliographical aid from Cuba. Dolores Martin, at the Library of Congress, solved many problems and sent me whatever I requested through interlibrary loan. At Cornell's Olin Library many employees were unselfish with their time and expertise, particularly Olivia Narins. In Paris I owe a debt of gratitude to my friends Severo Sarduy and François Wahl, and of course to Alejo Carpentier, who received me at the Cuban Con-

sulate and with whom I maintain an active correspondence. He
has graciously permitted me to print one of his letters in this book.
My friend from the University of South Florida, Carlos J. Cano,
procured books and journals for me during the last stages of the
preparation of the manuscript. At the Latin American Collection
of the University of Florida Library in Gainesville, Ariete Burch
helped me find several obscure bibliographical items. Isabel
Gómez, my wife, not only encouraged me with this work, but also
helped me translate sections of Chapter 3, originally written in
Spanish, and leafed through many a dusty volume in Caracas.
Bonnie Díaz typed most of the manuscript.

Financial and moral support was provided throughout by the
Latin American Studies Program at Cornell and its former director,
Tom Davis. John V. Murra, of the same program, lent me key
works of Fernando Ortiz and offered valuable advice on anthropological matters. In 1974 I was named Summer Fellow at Cornell's
Society for the Humanities, where I was fortunate to have as a
colleague Herbert Dieckmann, whose wise counsel and vast knowledge of the Enlightenment were invaluable. I wish to thank the
Society's director, Henry Guerlac, for such a rewarding summer,
during which I was able to write a large part of this book.

I owe my training in Latin American literature to José J. Arrom
and Emir Rodríguez Monegal, in whose classes at Yale I began to
ask myself some of the questions that I attempt to answer in this
book. I would like to thank them here for their selflessness and
encouragement. Finally, I would like to express my gratitude to
my good friend and teacher Willis Barnstone, who, when I was in
Bloomington, Indiana, around 1964, asked me if I had read a
certain Cuban novelist, considered by many to be the best writing
in Spanish.

R.G.E.

Anna Maria Island, Florida

Acknowledgments

Permission to reprint previously published material has been authorized by the following:

Alfred A. Knopf, Inc., for excerpts from Alejo Carpentier, *Reasons of State*, translated by Frances Partridge, copyright © 1976 by Victor Gollancz Ltd.; for excerpts from Alejo Carpentier, *The Lost Steps*, translated by Harriet de Onís, copyright © 1956, 1967, by Alfred A. Knopf, Inc.; for excerpts from Alejo Carpentier, *War of Time*, translated by Frances Partridge, copyright © 1970 by Victor Gollancz Ltd.; for an excerpt from the poem "The Comedian as the Letter C," in *The Collected Poems of Wallace Stevens*, copyright 1923, 1931, 1935, 1936, 1937, 1942, 1943, 1944, 1945, 1946, 1947, 1948, 1949, 1950, 1951, 1952, 1954 by Wallace Stevens.

Diacritics, for permission to reprint portions of my article "The Parting of the Waters," *Diacritics*, 4, no. 4 (1974), 8–17, which appears as part of Chapter 4 of this book.

Editorial Sudamericana, S.A., for excerpts from Jorge Guillén, "Más Allá," published in *Cántico* (Buenos Aires, 1950).

Faber and Faber Ltd, for an excerpt from "The Comedian as the Letter C," in *The Collected Poems of Wallace Stevens*.

Instituto Internacional de Literatura Iberoamericana, for permission to use my article "Isla a su vuelo fugitiva: Carpentier y el realismo mágico," which appeared in *Revista Iberoamericana*, 40 (1970), and which, translated and rewritten, is part of Chapter 3 of this book.

McIntosh, McKee, & Dodds, Inc., for excerpts from Alejo Carpentier, *The Kingdom of This World*, translated by Harriet de Onís, copyright by Alejo Carpentier; *Explosion in a Cathedral*, translated by John Sturrock; *The Lost Steps, War of Time,* and *Reasons of State.*

Alejo Carpentier: The Pilgrim at Home

1. Preamble: A Post-Carpenterian Reflection

> We are through a language that is our own while being foreign.
>
> Marinello, *Americanismo y cubanismo literarios*

> This is one of the strange social features of Cuba, that since the sixteenth century all its classes, races and cultures, coming in by will or by force, have all been exogenous and have all been torn from their places of origin, suffering the shock of this first uprooting and a harsh transplanting.
>
> Ortiz, *Cuban Counterpoint*

> "Empieza." —¿Por dónde empezar? ¿Por el comienzo? ¿Y dónde está el comienzo? ¿Dónde buscar el agua de Heráclito? ¿En el arroyuelo presocrático o en el brazo de mar hegeliano? ¿En el enunciado precursor, casi apólogo, célula primera pero ya explícita, o en el desarrollo de una dialéctica arrolladora?
>
> Carpentier, *La consagración de la primavera*

Alejo Carpentier's position in twentieth-century Latin American literature is no longer disputed. Along with Neruda and Borges, he is acknowledged as a key figure in a literary tradition of which he is one of the founders. Carpentier's contributions as a musicologist and as a scholar of Latin American history and art, and the decisive role he played in the beginnings of the Afro-Cuban movement and *vanguardismo* are also recognized. With whatever loss such enshrinement entails, Carpentier is already a classic; a perennial contender for the Nobel Prize and a writer whose importance is accepted even by those who are not in agreement with his political or literary beliefs. The time for panegyrics, first impressions, and partial readings has passed, creating the need for a more sustained consideration of Carpentier's works and their overall significance, both within the field of Latin American literature and in the broader context of contemporary literature. Because of

Carpentier's seminal position, any serious reading of his works implies coming to terms with the basic questions posed by Latin American literature, as well as with larger theoretical questions about literary modernity and literary history. Such a reading has been the task of this book, which is also an experiment in how to approach the entire work of a writer in the aftermath of a critical epoch that has liquidated the expedient of the author as origin and questioned many of the conventional practices of academic criticism.[1] A brief sketch of the history of that experiment may serve as an introduction both to Carpentier and to this work.

The book began as a study of a transition in Carpentier's writing, one leading from the unfinished *Libro de la Gran Sabana* (1947–1948), a travel journal of Carpentier's voyage through the Venezuelan jungle, to *The Lost Steps* (1953), an autobiographical novel in which a nameless protagonist travels to the jungle in search of self-knowledge and the origins of man's history. Carpentier's displacement of the autobiographical "I" of the travel journal onto the fictionalized "I" of the novel seemed worthy of analysis. Having found the published fragments of *El libro de la Gran Sabana*, I assumed that it would be a revealing, though not necessarily difficult, undertaking to reconstruct the process by which *The Lost Steps* was written, and to gain access to and knowledge of its creation. This search soon became problematic, for there appeared disturbing discrepancies between Carpentier's voyage, as reported in the *Libro*, and his published recollections about the composition of the novel (where the earlier book is never mentioned). Reconstructing the process by which *The Lost Steps* was written became as difficult a task as that of Carpentier's own narrator-protagonist in his search for origins. The obstacles encountered in that inquiry, which has become here Chapter 4, led to the study of Carpentier's entire work and to a recognition of his significance as a writer; to a revelation, as it were, of the complexity of his literary enterprise, which belies the overly simple explanations offered by critics and often by Carpentier himself.

1. See Eugenio Donato, "Structuralism: The Aftermath," *Sub-Stance*, no. 7 (Fall 1973), pp. 9–26.

As I read Carpentier—not only his novels, stories, and essays, but also nearly all of his considerable journalistic writings—a pattern began to emerge, a general critical insight of which my observations in the chapter on *The Lost Steps* appeared to be the unstable core. This pattern must be described negatively, for ostensibly it is based on disagreements between Carpentier's statements and his fictions—the discordant, even polemical relationship between essayistic pronouncement and novelistic writing. But the pattern is much less overt and much more encompassing than my reading of *The Lost Steps* suggested; indeed it constitutes a radical and pervasive discord at the center of Carpentier's production—that is, at the point where his work appears on the verge of attaining overall unity and coherence. The cohesiveness of the structure seemed to depend more on the repetition of a negative or contradictory set of relationships than on a positive, conceptual framework, and seemed to present the possibility of reading the works of a novelist without relying on the notion of a stable or progressively evolving presence. This reading of Carpentier seemed possible because, as a highly erudite and even academic writer, he often attempts to bring about a closure in his works, a synthesis between life and fiction, at a conceptual level.

But having noticed the recurrence of certain ideas, I pursued at first a well-worn path in criticism, which was to attempt to piece together a sharply defined profile of Carpentier, and to note its gradual evolution. Although the inadequacy of this procedure was soon evident because of the many contradictions and reversals that immediately surfaced, a good deal of it remains in the book. In order to trace the more erratic trail I was obliged to follow, I had to keep in mind the straight but delusory path that a reading complicitous with Carpentier's statements about himself would invite. Thus, pursuing clues that Carpentier had provided, I have delved into his indebtedness to Ortega y Gasset and Spengler, his fascination with Surrealism, his Sartrean "conversion," and his adoption of a Hegelian or Vicchian concept of history in his most recent fiction. Although at times the reader may wonder if I am not offering a sketchy version of the Latin American history of ideas, this has not been my aim: it is rather the residue of a critical itinerary. Instead of the sharply defined picture that I sought, tracking Carpentier took me through a series of multiple exposures, and my own work in deciphering them has assumed the form of a critical narrative. This preamble, which was written last and is in a way a conclusion, and the chapter on *The Lost Steps*, which was written first, do not occupy those original positions for reasons that I hope shall become clear in what follows.

The fundamental question that *The Lost Steps* raised concerned the relationship between the artist and his product. If our reading of that novel reveals that relationship to be based, at best, on discontinuity, or, at worst, on a mere convention of literary criticism, what is it then that binds Carpentier's work into an oeuvre? That is to say, if our reading of *The Lost Steps* is not to remain a mere assertion of the difficulties of linking the empirical writer and his texts, we must define the nature of the relationship between *The Lost Steps* and the rest of Carpentier's fictional and expository texts. The challenge was how to write—and indeed if it were possible to write—about Carpentier's entire corpus without taking recourse to a biographical unity that implies a notion of the self as origin, a notion that his autobiographical novel undermined: how to write, in brief, about a self that appeared not as an ordering or grounding principle but as a set of negative relationships. Two solutions were at hand. One would have been to note the contradictions found in that corpus of writing and to offer a series of disconnected readings of Carpentier's novels—to allow, that is, the multiple exposures to coexist, to reduce Carpentier's writing to a sort of typology, and to sidestep the question of authorship. Another would have been to dwell on each of those exposures and consider them as literary masks. But both solutions would have reintroduced the notion of unity, by compelling us to assume tacitly a continuous presence behind the masks. Besides, if ignoring the author would have afforded a comfortable methodological *découpage*, circumventing the authorial question would have also meant skirting the very problematics that Carpentier's works most insistently explore, which center precisely on that question. If *The Lost Steps* puts in doubt the relationship between author and work, it does so only in the process of suggesting that such a relationship is possible, and all of Carpentier's novels do the same—often by such blatant methods as "author's notes" and prologues, sometimes by less obvious strategies, such as having Esteban in *Explosion in a Cathedral* born on Carpentier's birthday. A more promising solution, drawn from our reading of *The Lost Steps*, was to dwell on the question itself and trace its history, for it seemed that the relationship between Carpentier's texts is found at the point where the issue about the existence of the relationship arises. But, since in Carpentier's texts, fictional and expository, this question always appears couched in terms of a broader inquiry about Latin American culture, history, and identity, the critical narrative had to delve into the aforementioned Latin American history of ideas, as well as into the vast scholarly background from which Carpentier draws the material for his novels.

It was somewhat disappointing at first to discover how ideas were abandoned by Carpentier without being explored to the fullest; how, in other words, philosophical positions were loosely and episodically taken in his journalistic work, often to explain or justify his fictions. How, too, hardly compatible systems of thought were at times mixed as in a broad mosaic of trivial allusions. Topics that criticism of Carpentier and of Latin American literature in general had already trivialized emerged raising the same questions, which were always left unsatisfactorily answered. Most of these questions were variations of the question about Latin American identity. Their stock answers floated about me: the universal in the local, the mestizo continent, crossroads of the great cultures and races of the world, the Faustian presence of Indians and Africans. All these answers spring from a denial of Western tradition and a desire to found an autonomous Latin American tradition—modernity's familiar cry for new beginnings.

But as Carpentier and modern Latin American writers denounced Western tradition, their search for a Latin American consciousness and mode of expression became, paradoxically, more European. And the idea that this or that system of thought, this or that artistic trend had to be adapted to the Latin American situation more often than not implied oversimplifying that system by inserting it into a familiar code of unanalyzed topics; or, significantly, making Latin America surreptitiously the natural or privileged object of that system or trend—whether it was Existentialism, because Latin America's "new" history makes it rootless by essence, or Surrealism, because Latin America is different and arcane.[2] Clearly, the charting of such a history offered little promise of yielding a reading of Carpentier that would not be the repetition of an uncritical gesture, an "interpretation" that would merely rewrite the sources of Carpentier and bypass the texts, by reducing them to a series of pseudo-philosophical a prioris. The tradition based on exploring the question of Latin American identity had to be subverted. Better yet, it had to be placed in a perspective that would allow it to subvert itself, since the very lack of originality of the question, as well as of the stock answers that it had elicited, supplied its own subversion. If Carpentier places the authorial question in the context provided by the issue of Latin American identity, then it is the rhetorical function of the question that is at stake, not the referential validity of the answers.

The search for Latin American consciousness or identity is a literary convention to which social and historical dimensions are simplistically attached—a gesture that is, of course, part of its rhetorical bases and the result of tradition—as if literature thus conceived could replace or in some way take precedence over the political struggles of often illiterate masses. Contemporary Latin American literature is, with few exceptions, a bourgeois, post-Romantic literature, not the direct descendant of an autochthonous tradition going all the way back to a primal birth in the colonial period. As a post-Romantic literature, it draws its thematics from the late eighteenth and early nineteenth centuries, the period when, coincidentally (but not accidentally), most of

2. One must agree with Edmundo Desnoes when he asks that this vast mass of people caught in such complex and tragic sociopolitical circumstances not be termed Surrealistic or Baroque; *Para verte mejor América Latina* (Mexico City, 1972), p. 31.

Latin America became politically independent from Europe. The question of Latin American identity has to be traced back to that second birth, propitiated by figures such as Andrés Bello.[3] Being bourgeois and post-Romantic, Latin American literature centers around a lack, an absence of organic connectedness, and its mainspring is a desire for communion, or, in a Hegelian sense, for totality through reintegration with a lost unity. That lack leads Latin American writers to invoke "culture" as the ontological and historical entity from which their works have sprung and to which they must return. But the lack is never overcome, for culture becomes in their works an entelechy (in its etymological sense of a finished teleology), a static, reified end product lacking a temporal dimension. Like the mothers in Carpentier's "Journey Back to the Source" and "Manhunt," culture appears as a dead, though always desired, source.

To read Carpentier without taking into account the contradictions of this dialectic would be naively to accept a fictional philosophy that allows for the coexistence of intolerable paradoxes. The problem is how to perceive in that philosophy not the order that it might claim but the underlying order of unresolved contradictions and the transformations that these generate within Carpentier's developing oeuvre. Since the relationship between Carpentier's works had to be placed within the history of these ideas about Latin American identity, their unity could only be gleaned by assuming a post-Carpenterian position—a position from which the rhetorical nature of the philosophical question, and the structure within which it is generated, could be seen in its double thrust toward and away from referentiality.

In a post-Romantic literature that must base itself in fiction (even while claiming the opposite), philosophical systems are not present in a radically coherent form but merely stand for what could be considered belief.[4] For this reason, philosophical systems

3. See chap. 2 of Emir Rodríguez Monegal's *El otro Andrés Bello* (Caracas, 1969).
4. M. H. Abrams writes in reference to the evolution of Romantic literature: "To put the matter with the sharpness of drastic simplification: faith

are dealt with here as metaphors or conceits—and I use "conceit" both in its present meaning and in its old poetic sense of binding image and concept. Carpentier's penchant for allegory stems from his persistent appeal to ideas, even in such fundamentally literary fashion. Though often reminiscent of Calderón (and the Spanish Baroque in general), Carpentier's allegory is the reverse. In Calderón conceptual meaning is attached to a series of interchangeable images, but the allegorical mechanism rests on the preliminary assumption of a meaning that is attached to signs by the unshakable certainty of transcendence. If allegory appears playlike in Calderón at times, it is because the end of the permutations is always known in advance and presented on stage at the end of his *autos sacramentales* as the irreducible symbol of the Eucharist. In Carpentier, as in most modern literature, allegory rests on the possibility of carrying the permutations further, to an idea of transcendence that is itself fictional and changeable.[5] That movement away from each metaphor or conceit (the system of ideas to which allegory refers, and more specifically that movable center on which it rests) occurs at the very moment when the implications of a given philosophy threaten the fictionality of the text, by upsetting the balance of the dialectical play.

The plot in Carpentier's stories always moves from exile and fragmentation toward return and restoration, and the overall movement of each text is away from literature into immediacy, whether by a claim to be integrated within a larger context, Latin American reality or history, or by an invocation of the empirical author. But because of the dialectics just sketched, the voyage always winds up in literature and remains as the reason for yet another journey. This process is akin to the one described by Paul de Man when he says that "literature is an entity that exists not as a single moment of self-denial, but as a plurality of moments that can, if one

in an apocalypse by revelation had been replaced by faith in an apocalypse by revolution, and this now gave way to faith in an apocalypse by imagination or cognition" (*Natural Supernaturalism: Tradition and Revolution in Romantic Literature* [New York, 1971], p. 334).

5. I have drawn here from Georg Lukács's discussion of allegory in "The Ideology of Modernism," *Realism in Our Time: Literature and the Class Struggle* (New York, 1964), pp. 40–46.

wishes, be represented . . . as a movement and is, in essence, the fictional narration of this movement. After the initial moment of flight away from its own specificity, a moment of return follows that leads literature back to what it is—but we must bear in mind that terms such as 'after' and 'follows' do not designate actual moments in a diachrony, but are used purely as metaphors of duration."[6] The unfolding of each of Carpentier's stories, as well as the unfolding of his writing as I describe it here, is evidence of such a process. Carpentier's expository texts are often designed to cover such reversals and thus become part of a broader intertextual play that I have attempted to plot.

In what on another level only amounts to a self-serving boutade, Guillermo Cabrera Infante pinpoints the crucial problem in Carpentier when he says: "Carpentier deals with contexts. I deal with texts. The context in Carpentier is well known in advance, not only territory explored, but even mapped out and illustrated."[7] But the question is whether a text can ever cease to be a context, that is, whether it can become independent of literature. Carpentier's texts demonstrate both the desire that Cabrera Infante so naively expresses, and the impossibility of its fulfillment. Obviously what led Cabrera Infante to make such a statement (aside from political rancor) is the enormous expanse of mapped-out territory within which Carpentier deploys his fiction, as if one of the strategies to counteract the imperialism of context would be to possess it all before setting out to discover uncharted routes. This dilemma, as shall be seen in Chapter 4, climaxes in "Manhunt" (1956).

Given Carpentier's penchant for allegory, for the codification of his symbolic universe through the repetition of scenes and plot structures, it was tempting to offer here what Roland Barthes calls "un reseau organisé d'obsessions";[8] in other words, to take that moment of which de Man speaks and expand it horizontally in a

6. *Blindness and Insight: Essays in the Rhetoric of Contemporary Criticism* (New York, 1971), p. 159.
7. Emir Rodríguez Monegal, "Las fuentes de la narración" (Interview with Guillermo Cabrera Infante), *Mundo Nuevo*, no. 25 (July 1968), p. 45.
8. *Michelet par lui-même* (Paris, 1965), first, unnumbered, page.

synchronic construct. I have chosen, instead, to use the metaphors of "after" and "follows" to chart the variations of that moment in time. I have attempted, therefore, to reconstruct as closely as possible the chronology of Carpentier's works and to set apart clusters of works that revolve around a particular conceit or philosophical position in the sense explained above. The metaphorical nature of such an unfolding as duration must be evident from the fact that Carpentier has said that he always works on two or three books at the same time.[9] Even so, each previously written set of texts constitutes an erasure over which Carpentier attempts to inscribe his "new" writing. His disavowal of early works such as ¡Ecue-Yamba-O! and his defense of the theories of the prologue to The Kingdom of This World years after its publication, while holding views blatantly opposed to them, is a clear indication that Carpentier is always a problematic but persistent context for Carpentier. Carpentier's views on his own works, then, must be incorporated into our reading of his works as productive misprisions that allow us to articulate his oeuvre, which he occasionally sees as a linear history.[10] The order in which Carpentier's works were written constitutes a way into the mechanics of the texts, a route, as it were, full of meanderings and retracings. The recharting of such a route is of necessity a charting of error, both in its connotation of mistake and in the etymological sense of wandering. But because of the nature of the route and the metaphorical quality of its temporal unfolding, such an itinerary cannot arrive at a synthesis, which would amount to a total and final fiction about Carpentier. At the same time, the diachronic unfolding of such a structure renders the very form of fiction unavoidable, and in a sense turns this book into a sort of metanovel. Given the perhaps inescapable danger of contamination by its object that criticism entails, I have chosen, at the risk no doubt of other errors, the contamination of fiction rather than that of concept. For this reason, I have bor-

9. Jacobo Zabludovsky, "Habla Alejo Carpentier" (Interview), *Siempre!* July 25, 1973, p. 44.
10. Miguel F. Roa, "Alejo Carpentier: el recurso a Descartes" (Interview), *Cuba Internacional*, no. 59 (July 1974), p. 51.

rowed Lope de Vega's title (*El peregrino en su patria*), since I follow the plot structure of the Byzantine romance more than that of the conventional novel. The protagonists, those conceits that represent Carpentier at various times, who are distinct but, as the characters in the Byzantine romance, related, meet and are separated in a series of anagnorises taking place over a vast and fictional geographical expanse—only to find, often, that their ultimate union is forbidden because of their consanguinity.

2

History is the main topic in Carpentier's fiction, and the history he deals with—the history of the Caribbean—is one of beginnings or foundations. It was in the Caribbean that Europeans first set foot in the New World, and it was there that the first European settlements were established. It was therefore in the Caribbean that the particular problematics of Latin American culture and history began to take shape. Colonialism, slavery, racial mixture and strife, and consequently revolution and independence movements all occurred first in the Caribbean. The Caribbean was the testing ground for the large-scale conquest of the mainland—the beachhead, as it were, from which the invasions of North, Central, and South America were planned and launched. The Caribbean was also the site of the first Indian and maroon revolts and where Toussaint Louverture carried out the first successful war of independence (other than that of the United States). The first American natives to set foot in Europe, sent to Spain by Columbus, were Taino Indians from the Caribbean, and it was in the Antilles that the great modern European powers first bickered and bartered over colonial territories wrested from the natives. Because the Caribbean was the proscenium of Latin American history, the area where the most overwhelming historical phenomenon in modern times—the conquest of America by Europe—began, Caribbean meditations on history have always had an apocalyptic quality, from Columbus to Carpentier.

It was therefore in the Caribbean that Latin American literature "began," for it is in Columbus's diary that we first encounter what will become the most persistent theme of Latin American literature: how to write in a European language about realities never seen in Europe before. And it was in Hispaniola that Fray Ramón Pané undertook the momentous task of writing a *Relación* about the myths of the known inhabitants of the New World. Pané's hesitations and apologies for the lack of order in his first-person account foreshadow those of the narrator-protagonist of Carpentier's *The Lost Steps*, and the polyglot mirages of his text remind one of Borges. Deep in what was then the thickly forested Hispaniola, living among people whose language he barely understood, Pané unknowingly faced dilemmas around which Latin American literature would weave its thematic core: writing in a language supposedly alien to the realities portrayed, unsure of his own situation as transcriber, torn between languages that betray him (he was a Catalan writing in Spanish and attempting to transcribe the names of Arawak gods).

What Fernando Ortiz has written about Cuba, which is of particular significance to Carpentier, is applicable to the entire Caribbean: "This is one of the strange social features of Cuba, that since the sixteenth century all its classes, races and cultures, coming in by will or by force, have all been exogenous and have all been torn from their places of origin, suffering the shock of this first uprooting and a harsh transplanting."[11] The keenness of this ultimately Latin American condition, of which Carpentier is a poignant embodiment, surely affects Caribbean literature, not by constituting a unique and decisive ontological factor, but by furnishing it with a compulsive thematics that magnifies and brings constantly to the fore a general condition of writing.

But if this origin-obsessed history is the theme of Carpentier's fiction, its deployment is more the product of Latin America's second beginning—that is to say, the eighteenth and nineteenth centuries—than of its remote origins in colonial times. The eighteenth and nineteenth centuries are also the historical setting of three of Carpentier's major works, *The Kingdom of This World*,

11. *Cuban Counterpoint: Tobacco and Sugar*, trans. Harriet de Onís (New York, 1970), p. 100.

Explosion in a Cathedral, and *Concierto barroco*, a fact that is clearly not accidental. The persistence of the structure and thematics of fall and redemption, of exile and return, of individual consciousness and collective conscience, stems from a constant return to the source of modern Latin American self-awareness within the philosophical coordinates of the transition from the Enlightenment to Romanticism. The origins of this concern in Carpentier are to be found in the dissemination of a strand of German philosophy throughout Latin America in the twenties, specifically the works of Hegel and Spengler. This philosophy, particularly Spengler's together with the avant-garde in the arts, rekindled reflections and polemics which certainly began in colonial times but which had taken on more urgency since independence. It is in this latter context, rather than in one extending back to the colonial period, that the various shifts in Carpentier's writing must be read. Since the eighteenth century the colonial period has been to Latin America more of a rediscovered past than a continued presence. It was, after all, in the Romantic period that precolonial texts, such as the *Popol Vuh*, as well as colonial ones, were rediscovered and edited, in a deliberate effort to make them a part of the cultural heritage that the fledgling self-awareness brought about by political independence laboriously nursed.[12] Carpentier's writing constantly reverts to that second birth, which is already a "reversion"; as such, his writing is always about the possibility of a Latin American literature.

Although always a search for immediacy or reality in a post-Romantic tradition, Latin American literature offers, from the very beginning—as we saw in reference to Columbus and Pané—the peculiar conceit of a double or meta-alienation. As Edmundo O'Gorman has toilsomely demonstrated, the discovery of Amer-

12. See the introduction by Andrián Recinos to the *Popol Vuh: las antiguas historias del Quiché*, 4th ed. (Mexico City, 1974), p. 12. Also see the extraordinary introduction (written by an 1812 committee charged with compiling all the knowledge available on the history and geography of Cuba) to José Martín Félix de Arrate, *Llave del Nuevo Mundo; Antemural de las Indias Occidentales; La Habana descripta; Noticias de su fundación, aumentos y estados*, 4th ed. (Havana, 1964), pp. xiii–xxii.

ica was a rediscovery, the revelation of a world already conjured up by the European imagination.[13] In this sense, the discovery of America was the actualization of a fiction, the founding of a world that had its origins in books before it became a concrete and tangible *terra firma*: thus the mythical and literary names in American topography, from the Antilles to California. The eighteenth and nineteenth centuries witnessed a second rediscovery. The New Continent became again the utopian world that the European could actually visit. This is the world of Romantic *Naturphilosophie*, of that indefatigable traveler and second Columbus, Alexander von Humboldt (who in his *Kosmos* made the most tenacious attempt at achieving a Hegelian totality), of countless other traveler-writers like Chateaubriand, and of fictional travelers like Candide. Within the topos of the rediscovery of America, America is a literary and fictional place, a new beginning that is already a repetition. In Latin American writing, the New World then occupies a doubly fictive space: the one furnished by the European tradition and the one re-elaborated by Latin American writers. Writing within a Western tradition and in a European language, Latin American writers feel they write from within a fiction of which they are a part, and in order to escape from this literary encirclement they must constantly strive to invent themselves and Latin America anew. The results of this peculiar conception of Romantic alienation have been both serious and slightly melodramatic, as Wallace Stevens noted in "The Comedian as the Letter C," when Crispin reaches Central America:

> In Yucatan, the Maya sonneteers
> Of the Caribbean amphitheatre,
> In spite of hawk and falcon, green toucan
> And jay, still to the night-bird made their plea,
> As if raspberry tanagers in palms,
> High up in orange air, were barbarous.[14]

13. *The Invention of America: An Inquiry into the Historical Nature of the New World and the Meaning of Its History* (Bloomington, 1961).

14. *The Collected Poems of Wallace Stevens* (New York: Alfred A. Knopf, 1954), p. 30.

Raspberry tanagers are not barbarous (i.e., foreign) in Yucatan, but for the Maya sonneteers of Stevens's poem, it is as if they were, bent as they are on repeating and asserting literary tradition by making their plea to the night-bird. As we noted, one of the strategies out of the imperialism of context is total possession of the code, a sort of atrophy by exaggeration. Larreta invents for himself an archaic, sixteenth-century Spanish and a Spain of Moorish princesses from bustling, modern Buenos Aires; Darío and the Modernistas become intoxicated with France, and their poems are often peopled by eighteenth-century courtesans. Borges creates a whole literature by manipulating sundry sources, a derisive erudition in which writing emerges after the whole of culture has been reduced to an encyclopedia. The opposite and correlative tendency is apparent in Neruda, who begins his General Song at a "minus zero" of history in which, according to the Blakean topos, he will name for the first time, like Adam in the Garden, the supposedly nameless reality of the New Continent.

Carpentier's work is inscribed precisely at the point where the desire for immediacy stumbles upon the fiction of Latin America; the "Caribbean amphitheatre" appears in his works as the stage where plays first performed in the Mediterranean area are replayed. The itinerary of Carpentier's works includes the invention of an archaic language, as in Larreta, an encyclopedic erudition, as in Borges, and the constant desire to inaugurate Latin American writing, as in Neruda. To come to know Carpentier's trajectory is to come to know the problematics of modern Latin American literature.

A sentence from an essay of Juan Marinello's (which is no doubt a version of Rimbaud's "I is another") kept coming back as this study progressed: "We are through a language that is our own while being foreign."[15] Marinello subverts the notion that Latin American identity can be found on an ideal level, where the stock answers will supply satisfactory solutions, and makes the language in which they are cast part of the problem itself. He also

15. Americanismo y cubanismo literarios (Havana, n.d. [signed 1932]), p. 6.

dispels the notion that the problem is exclusively Latin American, for language, to any writer, is always foreign, a given code within which he must labor. What is distinctly Latin American, then, is the double sense of otherness just observed, a double sense of otherness that mirrors and magnifies the initial otherness of language. It is in this context that Carpentier's work gains greater appeal and exemplariness, for he is a Latin American writer for whom Spanish is as close to being a foreign language as any since Garcilaso de la Vega el Inca. That double or meta-alienation of the Latin American writer vis-à-vis language and literary tradition is what characterizes Latin American literature.

Latin American literature is revolutionary and modern because it corrodes the core of Western tradition from its fringes, constantly reflecting back a distorted and denuded image of it—like Toussaint Louverture in the ill-fitting garb of a Napoleonic general routing the colonial troops. Rather than a radical, ontogenetic distinction, a perverse and exaggerated similarity often constitutes the difference in Latin American literature. If the main theme of Latin American literature is its newness and independence, its significance can only be gauged by its exaggerated topicality within the context of Modernity: born of Modernity, Latin American literature appears to be condemned to the delusions of newness in order to expose them.

3

Hampered by a speech impediment that gives his Spanish a strong French accent (as if his father's tongue and his mother tongue were at odds with each other), and having spent more than twenty years of his adult life in France, Carpentier could not easily satisfy his desire to assert the uniqueness and independence of a new Latin American beginning on a personal level.[16] But because

16. Luis Harss reported that Carpentier "would rather speak French than his peculiarly throaty, strongly French-accented brand of Cuban Spanish" (Luis Harss and Barbara Dohmann, *Into the Mainstream: Conversations with Latin American Writers* [New York, 1967], p. 45). The Venezuelan journalist Alexis Márquez Rodríguez, however, reports that Carpentier's guttural Spanish is due to a speech difficulty that prevents him from rolling the r's ("Dos

of the all-encompassing nature of his effort, the question of his own identity, even if subsumed within the larger framework sketched above, comes into play persistently in his writings. Just as the question of identity in the philosophical context noted could not be bypassed, neither can it be in the more specific one of Carpentier's own life. Again, the problem seems to be how to deploy the issue within the general strategy of our critical itinerary. A further problem is that while materials are available in the philosophical or textual context of the itinerary, there is really very little information about Carpentier's life, and then, most of it has been supplied by Carpentier himself. Yet, while the possibility of writing a rigorous, conventional biography of Carpentier is not near at hand, what is available suffices for our purposes here, since it is at the juncture where Carpentier's versions of his life and the various shifts mentioned are articulated that our itinerary ought to begin. These points of articulation, demarcating the various textual shifts, are also made up of contradictions, faults, as it were, where Carpentier has attempted to construct a synthesis of life and works. I have thus used the biographical material available, plus that which I have been able to gather, not to furnish a history that predetermines the texts, but to frame the itinerary of those textual shifts, those blind spots where a central conceit or meta-phor gives way to another. In his essay on Hölderlin, Heidegger writes that "in the very appearance of its outer fringe the essence of poetry seems to waver and yet stands firm. In fact it is itself essentially establishment—that is to say: an act of firm founda-tion."[17] Here, however, what is offered is the residue of the re-peated and strung-out returns to establish that foundation and in-stitute a history—both a personal history and a broader history within which it will be harmoniously set. Carpentier's choice of the narrative, and more specifically of the historical narrative, ap-pears to result from this desire, as do his historical works, such as

dilucidaciones en torno a Alejo Carpentier," *Casa de las Américas*, no. 87 (1974), p. 39.

17. "Hölderlin and the Essence of Poetry," in *Existence and Being*, ed. Werner Brock (Chicago, 1949), p. 286.

La música en Cuba. In a sense, as in *The Lost Steps,* Carpentier's entire literary enterprise issues from the desire to seize upon that moment of origination from which history and the history of the self begin simultaneously—a moment from which both language and history will start, thus the foundation of a symbolic code devoid of temporal or spatial gaps. The chapters that follow chart each of these reversions, encompassing various texts and various chronological periods.

The first two moments (in Chapters 2 and 3) are part of a single effort to constitute a sort of theology of narrative that will save the novel from the crisis of the twenties. The philosophical pretext is mainly Spenglerian. In the first of the two, extending from the mid-twenties to 1939 (Chapter 2), a unique and different form of narrativity is grounded in the symbolic plenum of Afro-Cuban religion. The second moment (Chapter 3), extending from about 1939 to 1949 and encompassing what has come to be known as "magical realism," centers on the conceit of the natural fusion of Latin American history and a process of writing that excludes the conscious author. It is a characteristically Nerudian movement to lay the foundation for a "residence on earth" (the major text of the period is *The Kingdom of This World*), still drawing heavily upon Afro-Antillian folklore. Because the works produced in this period are among Carpentier's most influential, we have had to correct major errors in their assessment by historical critics, who have been inclined to read all of Carpentier from the basis provided by "magical realism."

The third moment (Chapter 4), from about 1949 to the mid-fifties, questions the assumptions of the preceding one by inquiring about the situation of the modern Latin American writer vis-à-vis his sources, that is to say, the natural, autochthonous tradition celebrated in *The Kingdom of This World*. It is a Sartrean moment that includes *The Lost Steps* and "Manhunt" and in which the context of contemporary political history and the alienation of the writer corrode the assumed link between him and his product.

The fourth moment (Chapter 5), from the mid-fifties to the present, reassesses the previous three by undermining the notions of both author and history and positing the revolutionary nature of writing, its perpetual shifting around an absent source. This last moment, strongly inspired by the eighteenth century, includes *Explosion in a Cathedral* (1962) and Carpentier's latest novels, *Reasons of State* and *Concierto barroco* (both 1974), and appears to be a reversion to the avant-garde, particularly because of its recourse to the Kabbala and to a ludic conception of writing.

Because of the reflexive nature of these reversions we shall not begin with the first of those moments, but with the first remembered.

2. Lord, Praised Be Thou

> The first comprehension of depth is an act of birth—the spiritual complement of the bodily. In it the Culture is born out of its mother-landscape, and the act is repeated by every one of its individual souls throughout its life-course.
>
> Spengler, *The Decline of the West*

> A book found valuable at one time will pursue an author for the rest of his life, no matter what position he takes.
>
> Carpentier, in *El Nacional*, December 16, 1954

> Tylor already said it when dealing with this phenomenon: "this influence is so universal that the European established in Africa frequently experiences its assaults, and comes to accept the ideas of the Negro; or, to use an expression common in the Coast, he is apt to become a Negro."
>
> Ortiz, *Los negros brujos*

In 1939, Carpentier returned to Havana after having spent eleven years in Paris. Then thirty-five, he was the author of an obscure novel, a few poems, some stories, and several scenarios for Afro-Cuban ballets. At the time, Carpentier was known mainly as a journalist and critic.[1] During the thirties he had sent numerous articles to *Carteles*, a Havana weekly he had edited in the twenties, and to *Social*, a journal devoted partly to the arts. Through these articles the Cuban public had been kept abreast of the rapidly changing European artistic trends and fashions. In Europe, Carpentier had traveled to Berlin in 1932, to Madrid in 1933, 1934, and again in 1937 with the Cuban delegation to the Congress of Anti-Fascist Intellectuals, and to Havana in 1936 for a brief visit.[2] He came to know in Paris and Madrid some of the leading artistic

1. In 1939, in a note devoted to the Cuban composer Amadeo Roldán on the occasion of his death, Carpentier is mentioned as a music critic; *Estudios Afrocubanos* (Havana), 3, nos. 1, 2, 3 and 4 (1939), 110.
2. Testimony concerning his trip to the Congress appears in Carpentier's

figures—mainly the Surrealists—and was marginally involved in the disputes that erupted among them. Carpentier was also active in and indeed earned a living from the youthful art of radio broadcasting, directing the production of works such as Claudel's *Le Livre de Christophe Colomb*, Whitman's *Salute to the World*, and many others.[3]

In Cuba, Carpentier had been a member of the radical group that founded the *Revista de Avance*, had participated in some of the early skirmishes against the Gerardo Machado dictatorship, and had been one of the first advocates of the European avant-garde.[4] He spent forty days in jail for some of these activities in 1927, although he was then naive in political matters, unable to distinguish, according to his own testimony, between "a Socialist and a radical party."[5] His self-imposed exile to Paris in 1928 spared him the more decisive political confrontations of the thirties, when

"España bajo las bombas," *Carteles*, September 12, 1937, pp. 32, 52. The Cuban delegation was made up of Carpentier, Nicolás Guillén, and Juan Marinello. With them on the trip from Paris were Octavio Paz, José Mancisidor, Carlos Pellicer, André Malraux, Claude Oveline, Delia del Carril, and Pablo Neruda. See Neruda's account in *Confieso que he vivido: memorias* (Barcelona, 1974), pp. 180–85.

3. In "El radio y sus nuevas posibilidades," *Carteles*, December 17, 1933, pp. 14, 96, 98, Carpentier speaks of having directed more than forty-two broadcasts, with the support of Paul Deharme, a young French businessman who promoted him.

4. See *Orbita de la Revista de Avance*, ed. Martín Casanovas (Havana, 1965) and Carlos Ripoll, "La *Revista de Avance* (1927–1930), vocero de vanguardismo y pórtico de revolución," *Revista Iberoamericana*, 30 (1964), 261–82. Carpentier was a member of the board very briefly: "The first editorial group was completed by Alejo Carpentier, who because of professional incompatibilities left the board right after the appearance of the first issue and was replaced by José Z. Tallet" (*Orbita*, pp. 8–9).

5. "La Habana vista por un turista cubano," *Carteles*, October 22, 1939, p. 19. Carpentier signed the "Manifiesto Minorista" in May 1927. There is a specific study of this period of Cuban history: Luis E. Aguilar, *Cuba 1933: Prologue to Revolution* (Ithaca, 1972). See also Hugh Thomas, *Cuba: The Pursuit of Freedom* (New York, 1971), pp. 497–586. For an account of one of the participants and the text of the "Manifiesto," see Juan Marinello, "Homenaje a Rubén Martínez Villena," in his *Contemporáneos: noticia y memoria* (Havana, 1964), pp. 43–74. In "El escándalo de Maldoror," *Carteles*, April 20, 1930, Carpentier says that he spent more than a month in jail (p. 73).

many Cuban intellectuals—Juan Marinello, Nicolás Guillén, Raúl
Roa—had to define their political position. His involvement in the
beginnings of the Afro-Cuban movement was known since two
of his poems had appeared in Emilio Ballagas's widely circulated
Antología de poesía negra hispanoamericana.[6] His first-hand knowledge of European letters and native French were probably held in
awe. His musical expertise was acknowledged and respected. But
it was above all his work as a refined Parisian correspondent that
distinguished him in 1939. Upon his return to Cuba, Carpentier
was a minor literary figure, a well-known journalist, and a secondary cultural promoter. If in the twenties he had been successful
in organizing concerts of the new music, his attempt at editing a
literary journal (*Imán*, 1930) had floundered after one issue, and
¡Ecue-Yamba-O! (1933), his novel, remained largely unread.[7]
Carpentier's original intention had been to follow his father and
become an architect. But he was forced into journalism in his late
teens when his father abandoned his family (never to be heard
from again), leaving him to earn a living for himself and his
mother. Although his European refinement (he had studied at a
lycée in Paris from 1912 to around 1921) and musical talent had
made him a sort of *enfant prodige* of the Cuban *vanguardia*,
journalism turned him into a marginal figure—a commentator.[8] In

6. (Madrid, 1935), pp. 65–67 and 77–78.

7. Carpentier was responsible for the scenarios of two ballets composed by
Amadeo Roldán, staged in 1928–29, "La Rebambaramba" and "El milagro
de Anaquillé." For details see *Estudios Afrocubanos*, 3 (1939), 112–18.

8. Carpentier worked steadily as a journalist until 1959. Throughout the
fifties he wrote a column on music and literature, "Letra y Solfa," for *El
Nacional* in Caracas. Carpentier discusses his activities in music during the
twenties in the remarkably autobiographical essay, "La música cubana en estos
últimos 20 años," *Conservatorio* (Havana), 1, no. 2 (1944), six unnumbered
pages. In this essay Carpentier makes one of the very few direct allusions to
his father to be found in his writing. He notes, while mentioning the dearth
of musical activity in Cuba during the early years of the republic, that his
father attempted vainly to find a performance of Beethoven's *Fifth Symphony*
from 1902 to 1922. It must have been 1922 when Carpentier's father left
home. During the twenties Carpentier contributed to *Musicalia* a journal
directed by María Muñoz de Quevedo. When the second installment of an
article of his appeared in the second issue of this journal, the editors published

spite of ¡Ecue-Yamba-O!, or perhaps because of its failure, it is doubtful that Carpentier considered himself a writer in 1939. The eleven-year gap between the novel and "Journey Back to the Source" (1944) suggests that he did not come to assume that role fully until after his return. Carpentier came back to Havana as a journalist and an expert in radio broadcasting.

But his French origins—his parents had emigrated to Cuba in 1902, two years before his birth—and long stays in France placed Carpentier in a peculiar and difficult position, one from which he could bridge the cultural and historical gap that Latin Americans have always felt exists between the Old Continent and the New. It is a feeling that since the beginning of the century has provoked a pendular movement of attraction and rejection, of servile imitation of Europe and militant mundonovismo. Darío, Vallejo, Neruda, and many others had passed through Europe unnoticed. Others, like the Guatemalan Enrique Gómez Carrillo, had remained there, while still others, like the Cuban Augusto de Armas or the Chilean Vicente Huidobro, had written part of their work in French. But in Carpentier Latin Americans had an intellectual who was one of their own yet could claim to be almost French, one who had returned to America from the cultural promised land of Paris. Since 1939, Carpentier has always played that role of the prodigal son. Such an ambivalent position has been un-

---

a note that gives us a vivid description of the Carpentier of the twenties: "Alejo Carpentier has been in Paris now for a few months. In one of his last letters he sends us—with refined cruelty—an infinite number of programs from the concerts, exhibitions, and lectures that he has attended. Now he finds himself in a milieu favorable to his artistic ideals, his exquisite culture, and his dearest aspirations. He has already been made editor in chief of Gaceta Musical, and we have read some of his refined critical articles. He will begin to write for Candide, L'Intransigent, and other prestigious publications. Carpentier took with him to Paris a Cuban ballet, with music by Amadeo Roldán and stage design by Hurtado de Mendoza, for which we wish him the most generous reception" (1, no. 2, July–August 1928). Carpentier, incidentally, was never made editor in chief of Gaceta Musical, which was directed throughout its brief existence by the Mexican composer Manuel Ponce, though he did publish three articles in the journal. I have been unable to see L'Intransigent, but (at least between 1928 and 1930) Carpentier did not publish in Candide.

doubtedly a source of anxiety and has left a mark on his work; it has been at once a strength and a weakness. In 1937, Marinello already refers to Carpentier as a "cubano-francés" writer, and adds that in Havana, because of his accent, he was taken for a foreigner.[9] More recently, Neruda in his memoirs calls Carpentier a French writer.[10] Although today such statements seem unjust, in the early years Carpentier could very well have become a French writer, with as much of a claim on French tradition as Camus or Apollinaire. Carpentier allayed the anxiety inherent in his ambivalent position by reading everything he could find in Paris on Latin American history and literature. Carpentier prepared himself to become an American writer in Europe. Or, as he defined his role then, he attempted to become a "two-way translator of exemplary European techniques and American 'essences.' "[11]

Carpentier's return to Cuba in 1939 became for him a turning point, a symbolic Return. He has referred to it on many occasions, but never with as much poignancy as in 1945, in an interview with Juan Liscano (at that point Carpentier had moved from Havana to Caracas, but both he and Liscano speak as if Carpentier had just returned from Europe, skipping the six years in Cuba to dwell on the Return): "I was saturated with Europe. I felt that I was beginning to lose my footing. I was horrified of coming to look like one of those Latin American intellectuals who exile themselves and without ever succeeding in becoming Europeans cease being Americans. I did not want to become one of those hybrid products that so abound in the history of our arts."[12] Carpentier's literary enterprise is a search for that pied-à-terre that he felt he was losing in 1939: exile becomes a topic in his writing, both fictional and journalistic. His Return (and his several other re-

9. "Una novela cubana," in his Literatura hispanoamericana: hombres-meditaciones (Mexico City, 1937), p. 171.

10. Confieso, p. 175.

11. "América ante la joven literatura europea," Carteles, June 28, 1931, p. 30.

12. Lorenzo Tiempo [Juan Liscano], "Alejo Carpentier: un americano que regresa a América," Papel Literario de El Nacional (Caracas), September 16, 1945, p. 2.

turns) gave him the right to scorn those "hybrid products" whose specters he so ardently wanted to exorcise.

In 1941, two years after settling in Havana, Carpentier wrote a series of articles for *Carteles* that cast a retrospective glance on his first two decades of intellectual life. Confusing, but full of conviction and fervor, these articles are perhaps the most striking testimony of the problematic position which Carpentier occupied at that time. They are a manifesto of American autonomy and an attempt at a philosophical justification of the Return, a proclamation of Europe's demise that calls for a fresh American beginning.

The six articles, published under the general title "El ocaso de Europa"—"Europe's Decline," or literally "The Dusk of Europe"— are a diatribe against the Old Continent and a vehement defense of the New. Carpentier's assessment of the state of Europe in 1941, particularly France (German occupation, Vichy regime), is combined with personal reminiscences of his years in Paris and, surprisingly, an acrimonious critique of European art: "With how much cruelty did they always know how to throw in our faces our 'indigenism,' our 'lack of race,' our extreme youth; those very same superior spirits who today long to find themselves on our Continent—the last refuge of a freedom and joy of living that those who handed down to us languages, principles, and rituals have lost forever. I still remember a comedy that premiered with success at the Théâtre Montparnasse in which our countries appeared as fiefs of barefoot generals with parrots on their shoulders. . . . I still remember Marius André's books, in which he declared that the worst thing that we had ever done was to free ourselves from the Metropolis."[13] While European artists were deriding the New Continent, their own was in an advanced stage of decay, of which their art was but a faithful reflection:

The artists who lived in Europe between 1918 and 1939 projected the physiognomy of a world in which man had ceased to have faith in himself. Masreel's woodcuts, George Grosz's drawings, Rouault's terrible figures, the diabolic pictures of Balthus, were the plastic equiva-

13. November 16, 1941, p. 74. The points of suspension that often appear in Carpentier's writing are closely spaced in the Spanish and French manner. My own points of suspension are printed in the customary manner.

lent of the literature written by a Doeblin, a Ribemont Dessaignes, a Louis Ferdinand Céline... They unveiled all the infirmities, all the shameful baseness that the human soul can generate in times of confusion. An altar was erected to ugliness... The prostitutes with sagging breasts drawn by Grosz went hand in hand with novels in which whole chapters were devoted to secretions and excretions... Other artists, looking for ways of evasion, took refuge in the realm of dreams and pure imagination, creating one of the few Idealist schools to have flourished in those dark years: Surrealism! All mates in the same shipwreck.[14]

American art, on the contrary, is vibrant with optimism; the reflection of a young continent unencumbered by the past and aiming at the future: "Our entire Continent is characterized by an unlimited faith in itself. We know that we have done very little and everything remains to be done."[15] For one who had been a champion of the European avant-garde in the twenties, Carpentier's position seems odd. It was not taken without an attempt at a philosophical apology.

On the opening page of the first article, Carpentier makes an allusion to Hegel's *Philosophy of History* which appears to be the key to his thinking: "In its thousand-year displacement to the West, following the trajectory of the sun, the focus of universal culture has reached our latitudes. America, mature already for her own production, watches as everything worth rescuing from Europe's shipwreck arrives at her coasts."[16] But Hegel hardly seems to be the figure to choose in a defense of the New Continent, for he had spoken quite disparagingly of America and her indigenous cultures: "Of America and its grade of civilization, especially in Mexico and Peru, we have information, but it imports nothing more than that this culture was an entirely national one, which must expire as soon as Spirit approached it. America has always shown itself physically and psychically powerless, and still shows itself so. For the aborigines, after the landing of the Europeans in America, gradually vanished at the breath of European ac-

14. November 23, 1941, p. 37.
15. Ibid., pp. 36–37.
16. November 16, 1941, p. 74.

tivity."[17] Besides, if Europe had absorbed America, the end of history ("Europe is absolutely the end of History")[18] would also be the doom of the New World. But Hegel is not the only philosopher to whom Carpentier appeals. There is in the second article an equally disconnected statement of elementary Marxism: "An epoch is the product of material and economic circumstances, of collective impulses, which are beyond the reach of the artist."[19] It would be naive, of course, to speak in Marxist terms of the "dusk of Europe" and to state that the seat of culture was being removed from one continent to another. Although the presence of Hegel and Marx is significant, even if contradictory and confused, the key to Carpentier's articles is Oswald Spengler, to whom homage is paid by their very title.

The World War corroborates, for Carpentier, Spengler's prophecies about the decline of the West, but the holocaust does not announce a new and rejuvenated European order (as the Nazis proclaimed), but instead—here Hegel is the rhetorical bridge—a transfer of the focus of universal history to America.[20] Spengler's presence, however, goes beyond the title and the vulgarized notions about the decline of Europe; it is felt in most of the terms and concepts used by Carpentier: the cycles of culture, the physiognomy of culture, the law of necessity, and, above all, vitalism. But how can Hegel, Marx, and Spengler coexist? And how has Carpentier come around to such a negative view of Surrealism and contemporary European art?

The philosophical heterogeneity of the 1941 articles and the attack on Surrealism are indicative of some of the contradictions of Carpentier's early years as a writer. The problems faced by Carpentier and other avant-garde writers, particularly novelists, were radical ones. Not since the time of the Spanish colonization of America had the difficulties of writing from and about the New

17. *The Philosophy of History*, trans. J. Siebree, introd. C. J. Friedrich (New York, 1956), p. 81.
18. Ibid., p. 101.
19. November 23, 1941, p. 37.
20. November 16, 1941, p. 75.

World been posited with so much urgency. The uneasy coexistence of Hegel, Marx, and Spengler should not veil their fundamental affinities, particularly in the pattern of fall and resurrection, apocalypse and new beginning, that articulates their conception of history. The questions of writing, history, and culture confronting Carpentier could only be answered with such all-encompassing solutions, and it is because of this that heterogeneity occurs. Although by 1941 Carpentier was in search of other answers, Afro-Cubanism offered in the twenties an opportunity to make a clean break that would bypass the contradictions in such a holistic enterprise.

2

When Carpentier began to write, three issues preoccupied intellectuals in Cuba: the political problems of the fledgling republic (independent since 1902), the European avant-garde, and, after the midpoint of the twenties, the Afro-Cuban movement, which arose partly in response to the other two. These issues had at least one common denominator: the problem of assimilating a large and impoverished black population, the backbone of labor in the sugar industry, into the mainstream of political, social, and cultural life. The question was part of a larger one subtending Latin American thought since Romanticism: Is there a peculiar Latin American mode of being having its own, autochthonous mode of expression? In the twenties, the question became part of the well-known Western movement toward primitivistic utopianism, the desire to discover a new consciousness, devoid of the rationalistic strictures of European thought, which includes the Africanist movement.[21] If Modernity, as Paul de Man puts it, "exists in the form of a desire to wipe out whatever came earlier, in the hope of reaching at last a point that could be called a true present, a point of origin that marks a new departure,"[22] in Latin America (as in

21. See Roger Shattuck, *The Banquet Years: The Origins of the Avant Garde in France, 1885 to World War I*, rev. ed. (New York, 1968), p. 24.
22. "Literary History and Literary Modernity," in his *Blindness and Insight: Essays in the Rhetoric of Contemporary Criticism* (New York, 1971), p. 148.

Europe) this meant wiping out the European heritage. But what became particularly Latin American was the realization or hope that, because of its short history and the presence of non-European cultures, Latin America was already that new departure; in Cuba this meant embracing the cultural heritage of Afro-Cubans. The vexing sociopolitical and philosophical questions implicit in this proclamation of a new age soon became evident (as they did in Europe) and made for a particularly rich mixture of political commitment and aesthetic primitivism that is perhaps the trademark of the bulk of Latin American art in the twentieth century. But Afro-Cubanism did not discover the presence of blacks in Cuba; the movement was instead a radical shift in the position they were assigned in shaping Cuban culture. This shift involved a reassessment of what had been written about them before.

Since independence, the racial composition of Cuba had been a controversial issue. Blacks had filled the ranks in the wars of independence and demanded a better place in a society they had helped to forge, first as slaves and later as soldiers. In spite of the best intentions on the part of revolutionary leaders and some of the first legislators of the republic, the white majority was not eager to assimilate blacks into a society whose class divisions were largely (though not entirely) drawn along racial lines. Cuba's black population had tenaciously maintained its cultural identity, partly because many blacks were of recent arrival from Africa, but mostly because of the alienation to which slavery and later economic oppression had subjected them. African customs and religious practices thrived in the island. In spite of incipient racial mixing (which dates to the sixteenth and seventeenth centuries), blacks stood apart, not only by the color of their skin and general impoverishment, but because they clung to their ancestral traditions. Drums beat in the countryside and the outskirts of towns punctuating the social schism, and often calling to rebellion. The answer to that call took various forms as the political waters of the republic became more turbulent (there was a "Negro Revolt" in May 1912).[23] The presence of blacks in such an "uncon-

23. See Thomas, *Cuba*, pp. 514–24.

taminated" state provided intellectuals and artists with a domestic "primitive" population, in a country where Indians had not been a visible social and cultural force for a long time. The black became an alluring other, who was nevertheless there, close at hand and nominally a part of Cuban nationhood and could be claimed as the point of departure in establishing a radical new beginning.

Before and during the twenties, Cuba's black population was the object of earnest study by two men who left a lasting impression on Carpentier and all Cuban intellectuals since: Ramiro Guerra y Sánchez and Fernando Ortiz. Although not literary in the conventional sense, the texts produced by them are inscribed in Cuban literary tradition, for they provide the first significant approaches to the questions, Who were the blacks? What was their culture like? What role did they play in Cuban society? Their presence in Carpentier's work, as shall be seen, is polemical but crucial.

Guerra's *Sugar and Society in the Caribbean* (1927) outlines the social and demographic implications of the development of the sugar industry in the Caribbean. Guerra shows how Cuba was transformed from an insignificant sugar producer prior to the nineteenth century, with a relatively small slave population, into the world's principal sugar supplier, with a slave population that increased hugely in a short period of time. The main points in Guerra's book are: (1) the precipitous growth of the sugar industry in the last decade of the eighteenth century and its continuous growth during the nineteenth century were the direct result of the Haitian revolution, which by destroying the sugar industry in that country created a vacuum that Cuba filled; (2) large estates developed during the nineteenth century, particularly after 1880 and the coming of the railroad, and out of this liberal, anti-Spanish, landed aristocracy—from which latifundia emerged— came many of the leaders of the wars of independence; (3) between 1898 and 1927 (the present for Guerra) the enormous growth of the *centrales* (sugar factories) created a new and even larger demand for manpower. During the early nineteenth century this demand meant an increase in the slave trade. But from 1898 to 1927 (that is, after the abolition of slavery) black laborers were imported from the nearby islands of Jamaica and Haiti; this resulted in disastrous consequences for the economy and increasing social tensions. As Guerra's book demonstrates, blacks were the victims of a fatal socioeconomic process that brought them to Cuba whenever there was a sugar boom (usually precipitated by a European war) and kept them socially and economically alienated. Every new boom would bring new cheap labor, lowering the standard of living of blacks already on the island, many of whom eventually migrated to urban areas. Guerra added a new dimension to Cuban history by showing how the island was linked with the rest of the Caribbean by common economic and demographic structures and how the history of neighboring islands (as in the case of Haiti) could radically affect its own. There is a dramatic exactness to Guerra's book that was not lost to Cuban literature; nor was Guerra's identification of the central as the locus where the social, racial, and economic tensions in Cuba came into play.[24] *Sugar and Society* furnishes the socioeconomic setting for all of Carpentier's fiction whose scene is the Caribbean. Carpentier chose for the temporal setting of two of his novels, *The Kingdom of This World* and *Explosion in a Cathedral*, that historical break in Cuban history identified by Guerra, the last decade of the eighteenth century, when the Haitian revolution transformed Cuban economic and political life. All of the blacks in his fictions, from Menegildo to Filomeno, are in a constant state of mobility, propelled by the socioeconomic forces described in *Sugar and Society*. And the whites are often, particularly in Carpentier's

24. *Central* is defined by the editors of the English version of Guerra's book as a "large-scale sugar cane grinding mill, of the sort developed in Cuba after 1880" (*Sugar and Society in the Caribbean* [New Haven, 1964], p. 209). In *Cuban Counterpoint: Tobacco and Sugar* (trans. Harriet de Onís [New York, 1970]), Fernando Ortiz gives the following description: "It is a complete social organism, as live and complex as a city or municipality, or a baronial keep with its surrounding fief of vassals, tenants, and serfs. The latifundium is only the territorial base, the visible expression of this. The central is vertebrated by an economic and legal structure that combines masses of land, masses of machinery, masses of men, and masses of money, all in proportion to the integral scope of the huge organism for sugar production" (p. 52).

stories in *War of Time*, members of the nineteenth-century aristocracy created by the sugar boom following the Haitian revolution. In historical terms, Guerra provided Carpentier with the source of modern Cuban history—the point of origin of a new historical evolution and the structure of that evolution.

It is true that as economic analysis—Guerra points this out once or twice—*Sugar and Society* describes a phenomenon involving the rich and the poor, not the white and the black. But Guerra was nonetheless wary about assimilating a large number of blacks (mostly Jamaicans and Haitians) into the overtaxed fabric of the republic. In fact, one of the poetic qualities of *Sugar and Society*, and perhaps its flaw from a scientific point of view, is that the book is imbued with nostalgia for a golden age, visualized as that period in Cuban history when whites were the overwhelming majority and land was available to a stable society of small farmers. The urgency one feels in Guerra's book results from the desire to return to that moment prior to the historical break that he himself identified, and the fear that by 1927 the process begun by the Haitian revolution may be irreversible. *Sugar and Society* does not address the problem of what would be the fate of blacks already in Cuba.

The early works of Fernando Ortiz are more directly concerned with assimilation; that is to say, with blacks after they had undergone the process discussed by Guerra and wound up as a *Lumpenproletariat* in urban centers or as a rural proletariat in the *centrales* and small towns.

Fernando Ortiz's important role in the birth of Afro-Cubanism cannot be disputed, but stands in need of revision. A lawyer by training, Ortiz became interested in African culture for what it could reveal about crime in Cuba. In his early writings he is predominantly a criminologist, as the full title of his first book (1906) indicates: *Hampa afro-cubana: los negros brujos (apuntes para un estudio de etnología criminal)* [Afro-Cuban Underworld: Black Sorcerers (Notes for a Study of Criminal Ethnology)]. Prefaced by Cesare Lombroso, of whom Ortiz declares himself to be an admiring disciple, the book is a detailed study of witchcraft among Cuban blacks, undertaken with the avowed intention of understanding the phenomenon better in order to eliminate it quicker. Ortiz's interest is in the criminal side of witchcraft—the ritualistic killings, the necrophilia, the bizarre sexual practices—and its moral impact on society at large (since many whites were being converted). Ortiz's physiological conception of psychology and race viewed blacks as people with primitive mentalities and strong proclivities to lust and violence, people who must be civilized to insure Cuba's well-being and progress. Many of the elements of Afro-Cuban culture that the *vanguardistas* would later exalt Ortiz saw as socially detrimental. The sorcerer, for example, a figure whom Ortiz studied in detail and who became a central figure in Afro-Cubanism, is defined as "almost always a delinquent, a habitual swindler, often a thief, a defiler of tombs whenever he can. Lusty to the most savage sexual corruption, concubinary and polygamous, lascivious in the practices of the cult and outside of them, fostering the prostitution of others. A true social parasite because of his general exploitation of uncivilized mentalities and the particular exploitation of his several concubines."[25] The early Ortiz was a biological determinist and social Darwinist for whom human behavior was the result of physiological factors and genetic traits.[26] It is evidently for this reason that Carpentier evokes Ortiz with some reservations when he reminisces in *La música en Cuba* (1946) about the origins of the Afro-Cuban movement: "Fernando Ortiz, in spite of differences in age, used to mingle with the boys. His books were read. Folklore was acclaimed. Suddenly the black man became the focal point of all glances. Precisely because it displeased intellectuals of

25. (Madrid, 1906), p. 395.
26. In a little book of collected journalistic pieces, Ortiz wrote, discussing Cuba's demographic composition: "Evolutionism is today the law of life in all of its manifestations. . . . Perhaps our national future could in the end be nothing more than a complex problem of ethnic selection. [Humanity] continues abandoned to the most elementary sociophysical laws, struggling against the general biological promiscuity of inferior species, barely counteracted by the action of varieties coming from the cold countries with migratory storms and political hurricanes" (*Entre cubanos . . . [psicología tropical]* [Paris, n.d. (1914)], pp. 86–87).

the old school, one went with reverence to ñáñigo initiations and praised the *diablito* dance."[27] Ortiz was one of those intellectuals of the old school, a late member of the so-called First Republican Generation, whose main concern was the social and economic progress of the nation, within the framework provided by the recently established government. The fact that Ortiz suffered a radical conversion, probably brought about by the young Afro-Cubanists, has blurred his early years and the nature of his influence in the movement.[28] During his early period, Ortiz had much in common with Sarmiento; just as Indians represented for the Argentine an obstacle in his program of civilization, so did the blacks appear then to Ortiz as a regressive force. His work is important for the Afro-Cuban movement because it underlines the salient aspects of African culture in Cuba and constitutes the first systematic written account of its myths and beliefs. In this respect, Ortiz's work is to the *vanguardia* what Menéndez Pidal's work on the ballads was for the "generation of '27" poets in Spain: a source of scientifically gathered materials. Ortiz's work in the Afro-Cuban lexicon, in fact, owes a great deal to Menéndez Pidal in its positivistic methodology.[29]

But, paradoxically, Ortiz is also important because his early works represent in tone and philosophical orientation everything the *vanguardia* rejected: positivism, rationalism, progress as defined by the ideals of the republic, floundering already under the

27. *La música en Cuba* (Mexico City, 1946), p. 236. The *ñáñigos* were secret societies brought to Cuba by the slaves, where they were reorganized in various cities. The *diablito* was a particular kind of dancer in *ñáñigo* rituals who acted as a sort of sacristan. For details see *Los negros brujos*.

28. It was rumored that Ortiz actually converted to the Afro-Cuban cult, although Nicolás Guillén denies it in a eulogy published in *Casa de las Américas* when the anthropologist died (no. 53 [1969], p. 6). There are in this issue other useful texts on Ortiz by Juan Marinello, José Antonio Portuondo, and Miguel Barnet, as well as an unsigned biographical sketch (pp. 142–44). An encomium of some use may be found in Salvador Bueno, *Temas y personajes de la literatura cubana* (Havana, 1964), pp. 209–18. Carpentier wrote in homage to Ortiz in "Este gran Don Fernando," *El Nacional* (Caracas), October 3, 1951, p. 12.

29. See Ortiz's *Glosario de afronegrismos* (Havana, 1924).

double onus of sociopolitical chaos and the interventionist policies
of the United States.

Ortiz and Guerra had written about who the blacks were, where
they had come from and why, but their work was grounded in a
liberal bourgeois ideology that conceived of Cuban history as a
continuum, a progressive movement that eventually would neutralize African culture. Afro-Cubanism called for a radical break
and a new beginning. There was in it the sportive, frivolous élan
of the avant-garde, directly opposed to the mentality of the good
bourgeois for whom life was the performance of appointed tasks.
In the black, the new artists found, readily at hand, a being that
fulfilled all the requirements of the new spirit: the pure, primitive
way of expressing a simplified reality; his angular art; his jerky,
percussive music and dance; the unintelligibility of his religious
expression, which permeated all aspects of his culture. All this was
embraced as a redeeming cause and sometimes as a political program. But what predominates at the start of the movement is the
pour épater les bourgeois frivolity that characterizes their atten-
dance, "with reverence," at ñáñigo initiations and their praise of
the diablito dance. There is, after all, a striking resemblance between the diablito's costume and that of the harlequin, a figure
that Picasso popularized in his paintings at the time.[30] Carpentier's
second article for Carteles, significantly entitled "La banalidad en
el arte," is an account of the life of Le Douanier Rousseau. The
cult of the primitive, the unserious, the unintelligible, the euphony
of poetic language, led directly to African rituals, dances, and
songs that could be heard and seen all over the island. These were
the same rituals, dances, and songs that Ortiz in Los negros brujos
considered lascivious and socially pernicious.

A heightened sense of political mission eventually crept into
the Afro-Cuban movement as the situation in Cuba became intolerable, and made it pay for the original sin of its somewhat
frivolous birth. But politics was not the only factor that led

30. This similarity had been noticed years before by Pichardo: "[the
diablitos are] blacks dressed in the style of clowns or harlequins" (as quoted
by Ortiz in Los negros brujos, p. 184).

to the movement's demise. Another was contained in its very
dialectics: the phantom of its European origin and its claim to
autonomy, whose correlative set of opposing terms was self-consciousness and spontaneity. G. R. Coulthard addresses himself to
this when he says that the European influence is "recognized by
many Cuban writers, but they make a distinction. When they
took up the European fashion for Negro art, they claim, they did
so with more sincerity than Europeans, for Negro art had a deeper
significance for them. The Cuban Negro is Cuban and his art and
mode of being, his special sensibility, are part of the basic patrimony of the people of Cuba."[31] In 1935, Ballagas formulated the
problem in these terms: "That which is black has acquired of
late a surprising vogue. In this predominance of African art two
very different, we could say, antagonistic tendencies may be observed. . . . One is a superficial trend; the other deep. . . . That
which is black as a primeval cry, as something of the jungle and
of virginal nature, obviously became one of the ways of escape for
the exhausted European. Thus, Guillaume, Blaise Cendrars, Paul
Morand, Gómez de la Serna, and others search in the Baedeker
and the Kodak for what can only be found by looking at man
straight in the face: a new meaning for life and art. And besides,
this touristic African art is born in a time and space without historical dimension."[32] Earlier, Nicolás Guillén, the major poet in
the movement, had expressed the same feeling in these lines of
his "Ode to Kid Chocolate," the black Cuban world boxing
champion:

> And now that Europe's going naked
> to tan her flesh in the sun,
> and prowls Havana and Harlem
> for jazz and son,
> to be black and know it, as the boulevards cheer,
> and before white envy
> speak in real black.[33]

31. *Race and Colour in Caribbean Literature* (London, 1962), p. 29.
32. Ballagas, *Antología*, p. 13.
33. Quoted by Angel Augier, *Nicolás Guillén: notas para un estudio biográfico-crítico* (Santa Clara, Cuba, 1962), p. 99. I am indebted to Willis
Barnstone for substantial aid in translating these lines.

Since the beginning, every commentator on and practitioner of
Afro-Cubanism, particularly writers, has had to contend with the
problem of spontaneity and reflexiveness. For "to know yourself
black" is not to be black spontaneously, and "to speak in real
black" Guillén would have had to abandon Spanish and his own
impressive array of Hispanic poetic techniques. The leap out of
the European tradition was a perilous one, often taken at the ex-
pense of the dignity of the black man, as the humor in many of
the poems of Ballagas's *Antología* amply demonstrates. Juan
Marinello saw as early as 1932 the magnitude and complexity of
the problem:

The American writer is a prisoner. First, language. Later, the learned
fetters of Europe. In literature language is much more than the Gor-
dians [i.e., those who would cut off ties with Europe] imagine. If it
were only a means of expression, a translating medium, it would not
be a prison. It would be a slave, not a master. But language is a living
thing, with incoercible, immortal life. This is apparent in our Indo-
Hispanic lands as in no other place. Language is in us the strongest
Hispanic force, the thickest insulator from the vernacular. Since we are
born to language as to life, without the opportunity to choose, when
we think, when we exist, the language of Castille is already our only
language. We are through a language that is our own while being
foreign. Throughout our existence language will live its own life. We
will sweat trying to grind localisms into our native tongue, and whenever we attempt to renew speech radically, we shall produce modes of
expression that had a healthy life centuries ago in Andalusia or
Estremadura.[34]

Marinello laid bare the irony of poetic revolutions: that by attempting to raze what comes before them, they unwittingly privilege the past.[35] More importantly, he asked for the philosophical
justifications of the new beginnings that the *vanguardistas* were
heralding.

34. *Americanismo y cubanismo literarios* (Havana, n.d. [signed 1932]),
p. 6.
35. Michel Beaujour writes: "The radical break (a revolutionary one on
the level of language) conceals a bizarre return to origins whose reactionary
character cannot be mistaken" ("Flight Out of Time: Poetic Language and
the Revolution," *Yale French Studies*, no. 39 [1967], "Literature and Revolution," ed. Jacques Ehrmann, p. 42.

The missing link in nearly all commentaries of the Afro-Cuban movement and the *vanguardia* is perhaps the most important, for it is the one through which European Modernism was translated into Hispanic terms, and it provided some solutions to the questions raised by Marinello. This link is the *Revista de Occidente*, founded by Ortega y Gasset in 1923. It would be difficult to exaggerate the impact that Ortega and his magazine had on Spanish-speaking America. It was not only Ortega's thought that permeated the continent, but the many translations of (mainly) German philosophers that the magazine's publishing house and Espasa-Calpe (also under Ortega's aegis) disseminated: Spengler, Weber, Scheler, Hegel, Simmel, Frobenius, Husserl, Curtius. Their works were translated by important figures such as José Gaos and Manuel García Morente, their ideas glossed and commented upon by Ortega and others.

José Antonio Portuondo, one of the few critics to have taken note of this influence, says that the founders of the *Revista de Avance* were "profoundly influenced by Spanish culture, whose center was the *Revista de Occidente*."[36] And in a recent interview Nicolás Guillén answers the question "What books were you reading when you wrote *Sóngoro Cosongo* [1931]?": "Laugh if you want! A book that had nothing to do with my position then: none other than Spengler's *The Decline of the West*. I also read Ortega, who was much in vogue then."[37] But it is Carpentier who has most eloquently written about the impact that Ortega and the *Revista de Occidente* had on him and other members of the *vanguardia*. In 1953, Carpentier wrote: "What we had for many years been waiting for finally appeared: a true magazine, a real magazine, one that, to put it this way, would centralize the new Spanish thought: Ortega y Gasset's *Revista de Occidente*, better informed and more universal than all those being published in

36. *Bosquejo histórico de las letras cubanas* (Havana, 1962), p. 60. See also Barbara Bockus Aponte, *Alfonso Reyes and Spain: His Dialogue with Unamuno, Valle-Inclán, Ortega y Gasset and Gómez de la Serna* (Austin, 1972).

37. "Conversación con Nicolás Guillén," *Casa de las Américas*, no. 73 (July–August 1972), p. 129.

Paris, with its introduction of German philosophers and essayists, unknown to us until then, with the editions of the first Russian post-revolutionary novels, with its translations of Lord Dunsany, Worringer, Kaiser, O'Neill, Croce, Lenormand—everything we were anxious to read in our language."[38] And in 1955, upon Ortega's death, Carpentier wrote an entire column on the philosopher and his magazine, where he elaborated on what he had said previously:

The *Revista de Occidente* was for years our guiding light. It established a new order of intellectual relations between Spain and Latin America —relations from which very fruitful enterprises arose, such as the Institución Hispano-Cubana de Cultura, over which Fernando Ortiz presided. Its pages were like open windows to a thought only yesterday ignored by all those who were not specialized readers. . . . How many German, English, French authors, how many art historians did we not come to know thanks to the *Revista de Occidente?* Its issues revealed to us, in addition to the names of Lord Dunsany, of Georg Kaiser, of Franz Kafka, of the Cocteau of *Orpheus*—a whole new theater, a whole new line of short-story writing—not to forget, for those interested in music, the first essays of Adolfo Salazar. And what about the editions of the *Revista?* They were the first to offer us the novels of Vyacheslav Ivanov, of Leonov, of Babel, not to mention certain essential writings of Worringer and Vossler... I remember that some of our elders were alarmed by what they considered to be a "Germanization" of our culture, ever more given to the essay, to thoughtful studies, to reflection about everyday topics—a topic as simple as the frame of a picture, which had moved Ortega to one of his most interesting meditations.[39]

Ortega brought to the Spanish-speaking world an enthusiastic appraisal of the European avant-garde that is manifest in *The Dehumanization of Art* (1925), but more importantly he furnished an appealing philosophical justification for the new art, together with a conception of culture that denied ethnocentrism. The Ortega of the twenties, as Ciriaco Morón Arroyo has shown, is one who

38. "El por qué de cierta añoranza," *El Nacional*, September 26, 1953, p. 34. In "Fiebres de primavera," ibid., July 18, 1951, p. 12, Carpentier had also evoked Ortega and the *Revista de Occidente*.
39. "Ortega y Gasset," *El Nacional*, October 20, 1955, p. 16.

has veered toward a form of *Lebensphilosophie* in which pure, analytical reason is not the axis of human activity; life instead is the radical foundation of culture and civilization. It is an Ortega who is profoundly influenced by Spengler.[40]

In fact, despite its name, the *Revista de Occidente* disseminated in the twenties theories of culture in which Western civilization no longer occupied a privileged place. In an article published in 1924 on the occasion of Leo Frobenius's visit to Madrid, Francisco Vela summed up the various theories of culture then in vogue: "We have then three doctrines of culture. The doctrine of progress, in which there is only one culture that advances incessantly in a single direction. The doctrine of Spengler, for whom there are multiple cultures, closed, noncommunicating, of limited life and foreseeable phases, that die and never revive again. Frobenius's doctrine, according to which, in large territorial expanses, there exists, like a soil deposit, an unchanging reservoir of culture, a cultural predisposition; an 'original culture' that sometimes germinates and bears fruit in the form of temporal 'historical' cultures which pass as ephemeral vibrations, as a dream gives forth from itself various other dreams, to leave the earth again in its primeval stillness."[41] The last two doctrines are the ones obviously preferred by Vela and the magazine. But of those two, Spengler's had the greater appeal, and because he was of Ortega's predilection, his views were disseminated with greater intensity. If, as Carpentier says, he and his friends in the *vanguardia* were faithful readers of the *Revista de Occidente* from its inception, then one thinker they could not have missed was Spengler—and they had been reading him since 1923, four or five years before the date usually given as the beginning of the Afro-Cuban movement.

Just as it would be difficult to overemphasize Ortega's impact on Latin America, it would be difficult to do the same with Spengler's.

40. *El sistema de Ortega y Gasset* (Madrid, 1968), p. 80.
41. "León Frobenius en Madrid," *Revista de Occidente*, no. 9 (March 1924), p. 393. Frobenius had founded an institute for African studies in Berlin. His works were disseminated by the *Revista* and his impact on Afro-Cubanism was strong.

The Decline of the West appeared in Manuel García Morente's masterful translation (done with the assistance of Ortega himself) in 1923. It was an immediate best-seller whose impact on Latin America was instantaneous and pervasive. By 1924, Fernando Ortiz was lecturing in Havana on "la decadencia cubana" (Spengler's title had been rendered as *La decadencia de Occidente*), and Jorge Mañach spoke of the "physiognomy" of Cuban culture.[42] But if these are superficial signs of Spengler's presence (*decadencias* and *ocasos*, "dusks," proliferated), Vasconcelos's *La raza cósmica* (1925), one of the philosophical landmarks in twentieth-century Latin America, certainly is not; and the Mexican's essay is Spenglerian from its very title.[43] In the thirties there is no end to the allusions, replies, borrowings, and interpretations. In the case of Carpentier and Afro-Cubanism, Spengler furnishes some of the basic tenets for the postulation of a radical new beginning; but, paradoxically, his philosophy at the same time contradicted some of the fundamental assumptions of the avant-garde, specifically of Surrealism.

From its very introduction *The Decline of the West* speaks in terms that were very dear to Latin Americans: "As for the great American cultures, do we not, on the ground that they do not 'fit in' (with what?), entirely ignore them?" (I, 18). More impor-

---

42. Ortiz's lecture was published in a pamphlet, *La decadencia cubana* (Havana, 1924). Mañanch uses the term in a polemic with Enrique José Varona; see José Antonio Portuondo, *Crítica de la época y otros ensayos* (Havana, 1965), pp. 113–14.

43. "Race is something cosmic and psychic [*seelenhaft*], periodic in some obscure way" (*The Decline of the West*, vol. II, *Perspectives of World-History*, trans. Charles Francis Atkinson [New York, 1928], p. 114. Further quotations in the text are from vol. I [1926] of this edition, subtitled *Form and Actuality*). Spengler's impact was so pervasive that the *Revista* decided to publish authors whose work commented on or replied to him (see editorial note in no. 30 [December 1925], p. 331): Spangenberg, Weber, Scheler, and Valéry were among those published. And in 1928 Ortega's disciple José Gaos translated Hegel's *Philosophy of History*, obviously because in more than one way *The Decline of the West* was a refutation of Hegel's historicism. In that same year Ortega published an essay, "Hegel y América," that has had a sustained impact on Latin America. The essay may be found today in *Obras completas* (Madrid, 1963), II, 563–76.

tantly, Spengler offers a view of universal history in which there is no fixed center, and where Europe is simply one more culture. From this arises a relativism in morals and values: no more acculturation of blacks, no need to absorb European civilization. Spengler provided the philosophical ground on which to stake the autonomy of Latin American culture and deny its filial relation to Europe. Spengler's cyclic conception of the history of cultures kindled the hope that if Europe was in decline, Latin America must be then in an earlier, more promising stage of her own independent evolution. This, the most superficial and popularized idea generally derived from *The Decline of the West*, has some significant corollaries related to artistic activity.

Carpentier and the members of the *vanguardia* were not professional readers of philosophy, and Spengler, as C. J. Friedrich so aptly puts it, "speaks essentially as the *homme de lettres*."[44] *The Decline of the West* provided Latin American intellectuals with a synthesis of nineteenth-century philosophy, mainly German, going back through Nietzsche to Romantic *Volksgeist*: a leap back over Positivism and Neo-Kantism to a Romantic subject-object philosophy that spoke directly to the Latin American's wish to declare himself free from European tradition; a position, in short, that would allow him to bypass the reflexivity of European thought to reach a spontaneous culture grounded on the landscape—on the *terra mater*. A culture, according to Spengler, is not born out of a historical tradition, but from the perception of depth in a given landscape, a second birth which will generate the basic symbols of each culture in each individual. As the cycle of a culture progresses, such perception becomes reflexive, bringing about its death. Spengler conceived of culture as a living organism having a biography: "Every Culture passes through the age-phases of the individual man. Each has its childhood, youth, manhood and old age" (I, 107). Man's perception and expression of nature, of the landscape, varies according to the cycle in which his culture is found at a given moment, and his expression depends on his perception of the cosmos as fate, not as chance or causality.

44. First of five unnumbered pages of Friedrich's introduction to Hegel's *The Philosophy of History*.

Spengler divides these two modes of perception into two categories: that of the cultured man (the man who lives immersed in his culture) and that of the civilized man (what we would call cultured man). Spontaneity and the feeling of destiny (as opposed to chance or a mechanical causality), and thus the possibility of tragedy and faith, are the characteristics of a man whose culture is at its peak, a man who therefore produces an art in solidarity with that culture, where life, not its critical reflection, is the object. The inferences that may be drawn from this are clear. Latin America is in her period of culture, whereas the European man sees himself reflexively. Europeans see their history as a causal process; Latin Americans see theirs as destiny. The European experiences his culture intellectually; Latin Americans feel it. Thus the art of the cultured man of Latin America is endowed with a truth guaranteed by the fusion of his consciousness (wakeful individual consciousness, not a collective unconscious) with his culture.[45]

The Apollonian *élan* that Spengler advocates and his holistic concept of culture and man's role within it are on the surface akin to the spirit of the avant-garde, and of Surrealism in particular. Both Spengler and Breton speak in essentially theological terms; their systems demand not only conviction but a conversion. In spite of his protestations to the contrary, the admiration that Carpentier felt at one point for the Surrealist movement is incontestable, and it was obviously propitiated by the affinity between the movement and the *Lebensphilosophie* that he assimilated through the *Revista de Occidente*.[46] So it was in a sense not difficult for Carpentier to arrive in France impersonating a French Surrealist poet. After his arrest in 1927 Carpentier's situation in

45. Although Carpentier's debt to Spengler will be taken up again, it might be added here that some of the concepts put forth in *The Decline of the West* are still found in Carpentier's articles of the forties and fifties: "Giovanni Papini la emprende con América," *El Nacional*, June 1, 1947, p. 11; "Lo necesario en literatura," ibid., December 20, 1953, p. 58; "La técnica en América Latina," ibid., December 19, 1953, p. 56.

46. The most striking testimony of Carpentier's participation in Surrealist activities is found in a vignette that he sent to *Carteles*, recounting how he had produced the score for a Man Ray film shown at the Etude des Ursulines; "La música cubana en París," September 23, 1928, pp. 38, 74.

Cuba had become precarious and the Machado dictatorship (1925–1933) had intensified its persecution of students and intellectuals. When in 1928 he met Robert Desnos at a journalists' convention in Havana, Carpentier used the poet's papers to leave for France. Carpentier's acceptance of Surrealism was also facilitated by the fact that when he arrived in France, under the protection of Desnos, Surrealism was enjoying what Maurice Nadeau calls in his well-known history of the movement a "calm year," having already acquired a sort of *droit de cité*.[47] By 1930, however, when the notorious crisis erupted within the group, Carpentier was one of the contributors to *Un cadavre*, the vitriolic pamphlet published against Breton by the dissident group that Desnos led.[48]

The motives for this apparently radical shift have been variously discussed by Carpentier himself and by Klaus Müller-Bergh and Emir Rodríguez Monegal.[49] In summary, it may be said that the break with Surrealism came as a result of Carpentier's friendship with Desnos, who was one of the instigators of the partially political revolt against Breton, and of the intensified activism in Cuba against Machado, which rekindled Carpentier's political commitment. But this explains the break on a contingent, perhaps even anecdotal, level. In a 1928 article sent to *Social*, Carpentier defended Surrealism for "its aversion to skepticism," and added:

To the good bourgeois, the artists of my generation appear as playful iconoclasts; they seem like dangerously incredulous individuals, for whom life lacks any profound meaning... However, anyone who has even lightly examined the motives that subtend the system of ideas imposed by postwar mentalities will see that they owe their fresh flexi-

47. Nadeau, *Histoire du Surréalisme* (Paris, 1964), p. 107.

48. *Un cadavre* (Paris, 1930). Carpentier's note, relating a meeting of his with Breton in which the "Surrealist Pope" (as he was derisively called) attacked Paul Eluard, appears on the bottom right-hand corner of the fourth (and last) unnumbered page.

49. Müller-Bergh, "Corrientes vanguardistas y surrealismo en la obra de Alejo Carpentier," *Asedios a Carpentier: once ensayos críticos sobre el novelista cubano* (Santiago, Chile, 1972), pp. 13–39; Rodríguez Monegal, "Alejo Carpentier: lo real y lo maravilloso en *El reino de este mundo*," ibid., pp. 101–33.

bility to an intense faith, to a quasi-religious concept of intellectual activity. Although less confidence is placed on the creations of the spirit, a higher degree of purity will nevertheless be demanded of them... If the new ones turn their backs on the portentous banalities of Bordeaux, Echegaray, Bazin, if they abhor a theater fit for grocers, if they detest a miserably photographic painting, it is because they entrust to the works of the spirit an elevated mission as poetic vehicles exempt from stupidities... The entire effort of contemporary intellectuals tends to give greater affinity to aesthetic conception. In the end, those who accuse the new of dehumanizing art protest against the excising of a human trace—sentimentality, little domestic plots, kitchen psychology—which did not allow it to attain record-breaking heights.[50]

The echoes of Ortega's *Dehumanization of Art* and the insistence on faith hark back to Carpentier's years in Havana and to Spengler. Carpentier is justifying Surrealism in terms of that *Lebensphilosophie*, by appealing to the theological common ground and the holistic thrust of both Surrealism and German post-Romantic philosophy. But the faith of which Carpentier speaks is a telluric faith that cannot accept the universalist claims of Breton. For Spengler the mark of urban, civilized society is its reflexive search for universal values, while the man of culture possesses the specific values of his particular culture without knowing it. Breton's universalism would neutralize the new beginning that Carpentier seeks, by subsuming it in a European enterprise. This is the fundamental difference between Surrealism and Carpentier's position,

50. "En la extrema avanzada: algunas actitudes del 'Surrealismo,' " *Social*, December 1928, p. 38. In 1926 Carpentier traveled to Mexico to attend a journalists' convention. There he met many Mexican intellectuals and artists who had been involved in the revolution, among them Diego Rivera. One of Carpentier's contributions to the *Revista de Avance* was an article on the painter, full of political fervor. The article, which appeared in 1927, is now included in *Orbita de la Revista de Avance*, ed. Martín Casanovas (Havana, 1965), pp. 147–52. The first-person narrator of the published fragment of *La consagración de la primavera* describes a similar voyage, and the shock he feels upon viewing the works of the muralists, with their vigorous realism, after having been converted to the nonfigural art of the European avant-garde. Carpentier may very well be evoking here the confusion he felt in the twenties, which manifested itself in works such as *¡Ecue-Yamba-O!* See "De *La consagración de la primavera*," *Casa de las Américas*, no. 96 (1976), pp. 72–76.

and when years later (in 1941, for example) he undertakes a critique of the movement, it will be the foundation of his reasoning. Between 1928 and 1931 it is already, although perhaps he is not aware of it, an assumption in his assessment of the movement, and keeps him, although he feels its attraction, at a distance.

But ultimately it does not matter whether the contradictions between *Lebensphilosophie* and Surrealism were consciously apprehended or not by Carpentier at the time. In spite of them, it is their theological common ground that is important in connection with his early work. The new birth that Carpentier sought meant the accession to a new but complete system of signs, and in this Spengler and Breton are not at odds with each other. Such a process cannot fall short of a conversion, for, as Lévi-Strauss has argued when speculating about the birth of language, things cannot become progressively significant; all must become significant at once.[51]

The practice of Afro-Cubanism demonstrated that such a conversion was perhaps possible in media, such as music, dance, or even poetry (by "writing" in African languages), that did not depend on an extended temporal deployment of language. The scarcity of novels coming out of the movement is proof that in the narrative the problems were much more complex. The linear, temporal flow of narrative possesses a historical dimension that is contrary to the instantaneous, ahistorical nature of conversion. In this respect, Spengler had to be more appealing than Breton, for *The Decline of the West* attempts to articulate the history of such a conversion. But the problems remain, for the very existence of various stages in that process of articulation puts into question the source of its narrative, which must remain outside of it. Even though on the surface music, dance, and poetry have a more liturgical character, it is the narrative that demands a theology. Carpentier's narrative in the thirties and forties will be a struggle with this problem and a search for a theology of history, for a teleology that will endow the signs of his narrative with new

51. "Introduction à l'oeuvre de Marcel Mauss," in Mauss's *Sociologie et anthropologie*, 4th ed. (Paris, 1968), p. xlvii.

meanings within a continuum. Afro-Cuban religion offers itself as the symbolic plenum within which to inscribe the flow of such a history.

3

The works written by Carpentier during the twenties and thirties tantalize critics with the illusion of giving access to the birth of an oeuvre. Or, because they have been disavowed by their author, they seem to lie on the other side of a barrier erected by a conversion and a rebirth, and thus to be either worthless ruins of a past whose only function was ushering in the present or mere relics of an author who vanished upon reaching maturity. Seen from the perspective of his later work and judged by purely aesthetic criteria, there can be no doubt that ¡Ecue-Yamba-O!, "Histoire de lunes," "El milagro de Anaquillé," and other pieces of the period appear as hopelessly immature Jugendwerken, callow works in which only the barest outline of the future is discernible. Outside such a temporal chain, however, the works of the twenties and thirties constitute in themselves a fairly coherent nucleus, almost a single text wrought around one all-encompassing metaphor or conceit: the alluring otherness of Afro-Cuban culture, the cohesive religious force of which can become the source for a different writing, freed from the strictures of Western mentality. But whereas in Carpentier's later work that metaphoric center is strong, a dense and resilient structure that tenaciously preserves the illusion of unity, the nucleus formed by the early work is, overall, a distinct example of the impossibility for a fictional text to become an autonomous, self-enclosed unit. The "failure" of that early nucleus is not its falling short of accomplishing a closure, but the ease with which its openness is revealed. Carpentier's dismissal of ¡Ecue-Yamba-O! should not be taken as the final word on that novel; a novelist is wont to discard such obviously flawed products as an additional defense of his more strategically concealed and recent failures at achieving a closure. The dismissal must be linked to the constitution of another fiction, that of the later work. The texts of the early period, flawed though they may be, reveal much about the overall problematics of Carpentier's work.

Five texts remain of Carpentier's first two decades of literary production: ¡Ecue-Yamba-O!, published in Madrid in 1933; "Histoire de lunes," a short story published in the same year in *Cahiers du Sud*; "El milagro de Anaquillé," published in 1937 in the *Revista Cubana* but written ten years before (it is a scenario for a ballet); and two poems that were included in Ballagas's *Antología de poesía negra* (1935), "Liturgia" and "Canción."[52] ¡Ecue-Yamba-O! was first written from beginning to end in only seven days, during Carpentier's stay in jail in 1928, but rewritten later in Europe. The poems and the scenario also date from the twenties, and, in fact, the poems may be fragments of other unpublished scenarios for ballets. "Histoire de lunes," although published in the same year as the novel and four years before "El milagro de Anaquillé," was probably the last of these texts to be written, and

52. ¡Ecue-Yamba-O! *Historia Afro-Cubana* (Madrid: Editorial España, 1933); "Un ballet afrocubano" ["El milagro de Anaquillé"], *Revista Cubana*, nos. 22–24 (1937), pp. 145–54; "Histoire de lunes," *Cahiers du Sud*, no. 157 (1933), pp. 747–59. For the poems see n. 6 above (quotations from ¡Ecue-Yamba-O! are from the 1968, Montevideo edition). There are, in addition, the two series of poems written in collaboration with the composers Marius-François Gaillard and Alejandro García Caturla respectively. These poems are more substantial than the ones published in Ballagas' *Antología*, but are beyond my competence to discuss. They seem, however, to fall within the context outlined here, and in some cases repeat parts of ¡Ecue-Yamba-O! The nine poems written with Gaillard appear to form a unity. In the last, the Cuban landscape suddenly changes to Paris, and Carpentier addresses the composer: "Nous ne verrons donc jamais ton village, ta fanfare, ton sorcier. La Seine coule dans la brume. La pluie glisse sur les toits gris. Si nous savions ton rosier épargné par tempête, il ferait peut-être moins froid ici. Nous ne verrons donc jamais ton village, tes palmiers, ta colline. Gaillard, allumons le feu. . . ." "United Press, Octobre," *Poèmes des Antilles: Neuf chants sur des textes de Alejo Carpentier, musique de Marius-François Gaillard* ([Paris], n.d. Copyright M-F Gaillard, 1931), p. 36. Besides the note of acute nostalgia, it is interesting to note that this is the first time that Carpentier openly introduces in a text the problem of autobiography, by abolishing the distance between narrative voice and his own situation in the present. Printed as sheet music, the only copies of these two series of poems I have been able to see are at the Performing Arts Library of the Lincoln Center, New York City.

it is the only one known to have been composed and published in French.

¡Ecue-Yamba-O! has often been taken as Carpentier's contribution to the *novela de la tierra*, to *costumbrismo*, or as the Caribbean equivalent of *indigenismo*, tendencies that he is supposed to have overcome later and against which novels such as *The Kingdom of This World* are pitted. But this is an illusion created in part by the date of the novel's appearance and by Carpentier's own statement years later when he dismisses it.

> In a time characterized by its great interest in Afro-Cuban folklore, recently discovered then by the intellectuals of my generation, I wrote a novel—¡Ecue-Yamba-O!—whose characters are blacks of the rural classes of the period. I must explain that I was brought up in the Cuban countryside, in contact with rural blacks and their sons, that later, very interested in *santería* and *ñañiguismo*, I attended innumerable ceremonial rituals. With this "documentation" I wrote a novel published in Madrid in 1932 [sic], during the apotheosis of European nativism. Well, twenty years of research about the syncretic realities of Cuba made me realize that everything profound and real, everything universal about the world that I had pretended to portray in my novel had remained outside my field of observation.[53]

In that statement of rejection Carpentier speaks of European nativism, not of Latin American *nativismo*. The distinction is important. European primitivism, as we have seen, coincided with the emergence of the avant-garde in the twenties and earlier, whereas Latin American literature of local color dated back to Romanticism and Realism. From the very start, Carpentier is experimenting within an aesthetic movement that rejected the tenets and practice of Realism and the classical nineteenth-century novel. The elucidations offered above in regard to the Afro-Cuban movement are pertinent here. Just as Carpentier and other members of *vanguardismo* rejected the ideological stance of the members of the First Republican Generation, so will they reject their aesthetic

53. I am translating from *Tientos y diferencias* (Montevideo, 1967), pp. 11–12. Carpentier had said more or less the same in various articles in *El Nacional* during the fifties: e.g., "Perfiles del hombre americano," April 30, 1954, p. 44.

assumptions. The parallel between *indigenismo* and the Afro-Cuban movement, on the other hand, is too facile. Indians did not enjoy the vogue in the European avant-garde that Africans and their American descendants had. Just because they were the two most representative "primitive" races in the New World, they need not necessarily have become the object of the same literary movement, even if their sociopolitical futures could be encompassed by the same broad political movement. Perhaps because their history in the continent was longer and the richness of their culture a known fact for centuries, Indians could hardly have become the symbol of primitivism. With the notable exception of Asturias's *Leyendas de Guatemala*, they have rarely played a prominent role in avant-garde narrative. Novels dealing with Indians have generally followed a realistic model, as in Ciro Alegría's *El mundo es ancho y ajeno* or Jorge Icaza's *Huasipungo*. Carpentier will eventually disavow *¡Ecue-Yamba-O!* and he will never reissue "Histoire de lunes" in Spanish, but not for the reasons usually given. There is no break of major consequence between his work of the thirties and that of the forties, but rather a continuation, an attempt to solve the questions that *¡Ecue-Yamba-O!* and other works of that period had posed. If the articles on Europe's decline sum up Carpentier's years in Europe, they do not close a chapter of his work. They are in fact a manifesto that will be repeated with minor variations until after the publication of *The Kingdom of This World* in 1949. As the most ambitious of the works published during the twenties and thirties, *¡Ecue-Yamba-O!* is the best available access to the problematics posed by that first era.

As an object in its most tangible form *¡Ecue-Yamba-O!* is baffling. Anyone leafing through its pages in 1933, when the book appeared in limited quantities in the bookstores of Madrid, must have been surprised by its very appearance, as well as by its strange-sounding title (which means "Lord, Praised Be Thou" in ñáñigo dialect, one of the African languages still spoken in Cuba). Here was a book subtitled "Historia Afro-Cubana" (even the word

"Afro-Cubana" must have seemed odd at the time) and containing, in addition to the text, photographs and drawings of extremely weird objects and beings—the drawing of a Chinese with a tiny horse galloping on his head, a pipe in his left hand and a fish dangling from his right, a snake painted on his right ankle and a mouse on his left, dressed in the loosely fitting shirt and pants worn by Chinese coolies but with kabbalistic figures (turtles, frogs, birds, dogs, roosters, goats, skulls and bones, a monkey) scattered in no apparent order over the entire garment. Another drawing shows what appears to be an altar with the figure of a virgin standing on a set of bull's horns, flanked by, on one side, a black man brandishing an axe and accompanied by a woman and, on the other, a roughly constructed rag doll without a face and with what look like rosary beads wrapped around its body. Yet another drawing depicts a man or mannequin with a triangular mask, puffs of straw on its feet, feathers in what appears to be a hand, and a stick in the other. The book itself is composed of very brief chapters, followed by a glossary of Afro-Cuban terms.

The surprise felt by that early reader was fully justified. ¡Ecue-Yamba-O! does not fit within the scheme of Latin American literary history. It appeared in 1933 when the novela de la tierra was enjoying its heyday, but it is contemporary and akin to novels that had already broken with the mold of that form of narrative, although they would not be published, in most cases, until later.

¡Ecue-Yamba-O! is contemporary with Valle-Inclán's Tirano Banderas (1926) and with Asturias's El señor presidente, which was not published until 1946. The novela de la tierra continued the tradition of the nineteenth-century novel; it was essentially a bourgeois novel written within realistic conventions. Thematically it protested against social injustice and made a plea for progress in positivistic and liberal terms—the same position taken in Cuba by the First Republican Generation and that one finds in a novel such as Juan Criollo. If one takes as the paradigm of the novela de la tierra a text such as Rómulo Gallegos's Doña Bárbara (1929), one sees that the main characters, Santos Luzardo and Doña Bárbara, represent the two forces that are presumably at odds in

Latin America; civilization, personified by the young lawyer whose answer to the rural problems of Venezuela is legality and barbed wire, and the mysterious telluric forces that conspire against progress, personified by the romantic figure of the heroine. The inner dynamics of the text are conceived within this ideological framework. Time is seen as a continuum, character and setting blend according to the established rhetorical norms of the nineteenth-century novel, and the narrative is given from the perspective of an omniscient narrator whose academic, standard Spanish gives the novel an even texture in which all differences are subsumed. History is an outside force that, just as the narrator's voice gives an even tone to the text, will eventually create order out of all the disparate forces that occupy the present. ¡Ecue-Yamba-O!, on the other hand, was written at the height of the crisis of the European novel, when all of these conventions and rhetorical devices had come to be questioned, not only in the practice of novelists such as Joyce or Huxley, but in theoretical texts such as Ortega's *Dehumanization of Art* and *Ideas on the Novel*, as well as in Breton's *Surrealist Manifesto* of 1924. Carpentier, then, does not write directly against the conventions of the realistic novel, but in response to the crisis created by their crumbling. The failings or successes of his text must be seen within that moment of crisis, when fragmentation and dispersal were the order of the day.

Years later, Carpentier would remember and synthesize that crisis in one of his journalistic pieces for *El Nacional*:

The novel as a literary genre did not suffer a visible evolution with respect to form during the entire nineteenth century. . . . Until well into the twentieth century, the novel will be developed through a well-wrought succession of events, alternating descriptions and dialogues— with a very carefully measured dose of each. . . . One began by describing in detail the scene of the action, just as one set a stage and turned on the lights appropriate to the spectacle, and then allowed the characters to enter. Or, if one wanted to capture the reader's interest from the start, the First Chapter began with a very interesting and active first scene, with a hellish rhythm, followed generally by a long exposition of its antecedents. Genealogical trees and references to the origins of the hero also appeared in Second Chapters, which were frightful if the author had a tiresome pen. Parallel actions were also employed, asking the reader for permission to leave Luisa crying for a while, to return to Gerardo's meeting with his lawyer, and to skip from that to grandfather's deathbed. The dialogue was in the realistic style, although lacking obscenities, with little pauses to light a cigarette, open a window, furrow a brow, or look fixedly at the other speaker... From the 1920's on, the novel thus conceived comes into crisis. A severe crisis, as all crises are, is created to solve a difficult situation—a grave illness—and prepare the way for relief and renewal. Suddenly, all eyes turn to France, the United States, England, or Germany, and a desire to pull the novel out of the molds that had shaped it during the entire nineteenth century may be observed. Temporal scales are modified (Proust, Joyce), counterpoints are established (Huxley), dialogue techniques and even their style are renewed (Raymond Queneau), evocative elements are used, dated, which perform in the narrative the function of Picassian collages (the songs, the commercials inserted by Dos Passos in *Mahattan Transfer*), parallel lives that never meet are recounted (*42nd Parallel*), recurrent action, reversible action is invented, with "times" freely shuffled through time (Guilloux, *Jeux de patience*).[54]

Carpentier wrote this in 1953, when he had far more insight than during the crisis itself. The examples given, furthermore, are clearly more related to his later novelistic efforts than to *¡Ecue-Yamba-O!*, the allusion to the parallel lives that never meet and the shuffling of times seems to point to "Manhunt," and the discussion of regressive action to "Journey Back to the Source." Nevertheless, his views are not only pertinent but crucial for a reading of *¡Ecue-Yamba-O!*: they show Carpentier's keen awareness of a breakdown in the traditional novel and explain his desire to incorporate into his writing many of the techniques mentioned. The clearest sign of the involvement of *¡Ecue-Yamba-O!* in that crisis comes precisely from Carpentier's attempt to incorporate too many of those techniques into his text. For if there is one way to characterize *¡Ecue-Yamba-O!*, it is as a heterogeneous text, where a series of contradictory forces meet and remain unresolved.

Because of Carpentier's allegiance to the avant-garde and to Surrealism he could not be content with writing a story, in the

54. "Renuevo de la novela," *El Nacional*, October 14, 1953, p. 30.

sense of relating a series of incidents about a set of characters in
their social and domestic milieu. With Ortega, Carpentier has
come to accept the idea that art, that the novel, cannot dwell upon
the particular and sentimental aspects of existence. In addition,
Carpentier seems inclined toward an art devoid of transcendental
pretensions—a literature that by its free play of metaphors uncovers its own game of illusion. For these reasons, Carpentier will
be wary about creating a text in which descriptions and characters
will blend in a continuum. Breton had categorically rejected such
novelistic procedures in the first *Manifesto* (1924), which had
been highly praised by Carpentier in 1928. Breton's rejection of
the continuity of life spelled doom to the novel, for it withdrew
the basis for its very construction and also opened a rift between
the narrative and history.[55]

On the other hand, because of his association with the Afro-
Cuban movement and his immersion in Spengler's *Lebensphilosophie*, Carpentier was also inclined toward a different sort of
artistic credo. There was an obvious opposition between the
frivolity of the new art and the religious, transcendental view of
art that Spengler's system advocated, not to mention the political
commitment that Afro-Cubanism soon demanded. In 1927, participating in a polemic about whether Madrid ought to be considered the intellectual center of the Hispanic world, Carpentier
wrote: "It is difficult [in Latin America] for a young artist to think
seriously of creating pure art or dehumanized art. The desire to
create a native art conquers all wills . . . our artist finds himself
forced to believe, a little or a lot, in the transcendence of his
work."[56] It will be recalled that in his 1928 defense of Surrealism
and new art in general Carpentier had insisted on "the quasi-
religious concept of intellectual activity" of the young generation
—an implied criticism of Ortega that appears to contradict Car-

55. *Manifestes du surréalisme* (Paris, 1971), pp. 16–17.
56. "Carta abierta a Manuel Aznar sobre el meridiano intelectual de
nuestra América," *Casa de las Américas*, no. 84 (1974), p. 148. The letter
appeared originally in *Diario de la Marina* (Havana) in 1927.

pentier's enthusiastic endorsement of *The Dehumanization of Art*.[57]

These two tendencies raised not only the problem of transcendence versus frivolity, but also the specter of history. If writing is a game, then it remains outside of history; if it is serious and transcendental, then it has to have a place in the general flow of events (mainly political events). If the initial impulse toward African art was frivolous, the fact that Afro-Cubans were an important part of Cuban political life made the writers' involvement serious. Carpentier, who on the one hand defends the banality of art as represented by Le Douanier Rousseau and on the other insists on the commitment of new artists, is treading a very thin line. These contradictions may not have affected him consciously, but the text of *¡Ecue-Yamba-O!* is fraught with them. Not until the forties did Carpentier come close to formulating a viable solution to the dilemma they posed, but the works of the twenties and thirties show evidence of a continuing effort to overcome them.

That no solution had been found at the time *¡Ecue-Yamba-O!* was written may be gleaned from the most cursory perusal of the text, for, if the book as an object was strange, the novel that it contained was no less odd. *¡Ecue-Yamba-O!* tells the story of Menegildo Cué, a black man born on the grounds of the San Lucio sugar mill who, involved in a lovers' triangle, kills another man and is sent to jail in Havana. After his release he joins one of the urban criminal societies and dies in a gang war. In terms of its plot, the novel assumes the form of a biography, and more specifically of a *Bildungsroman*. Menegildo's physical and spiritual development is observed from the cradle, through his adolescence crisis, various

57. Ortega's five characteristics of the new art were: "When we analyze the new style we find that it contains certain closely connected tendencies. It tends (1) to dehumanize art, (2) to avoid living forms, (3) to see to it that the work of art is nothing but a work of art, (4) to consider art as play and nothing else, (5) to be essentially ironical, (6) to beware of sham and hence to aspire to scrupulous realization, (7) to regard art as a thing of no transcending consequence" (*The Dehumanization of Art, and Other Essays on Art, Culture, and Literature* [Princeton, 1968], p. 14).

initiation rites, his clash with the dominant white society, and his
assimilation by the black, which demands his allegiance to the
death. Menegildo's legacy is his son, born after his death and
named after him. Interspersed through the text are chapters that
contain stylized descriptions of the various settings of the action,
wrought in the "higher algebra of metaphors" that the new poetry
had become, according to Ortega.[58] These chapters are generally
devoid of action or dialogue; they pretend to be settings in the
theatrical sense, slipped between the action scenes but not blend-
ing with them in a continuum except in very exceptional cases.
Whereas the action is conveyed by means of dialogues imitating
the speech patterns of rural blacks, and by a voice that wavers between conventional omniscient narrator and commentator who
passes judgment on events, these descriptions are given in an impersonal, pictorial style, in a prose characterized by metaphoric
play and the rhythm and onomatopoeic euphony of Afro-Cuban
poetry. In some sections the narrator assumes a critical stance in
describing the social and political aspects of a setting that is im-
personally described in others. Moreover, the setting itself, from
the sugar mill to the scenes in Havana, faithfully mirrors Guerra's
and Ortiz's analyses of those milieus. It is in connection with the
latter's theories and descriptions that the novel assumes that
"scientific exoticism" that Fernando Alegría has seen in ¡Ecue-
Yamba-O! and that accounts for the photographs included in the
book, as well as for the descriptions of the various rituals.[59] In
Menegildo, Carpentier offers the life of a criminal, in the manner
studied by Ortiz in Los negros brujos, except that his criminality
is not seen completely as an evil, but as the result of the oppression
to which the black man is subjected by white society, and by the
tragic nature of the African world, which, in Spenglerian terms, is
ruled by fate. This "documentary" aspect of the novel, however,
cannot be confused with the descriptions of the realistic novel.
Within the conventions of the latter, descriptions, plot, and

58. Ibid., p. 32.
59. *Historia de la novela hispanoamericana*, 3d ed. (Mexico City, 1966),
p. 276.

characters are made to blend in one continuous textual flow. What is striking about the documentary tendency in ¡Ecue-Yamba-O! is the relative independence of these elements, their unmediated incorporation, as in an anthropological treatise—witness the photographs, the "Anima Sola" prayer, the quotations of ritualistic songs. This bringing together of concrete slices of the real world has more in common with the syncopated rhythm of the collage than with the realistic descriptions of the classical novel, partakes more of the *objet trouvé* than of the integrated texture of a Balzacian or Galdosian description. (The fact that the subtitle of the novel in the original edition says *novela* on the cover and *historia* on the title page may be a reflection of this heterogeneity.)

The relation between all these elements, moreover, is not a stable one; the text of the novel seems at times like a series of scenes and tableaux written separately and shuffled at random like a deck of cards. It is not stable even in a diachronic sense, for toward the end of the novel the texture of the prose becomes more even, losing some of the metaphoric impetus found at the beginning. This occurs, significantly, at the point when Carpentier is describing not the countryside but the city, in other words, when a landscape other than the one preferred by the *novela de la tierra* is the setting.

The metaphoric play in the novel can be attributed to Carpentier's imitation of the Futurists (as he has acknowledged) and of some of the mechanical tics of the Cubists. The very first sentence of the book establishes the tone: "Angular, of simple lines like the diagram of a theorem, the block of the San Lucio sugar mill rose up in the middle of a wide valley, bordered by a crest of blue hills" (p. 7). This sort of description, insisting on angles, lines, cylinders, and planes, prevails, but the most striking and now dated topoi are those derived from the Futurists, in which inanimate objects are given animal characteristics, or vice versa. Oxen let out steam "like overheated engines" (p. 15), a phonograph "ejaculates love songs" (p. 12), tubes and rods suffer contractions "like metallic intestines" (p. 13), the sugar mill is a "diabetic giant" (p. 12), a siren "moans" (p. 18), a peacock sounds its "claxon" (p. 59), and a full moon appears to be "screwed, very low, in a socket of the nocturnal dome" (p. 71). In addition, there are innumerable mentions of trademarks and commercial objects, strewn in disarray, creating by the bizarre signs of their labels an explosion of multiple meanings. The text becomes the meeting place for a meaningless plethora of signs:

At the inns, slices of dried beef and cod were being unloaded; a torn sack pours a cascade of chick-peas on a screaming pig. On a corn-meal label, two natives of the Canary Islands wrestle. The American hotel has its bar stained in false mahogany. There are foreign cigarettes with pictures of cross-eyed princes. Bricks of chewing tobacco wrapped in silver paper. Fatimas with odalisques. Brands that display royal emblems. Khedives or Indian moccasins. Taverns and little cafés primp up. A hundred beverages are placed on the shelves. Earth-smelling caña santa. Rums "on tap." The turbid escarchados, whose aquarium bottles contain a sprout of candy-sugar. On some labels, soldiers in Scottish kilts. White Label. Gold Label. The stars in brandies become constellations. There are Torinos made in Regla and Anisettes in patriotic bottles with laces. Medals. Paris Exhibition. The Preferred One. A lithograph that shows an écuyère with spangled dress and long boots, sitting on the lap of a bemedaled and lewd old man. There is even rice Mu-kwe-ló, imprisoned in big-bellied earthen jars that came to the village, after fifty days of travel, via San Francisco, wrapped in manifestoes of the Chinese Nationalist Party.   [Pp. 11–12]

It is in these descriptions, and in those of the hurricane where the violent winds bring together all manner of disparate objects, that Carpentier pays homage to Surrealism. However, instead of the umbrella and the sewing machine meeting on the operating table, here we have écuyères and Scottish soldiers, or, in the hurricane scene, "a sloop on the roof of a cathedral" (p. 43). It is also in these Surrealist descriptions that Carpentier's prose breaks into the onomatopoeic and alliterative rhythms of Afro-Cuban poetry: "Ronda que ulula, derriba e inunda" (p. 42), and during Menegildo's feverish dream after he is wounded in his first fight with Napolión: "El jarro de hojalata. Jarro, carro, barro" (p. 109).

Among the Surrealistic descriptions, however, are authorial statements such as: "The Norwegian fisherman in an Emulsion sign woke up, with his heraldic cod on his back, the rosy-cheeked smoker of Virginia cigarettes, planted on Cuban soil by the commercial imperialism of the North, became visible" (p. 170). There are also incursions of the narrator into the minds of his characters to expostulate and explain: "Today—as it sometimes happened to him in the hut that sheltered him with his parents and brothers— he thought vaguely about the things that others who were no better than he enjoyed" (p. 60). And, after explaining the beliefs of the blacks in matters of magic and sorcery: "It is enough to have a conception of the world different from the one generally taught, in order for prodigies to cease being so, and become part of the normally verified order of events" (p. 56). And, soon thereafter, the black man's conception of the cosmos is justified for having allowed "naked man, on an earth badly recovered from its last convulsions, to find within himself instinctive defenses against the ferocity of creation" (pp. 56–57). It is not the political intention of some of these statements that clashes with the rest of the novel so much as the texture of the writing. In the Surrealist and Cubist descriptions, writing is entirely depersonalized, disinterested, devoid of intentionality; the speech of the characters is made to be an imitation of the rural speech of Cuban blacks (or, when in Havana, of urban blacks) that precludes consciousness of itself, and would belie the oratorial tone of the pronouncements just quoted. In addition, the Surrealist descriptions in particular absorb the language and signs of publicity as part of a chaos of latent signification, which is without direction, without a fixed meaning, while the political statements, particularly the one appended to the description of the smoker in the tobacco ad, assigns language an origin and an order. In the market all the labels live in the joyous complicity afforded by the text, in spite of their multiple origins; the sign in the field is not merely juxtaposed with the cod in the Scott Emulsion ad; they are brought together by the economic imperialism of the United States. Because of the mixture, neither conception of origin or idea of order prevails. This clash is merely the symptom of broader oppositions.

In its plot, ¡Ecue-Yamba-O! is faithful to the sociopolitical analyses of Guerra and Ortiz. The world first inhabited by Menegildo Cué is the chaotic *batey* of the San Lucio sugar mill: a world populated by a sundry collection of immigrants brought to the island by the sugar boom created by World War I and the need for labor that it brought about. The *batey* is the meeting point of Haitians and Jamaicans who have been imported as cheap labor, Polish Jews and Spaniards who have come to sell their wares to the growing population or to work as laborers, American technicians sent by the company that owns the factory, Chinese workers, white *guajiros* (poor, rural whites), Cuban blacks of various generations, some born in Africa, others who had gone to the city and are passing by with a political campaign. The Cué family has been forced to sell its land to the American company for reasons explained by Guerra in *Sugar and Society* and repeated in the text of the novel: "As sugar went up, as its indices grew on the boards of Wall Street, the lands acquired by the *central* became a larger blot on the map of the province. A series of small farmers had allowed themselves to be persuaded, by the tempting offers of the American company, to turn over titles and deeds that dated back more than a century" (p. 27). Those who did not sell fell prey to the problem of transportation also analyzed by Guerra: "The company would declare that it had enough sugar cane with that of its own fields, and refused to buy it from his. And one could only count on the San Lucio to grind it, since the other factories were too far away and the only available railroad belonged to the company itself!" (p. 28). After the sale of the land the fate of the family is sealed; they buy oxen and work transporting sugar cane, but their dependence on salaries assigned by the company makes them prey to the circle of exploitation noted in our discussion of Guerra's book. The next step, Menegildo's voyage to Havana (as a prisoner, but he later decides to settle there), and his staying in the city, where he falls in with the *ñáñigo* groups and the underworld, is also patterned after Guerra and Ortiz. The pattern is clear. Because of the drop in sugar prices, or because new shipments of blacks are brought over to further cheapen labor, many blacks (as well as some of the other immigrants) set off for the city, where they lead a precarious existence on the outskirts, forming rival criminal societies and various kinds of underworld clubs. The growth of this underworld is what led Ortiz to write *Los negros brujos.* In Carpentier, however, for reasons already discussed, this world is seen only partially as negative, for, although it is the corrupt place where Menegildo's life ends, it is also the privileged place where magic and belief rule man's existence. The sociopolitical pattern derived from Ortiz and Guerra is clearly part of *¡Ecue-Yamba-O!*, but the prime mover of the action is found elsewhere.

Menegildo's life is punctuated by a series of initiations, omens, and repetitions. When he is a new-born baby a lizard falls on his abdomen; later, the family is cursed by Paula Macho, a widow who roams around the town casting spells and sexually initiating all the young men in ditches; finally, Menegildo is initiated into the ñáñigo group by means of an elaborate ritual. There are, in fact, three different chapters entitled "Iniciación" (labeled *a*, *b*, and *c*): the first describes Menegildo, as a baby, crawling around his house until he reaches a small altar the family keeps, which he significantly topples; the second describes Menegildo's first sexual encounter with Longina, and the third describes the final rituals in Menegildo's initiation to the ñáñigo group. The progression of the plot must be seen within the pattern of repeated initiations that these scenes establish. Menegildo's story within this pattern is a tragic one, a quality that the broader context of his life, white society, lacks. The novel portrays two worlds: a black world ruled by magic and fate, and a white world where history and politics prevail. As Pedro M. Barreda-Tomás has put it, quite rightly: "The black seems to remain outside the avatars of history, to be a purely natural entity."[60]

At the beginning of chapter 27, entitled "Politics," Carpentier adds a footnote: "In this chapter I commit willful anachronisms, placing on the present time and in one same temporal level some elements of creole political mythology that were revealed to us in the course of three different electoral campaigns. But the dates and

60. "Alejo Carpentier: dos visiones del negro, dos conceptos de la novela," *Hispania,* 55 (1972), 35.

the candidates are of less consequence in this case than the in-credible atmosphere of that political world—a prelude to yet worse plagues" (p. 121). The electoral campaigns to which Carpentier refers are those that preceded the accession to power of Gerardo Machado in 1925 (he is clearly one of the "worse plagues"). The allusions at the beginning of the novel to a decree by "Tiburón" (José Miguel Gómez, president from 1909 to 1913), permitting the immigration of Haitians into the island, places the action in 1914. The action begins, that is to say, in the same year that World War I and the sugar boom began ("There's war over there in Europe," someone says in the first chapter; p. 13). The three electoral campaigns, then, must be those of Mario García Menocal (1913–1921), Alfredo Zayas (1921–1925), and Machado (1925–1933). But chapter 27 also contains allusions that go as far back as the 1908 campaign.[61] There is no clear or real correspondence be-

61. For details, see Thomas, *Cuba*, pp. 497–586. In "Lettre des Antilles" (*Bifur* [Paris], no. 3 [1929], pp. 91–105), Carpentier gives a very good ac-count of the anthropological, social, and political background of *¡Ecue-Yamba-O!* Besides giving details of the various religious ceremonies that ap-pear in the novel, Carpentier furnishes evidence about the differences between the various groups of blacks—Jamaicans, Haitians, and Cubans—present in Cuba at the time. *Bifur*, by the way, was edited by G. Ribement-Dessaignes with James Joyce, William Carlos Williams, and Ramón Gómez de la Serna among its "foreign advisors." Miguel Angel Asturias, Vicente Huidobro, and José Eustasio Rivera were the other Latin Americans who published in the journal. Carpentier's only other contribution was a French translation of a piece by Gómez de la Serna on Spanish dancing (no. 2 [1929], pp. 69–84). Although Carpentier attacks Ribement-Dessaignes in his *Carteles* articles on the decline of Europe, he published him in *Imán*, which might indicate that they were friends at some point. But the presence of Carpentier and the other Latin Americans in *Bifur* is due to the cult of the exotic practiced by the Parisian avant-garde: "During this year [1929] the Italian writer Nino Frank persuaded Joyce to do something unprecedented for him; he allowed his name to appear as one of the editorial committee [actually *conseilleur étranger*] of the review *Bifur*, which G. Ribement-Dessaignes was about to launch. Joyce's suggestions for material were all, to Frank's mind, bizarre: he proposed translating Dunsany, the Irishman, Hamish Miles, the Scotsman, or various Australians and Afrikanders, but no English writers." Richard Ellman, *James Joyce* (New York, 1959), p. 628. I am not suggesting, of course, that Joyce proposed that Latin American authors be published, though there is a striking parallel between the situation

tween the story told in the text and history, although on page 53
we are told that Menegildo is seventeen years old, which would
put the action in 1931, a feasible year for the present time of the
narrative, within the flow of events mentioned in the novel. But
the décalage between history and the story is significant, as is
Carpentier's disdain of chronological precision (something that
will change radically in the forties). The reason for it is to be
found in the separation of the world of the whites and that of the
blacks, which was pointed out above and which may be clearly observed in the following passage from that same chapter: "The
Cuban countryside already showed pictures of foreign fruits, ripen-
ing in soda-pop commercials! *Orange Crush* became the instrument of Yankee imperialism, like the memory of Roosevelt or
Lindbergh's airplane! . . . Only the blacks, Menegildo, Longina,
Salomé and her children, jealously preserved an Antillian character and tradition. The *bongó* was the antidote to Wall-Street!
The Holy Ghost worshiped by the Cués did not allow hot dogs
on its sacred bread! . . . No hot dogs for Mayeya's saints!" (p.
125–126). The story of Menegildo is developed within that black
world, which opposes the white world of politics and history that
envelops it by adhering to religion and tradition rather than to
change and progress. Time and history follow a different rhythm
in that microworld of the blacks, which may explain the subtitle
of the original edition of the novel: *historia afro-cubana* (the 1968
edition has *novela*). Subject to history, the white world is caught
in a process of decay, invaded as it is by the effluvia of American
products and customs that pollute the countryside. The white
world is one of time and gradual decay; the black world has the
strength of permanence. Within the context of the white world

---

of Irish writers having to use English as their means of literary expression,
and therefore being reluctant heirs to English literary traditions, and Latin
Americans writing in Spanish. It is possible that Carpentier read Joyce in
the twenties, since *The Portrait* had appeared in French in 1924, and *Ulysses*
in 1929 (Carpentier has told me that his English is not up to reading
literature, and that he read Faulkner, for example, in French). But the presence of Joyce is not felt in Carpentier's work until "Manhunt" (1956) and
Explosion in a Cathedral (1962).

only comedy is possible (the pimp wars), whereas tragedy is the
trademark of the black.[62] The signs generated by white culture
(read politics, change) are comical, ephemeral, meaningless; those
of the black world are permanent and full of meaning. The contrast between white and black rituals is one of the main devices
by means of which this difference is established: the New Year's
party at the house of the sugar-mill manager, for example, is set
against the various black rituals.

Whereas the white world is caught up in the broad flow of history (world war, fluctuation in sugar prices, elections), the black
world is seen from the perspective of the family unit and the individual. We are told the story of the Cué family, from Luis, the
grandfather, a *negro de nación* (a former slave born in Africa); to
Usebio, Menegildo's father, a landowner owing to the generosity
of his father's former master; and finally to Menegildo's own son,
named after him, the beginning of whose life is told, appropriately,
at the end of the novel. The novel proper is the biography of
Menegildo, but his biography must be seen within the continuity
of the family, a continuity underscored by the birth of a new
Menegildo after his father's violent death—a biological and cultural continuity. It is not by chance that the chapter tracing the
Cué lineage comes after Menegildo's first sexual encounter with
Longina; sexuality, within the black world, is not an independent
activity but part of a permanent framework of physical and cultural
relations that ensure the permanence of that world. Furthermore,
because Menegildo's life is structured by a series of rituals and
repetitions, it is seen not as a linear progression but as the fulfillment of a predetermined set of events. All of Menegildo's initiations are important. The first, when he crawls around the family
home and stumbles upon the altar, is an omen that his life will
take a certain direction within the established patterns of black
culture. Later, he is allowed to participate in ritualistic dances,
where he begins to play drums and is initiated into the beliefs that
support his culture. Those beliefs, according to the narrator,

62. On Spengler's idea of destiny see pp. 56–57 above.

hinge upon "the vast harmony of occult forces . . . In this world the visible was insignificant. Creatures lived deceived by the accumulation of gross appearances, under the condescending gaze of superior entitities" (p. 54). According to the wiseman Beruá, "what really counted was the apparent void. The space between two things, between two sexes, between a she-goat and a girl, revealed itself to be filled with latent powers, invisible, very fertile, which had to be set in motion in order to obtain any desired end" (p. 54). In short: "Just as the white man has populated the atmosphere with coded messages, symphonic time and Basic English courses, colored men were capable of making endure a long tradition of science handed down for centuries from fathers to sons, from kings to princes, from initiators to initiated, knowing that the air is a seamless fabric made of threads that transmit powers invoked in ceremonies whose role is in essence that of condensing a superior mystery to direct it for or against something . . ." (p. 55). Later Menegildo will set those powers in motion when he falls in love with Longina and wants to possess her. Finally, he is invited into the ñáñigo power, for which he gives his life in a brawl at a dancing session at the home of Cristalina Valdés, a medium.

In addition to such initiations, Carpentier endows his character with an innate inclination to the forces of his culture, a culture that he absorbs as an alternative to the knowledge and consciousness offered by Western society: "It was true that Menegildo could not read, being even ignorant of the art of signing with a cross. But, on the other hand, he already had a doctorate in gestures and rhythms. A sense of rhythm beat in his veins. When he beat on a box or a tree trunk hollowed out by termites, he invented man's music anew" (p. 31). Further on, when Menegildo is free in Havana and living with Longina, Carpentier describes him thus:

Lacking all class-consciousness, Menegildo had on the other hand consciousness of his capacity to exist. He *felt* himself full and hard, filling his skin with no waste of space, with that essential reality of cold or heat. As long as he was allowed to take a stroll, smoke a few cigars, or make love, his muscles, his bronchia, his genitals gave him a sensation of living that excluded all metaphysical anguish. Not even scruples about his idleness managed to upset him, for, since his initiation, the *ecobios* [friends, in *ñáñigo* dialect] gave him from time to time the chance to show the people of the boarding house that he worked, and that the child beginning to grow in Longina's womb would be free from penury.   [P. 188]

The course of Menegildo's life is determined by the beliefs and supernatural forces that control it, and also by nature, which endows him with an unreflexive *feeling* for life, a knowledge from within that set of beliefs that manipulate his destiny. This nexus between Menegildo's consciousness and nature is also made clear by the complicity that exists between the incidents of his life and the cycles of nature. His sexual awakening, for example, is accompanied by the arrival of spring: "A peculiar vibration in the atmosphere proclaimed the arrival of spring, with its secretion of saps and elaboration of seeds" (p. 89). These vibrations are paralled by Menegildo's longings, which make him irritable and intractable, until he manages to seduce Longina in a violent encounter in the bush, under the stars, which in her, at first, "rekindled a primeval ritual of escape" (p. 91).

Menegildo's life is not only foreordained, but it appears in the novel as an archetype, a quasi-allegorical representation of the black man in the Caribbean. The text suggests this allegorical reading because of the family structure within which the protagonist's life is told and because of the cycles into which the story falls. Menegildo is not important in himself; he is one of a series of individuals, one of many—all. Barreda-Tomás correctly sees that Menegildo "is not an individual, but a species."[63] The division of the novel into three parts, "Childhood," "Adolescence," and "The City," is also significant in this regard. Although the last title seems to break the set (one would expect "Adulthood"), Carpentier has merely followed in his progression the stages of culture's evolution in history according to Spengler's system. Within that conception, the final stage of development of a culture is the city, which represents the moment of corruption before dissolution,

63. "Alejo Carpentier," p. 35. Alegría also mentions this; *Historia*, p. 277.

when natural values are eschewed and faith is replaced by deliberateness and reflexiveness. The parallel with Spengler's system strengthens the allegorical arrangement, but it also creates ambiguities and contradictions. On another level, as we have shown, the plot of ¡Ecue-Yamba-O! follows the sociopolitical theories of Guerra and Ortiz, and seen in this context the city would be the end result of a historical process in which black culture could be seen as being on the wane. But Longina returns to San Lucio to give birth to a new Menegildo and begin another cycle. The opposition between history and permanence already observed is evident here again.

That the city assumes not only a Spenglerian but a traditional role as symbol of corruption there can be no doubt. In the episodes when Menegildo is in jail there are descriptions of homosexuals who put on group performances in the prison yard, of gambling, pimp wars, Communists who do not know the International and are in the dark about "historical materialism." It is the world of the picaresque novel, a topsy-turvy world of inverted values. The Sevillano (Seville was the traditional center of picaresque life), one of the pimps spending a season in jail, sums up his life in this self-deprecating quatrain—a sort of manifesto of corruption:

> My mother died [of a venereal disease] in a hospital,
> My father was executed,
> My sister is a whore
> And I'm here in jail. [P. 141]

There is in all this a lot of Cervantes, particularly the Cervantes of Rinconete y Cortadillo and El casamiento engañoso, and of Mateo Alemán, as well as of the traditional view of the city as the center of corruption, decay, and chaos, as opposed to the pastoral virtues of the countryside. But the link with Spengler's theories is much more precise.

Menegildo undergoes a conversion in jail. When his cousin Antonio, who is his idol (he is a great baseball player, a ñáñigo, and a political operator) comes to see him, he is astonished by the transformation undergone by his rural relative, who was a naive country bumpkin when he went in. Menegildo is now proud of

having stabbed Napolión, brags about his courage, and has bought
a loud shirt with money he earned by gambling. Menegildo has
become a *pícaro*, but more importantly he has objectivized his
former behavior, which had been spontaneously motivated by passion, and deliberately turned himself into a reflection of Antonio
and the other underworld figures surrounding him in his new
environment. Reflexiveness, in the form of image making, of
specular repetitions and duplications, has replaced spontaneity.
But there are specific scenes which establish even sharper contrasts
between city and country life and consequently between spontaneous communion with nature and culture and a reflexive and deliberate posture before life—for example, those in which the life
of children in the city is portrayed, which contrast with Menegildo's upbringing in San Lucio, and in which the authorial voice
that occasionally appears to expostulate says things such as: "The
essentially sickly character of creole children came to the surface,
with its lack of respect for property, for modesty, for trees or
animals" (p. 186); and when Menegildo's conversion is justified:
"Now that the city managed to erase in him all remembrance of
rural life, with disciplines imposed by the sun, by saps and moons,
the young man adapted himself marvelously to an indolent existence, the idleness of which penetrated his flesh" (p. 188). This
opposition between country and city is made more striking, however, in scenes where a less direct intervention of the authorial
voice permits a vivid portrayal of the deviant and corrupt practices
of city life. The most notable is the following, in which the
prisoners ogle a couple in a hotel room across the street:

The prisoners got up in a rush to go frame their faces between the bars
to be able to contemplate the inside of a lit room. Separated from
them by a few meters of asphalt-smelling air, a blond woman, an American no doubt, was slowly taking off her embroidered brassiere. Her
hands, going to meet between her shoulder blades, sketched an ara-
besque of wings. Later, with the gestures of someone attempting to
rid herself of her hips, the woman began to escape from a broad girdle
that fingers threw to the floor. She closed the wardrobe, and its mirror,
placed now at a different angle, revealed the presence of a man lying
down reading a newspaper. The blonde, totally naked, placed herself

at his side with a sudden shudder of the mattress. Fifty anxious looks converged on a thigh being lightly scratched by a thumb. A breast several times brushed the man's elbow without his turning from the printed page. "Disarmament conference?" "Cooperativism?" The woman's fingers outlined caresses that elicited no response. They then turned toward a candy jar that rested on the night table. The prisoners howled in unison: "Take her now, dummy! What are you waiting for?" [Pp. 151–52]

Whereas sex between Menegildo and Longina is a productive and passionate ritual in the bush, under the moonlight, tied to the cycles of nature, and is portrayed directly in the text by means of animated dialogue, this scene of sex in the city between two distant and silent partners is framed by a window, illuminated by artificial light, and seen through a series of mediating objects (bars, the street, a mirror). Sex between Longina and Menegildo is a cosmic, total act, while here its fragmentation is underlined by the prisoners' partial view of the partners, seen as fingers, thighs, breasts, and other parts of the body disconnected from each other. The love between Longina and Menegildo occurs outside of history; it is a ritual within a broader context of repetitions. Here, on the other hand, it is precisely history (the newspaper read by the man) that impedes sexual fulfillment.

The woman's heavy inner garments bring out the theatrical side of city life, where the characters appear wearing disguises that conceal their true identity, or exaggerate it to the point of dehumanization (the homosexuals in their shows, the pimps in their outlandish garb). In the city Menegildo even works in a circus, playing the role of John the Baptist's executioner. When Antonio first appears in San Lucio, he is dressed in his garish baseball uniform, and the sign of Menegildo's conversion is his new shirt. Descriptions of the city, as a matter of fact, often assume the character of a tableau: "The funeral home *La simpatía* boasted an almost obscene angel wrapped in transparent gauze. In a corner fruit stall three Chinese fanned themselves among red *mameyes* and banana bunches" (p. 136). In view of this, it is significant that the ñáñigo initiation takes place outside the city, and that the house of Cristalina Valdés (her name suggests the transparency of air), the medium, is located on the borderline between city and country.

By means of this separation Carpentier keeps black culture outside of history, or within its own separate history. The city may be the end of history, the apocalyptic moment of dissolution, but Menegildo manages to escape that linear thrust of time by remaining, eventually, within the confines of the black world. His life ends, as natural cycles come inexorably to an end, but is renewed by his son. In the black world, time is subject not to history but to liturgy, ensuring the rhythmic processes of life and preserving them. The omens of Menegildo's fate come true—the lizard that falls on his body as an infant, the curse of Paula Macho, Beruá's reading of his future. But the curses can only abolish him, not his kind. Meanwhile the white world that surrounds him continues to be reduced by the erosion of history and the proliferation of meaningless signs, masks, and costumes.

In 1937, Juan Marinello made a series of very perceptive objections to ¡Ecue-Yamba-O! Marinello's criticism cannot be disputed, although he concludes his article by contrasting Carpentier's novel with the novela de la tierra. But Marinello's perception of the presence of various forces at odds with each other in the text is flawless. Nothing better has been written since on ¡Ecue-Yamba-O!, and Carpentier's eleven-year silence between that text and "Journey Back to the Source" may very well have been the result of the reception that Marinello, a man much admired among left-wing intellectuals in Cuba, gave his Afro-Cuban novel. Marinello objects to what he considers to be two contradictory forces: Carpentier's literary "ambition," his desire to subject the Afro-Cuban world to "the last literary wisdom," and the desire to "touch the inner core" of the Cuban black.[64] Marinello considers that Carpentier has attempted to portray Afro-Cubans from the inside and from the outside simultaneously, thereby creating a "crack" at the center of the novel—a cleavage between the black world and what is essentially a white perception of it.

64. "Una novela cubana," p. 171.

Marinello is right when he says that there is a "crack" in ¡Ecue-Yamba-O!, and we have observed some of its results. But the reason for that lack of unity is not as simple as Marinello perceives it. Carpentier was grappling with a complex narrative problem created by the crisis in the novel and the desire of the avant-garde to produce art from a consciousness that would not be supported by the *idées reçues* of the West. Nowhere is the lack of unity more visible in ¡Ecue-Yamba-O! than in chapter 12, where the theology of Afro-Cubans is explained by the narrator: "It is quite possible that the saint will never speak, but the profound exaltation produced by an absolute faith in his presence confers upon the word the magic creative power of primitive eras. . . . Without suspecting it, Beruá [the sorcerer] knew practices that excited the deepest and most primitive centers of the human being. He dealt with the power of conviction, the power of contagion of a fixed idea, the prestige surrounding a taboo, the effects of an out-of-kilter rhythm upon the nervous centers . . ." (pp. 55–56). As in other passages of authorial overview, the tone of the narrative is broken, not so much by a clash between black and white views, but by having the former explained by the latter. Here a pseudo-scientific discourse is inserted to justify the theology of Afro-Cubans and in a sense to usurp its claim to priority. But because the source of the narrative in ¡Ecue-Yamba-O! appears to be more systematically and avowedly Afro-Cuban theology, the authorial voice, which conveys Western ideas and a historical rationale, is shifted within the text to that degraded code in which the white world manifests itself in the novel—a world which, as we have seen, is lacking what might be called a liturgical permanence that the text seeks from its very title.

The only section of the novel that does not manifest this lack of centering principle is the last part, portraying the pell-mell world of the city, but only because it does not make an appeal to theology. Here, as opposed to the rest of the text, neither the black nor the white world claims priority, since all cultural codes seem to be caught in the same process of amalgamation and decay. But this apocalyptic world is clearly not the one within which

Carpentier wishes to deploy his narrative, and the ending of the novel seems to cancel its potential as a solution to the crisis of the novel from which ¡Ecue-Yamba-O! issues. It is obvious from Carpentier's statements, even those acknowledging the novel's flaws, that he aspired to the constitution of a well-centered and self-contained system of signs, distinct from that provided by Western culture—a system of signs positing a relation between history and the narrative in which their unity could be recuperated.

Although "El milagro de Anaquillé" and "Histoire de lunes" are less flawed attempts at achieving that new relation between history and narrative, they pose the same problems as ¡Ecue-Yamba-O! Besides, precisely because the scenario does not require an authorial presence in the same manner as the novel and the story was originally written in French, both texts seem to evade or displace Carpentier. If the "crack" at the center of ¡Ecue Yamba-O!, as Marinello strongly suggests, is produced by Carpentier's own "indefinition," then these texts avoid that rupture by instituting, from the beginning, an absence. Both are, however, closely related to the novel.

"El milagro de Anaquillé" is composed of eight brief scenes. The décor prescribed by Carpentier consists of two bohíos (rural Cuban dwellings), one on the left typical of the white peasant, and one on the right, made of straw, belonging to an Iyamba (a high priest in Afro-Cuban religion). The backdrop has painted sugar-cane fields and palm trees to suggest the archetypal Cuban landscape, and, in the distance, "the angular mass" of a sugar mill. The action begins with the entrance of a guajiro pulling a toy wooden horse. He is followed by three guajiras, who dance to the music that the man has begun to play on a guitar. The guajiros have very pale faces and do not wear masks. As they dance, the Businessman appears, with a huge mask that doubles the normal size of his head, a checkered coat, golf pants and socks, and an enormous cap. He carries some posters, a bicycle-tire pump, the tripod for a movie camera, and several packages. He dumps everything in front of the house of the Iyamba, moves around inspecting the *guajiros*, feeling their muscles. A Flapper and an American Sailor come on stage furiously dancing a "black bottom." As they dance, the Businessman begins hanging his posters—for Wrigley's Gum, Ice Cream Soda, Church of the Rotarian Christ—and connects his pump between some sugar-cane stalks. He pumps madly and a skyscraper begins to grow in the background until the pump blows up, and with the explosion the "black bottom" ends. Then the Businessman sets up his camera, pulls from one of his packages shawls and other costumes with which he dresses the Flapper as a Spanish dancer and the Sailor as a bullfighter, and gives the *guajiros* tambourines, which they begin to play timidly as the two dancers perform a grotesque number mimicking a bullfight. As the Sailor threatens the Flapper with his sword, the black sugar-cane cutters enter the stage, following the *Iyamba*, and cut in front of the Businessman, ruining his shot. The Businessman protests, but is stared down by the blacks. The *Iyamba* then sets up the various things needed to perform a ritual. A *Diablito* runs onstage, jumping around with a black rooster in his hand. The black men observe with reverence and later begin to dance frenetically. As this has been taking place, the Businessman has pulled out a director's folding chair and has been observing the scene with increasing interest. He gets up, points the camera in the direction of the black man's hut, dresses the Sailor in a tiger skin and the Flapper as a Hawaiian hula dancer, and urges them to join the black dancers, who repel them violently; the Businessman, in anger, destroys the *Iyamba*'s altar with his tripod. As the blacks are about to attack him, the *Jimaguas* (twin deities) appear. These are dressed as two enormous round dolls with cylindrical heads, huge protruding eyes, and short red skirts. They are tied to each other by the neck with a rope, which they wrap around the Businessman's neck without using their hands. The skyscraper deflates, the sugar-mill's siren lets out a long lugubrious whistle, and, as the sugar-cane cutters raise their arms to the sky, the remaining figures freeze like statues. A slow curtain ends the ballet.

The intended sense of the "miracle" could not be clearer: the opposition to American imperialism can only be carried out by the blacks. These, armed with their faith, will not allow the white man to make them dance to his tune, as the *guajiros* do, nor allow him to alter their culture. The important weapon, again, is religion, the belief in the "vast harmony of forces" that binds the cosmos and is impervious to the fraying of history. The objects and signs of the white man's culture are, as in *¡Ecue-Yamba-O!*, a collection of meaningless and ephemeral artifacts that vanish once they come into contact with the powers of African culture. The signs of Western culture are comical because they lack internal coherence and have no stable relation with the environment in which they are deployed. To the Businessman, Cuba is a combination of the Spain of travel-poster lore (bullfighters and flamenco dancers) and an island of the South Pacific.

Given the absence of language as a primary medium of composition, Carpentier avoids in "El milagro de Anaquillé" some of the traps into which he fell in *¡Ecue-Yamba-O!* One has to ask, nevertheless, the obvious question: Is not the position of the audience and of the composer basically the same as that of the Businessman? Medieval "miracle plays" and seventeenth-century *autos sacramentales* were communal ceremonies in which the faith and participation of the audience were major ingredients of the representation, and because they were staged on religious holidays, they belonged both to a specific liturgy and to the liturgical year; each re-enactment of sacred history had a clear place in a sacral time sequence. In "El milagro de Anaquillé," on the other hand, there is an aesthetic portrayal of Afro-Cuban religious practices, or, at most, a political statement about them. Even if the latter were true, making Afro-Cuban religion an agent of political history violates its atemporal quality, allows it to be placed outside its own liturgical time. Essentially, then, the problem is similar to the one encountered in *¡Ecue-Yamba-O!*: a *décalage* between History and black history, and the insertion of the latter into the former. In other words, how is writing to be incorporated into the "vast harmony" of forces of that world it presumes to represent if within that world writing is condemned to marginality, or, more precisely, to otherness?

Although published in the same year, "Histoire de lunes" was most probably written after ¡Ecue-Yamba-O!, since it already offers solutions to the problems posed by the novel and "El milagro de Anaquillé," solutions that Carpentier will experiment with more fully after his return to Cuba in 1939. Unlike ¡Ecue-Yamba-O!, "Histoire de lunes" is devoid, for the most part, of Futurist and Cubist tics, and there is a sustained attempt to achieve a synthesis of Afro-Cuban and white history.

A first reading of the story, however, tends to reveal above all its parallels with ¡Ecue-Yamba-O! Carpentier has, in fact, used in the story a few scenes from the novel, and Atilano, the protagonist, has the same name as Paula Macho's dead husband in ¡Ecue-Yamba-O! (although the two texts do not make a continuous fictional world). The description of a train station, when Menegildo travels to Havana, is given thus in the novel: "Vendors of small cakes, fruits, and newspapers cried out. Under the broad rims of their blue hats, the girls of a Conservatory awaited the arrival of a professor from the capital, displaying velvet ribbons across their chests with the words 'Long Live Music' inscribed in silver letters. Cock-fighters with their shaved Malaysian roosters in their hands. Beggars and unemployed men with a piece of straw in the mouth. Plantation owners in white suits and bony guajiros saying good-bye to a children-ridden cousin. In the midst of all the bustling, several shirtless men hailed a fish-faced Representative who pompously descended from one of the first-class cars, wedging his holster against a buttock" (p. 139). In "Histoire de lunes," Carpentier has made the train station the most important locus of the narrative and describes the scene in these words: "And the beggars, the vendors of fritters and of prayers engulfed the platform . . . Often, the train brought passing visitors. A politician dressed in a white suit, a captain of the rural police, an animal trainer, or several girls from a nearby conservatory, going on an excursion, displaying on their chests a red velvet ribbon with the words 'Long Live Music' inscribed in golden Italic letters . . ." (p. 747). There are other borrowings, particularly in the scenes describing the ñáñigo ritual, that are equally concrete and obvious. But the most salient and relevant parallels are those of the historical and sociopolitical setting. "Histoire de lunes" takes place during the same years of Cuban history as ¡Ecue-Yamba-O!, although there are less direct references to specific events and personalities, and the setting is also a rural town where people of the most varied backgrounds—Chinese, whites, blacks—live together in precarious harmony.

The significance of these borrowings, however, can be assessed only in view of the differences between "Histoire de lunes" and ¡Ecue-Yamba-O! Carpentier is not merely economizing when he borrows from the novel. He is reworking the same materials as part of the process of finding a solution to the dilemmas that ¡Ecue-Yamba-O! had responded to. Carpentier is, in a sense, rewriting. In The Kingdom of This World and Explosion in a Cathedral, which also share the same historical period and some of the settings, we shall find the same procedure, and Reasons of State returns to the era covered by ¡Ecue-Yamba-O! and "Manhunt." From "Histoire de lunes" on, rewriting will be one of the constants in Carpentier's work, the most significant and revealing instance of which is his turning of El libro de la Gran Sabana into The Lost Steps. Observing the changes that "Histoire de lunes" effects upon the material present in ¡Ecue-Yamba-O! offers the first possibility of analyzing that process.

The most striking feature of "Histoire de lunes" is its careful temporal arrangement. The story opens: "It was at 12:28 pretty much on the dot that the train with the long yellow cars stopped at the village station" (p. 747). The second section begins, "Now at 12:28, only the children went to the station" (p. 749). Other sections open, "On that day," "Now," "The next day," and there is mention of Mondays, Tuesdays, Sundays, as well as reference to Carnival time and other rituals dependent on the specificity of certain dates. The obvious justification for this insistence on the exactness of dates and times is the repetitive nature of "Histoire de lunes." The locus of the narrative is the train station, a place of chronometrically determined passage and repetition, and the story, as the title indicates, hinges on the repetitive cycles of the moon. The vague complicity between the cycles of nature and

events in ¡Ecue-Yamba-O! has become more precise in "Histoire
de lunes." But there is more, even in the opposition between the
two nouns in the title itself: "history," implying a linear development, and "moons," involving a series of cosmic repetitions. The
complex game of times, dates, and the cycles of nature begins to
form a system of correspondences in this story that was not present
in the other texts of the period.

There is what might be called a surface level where repetition
is not only obvious but stressed in "Histoire de lunes." The train
arrives at a certain hour and sets off a series of events that occur
without variation every day: the fan in the café The Three Magi
is turned on, the Fords are started, the vendors go to the platform
to sell their snacks. Once the train leaves, everything ceases. With
every arrival of the train Atilano begins to feel a tree growing
inside of him, penetrating his every limb with its roots. He goes
to the café to lie under the shade of a tree but cannot calm himself
until evening, when, covered with lard and naked, he goes into
the town with the intent to rape as many women as he can. Seven
days after the first rape the news of the activities of "The Slippery
One" is uncovered and the rhythm of the repetitions is broken.
The men gather at The Three Magi and plan to hunt down the
rapist. This is followed by two opposing ceremonies: the sermon
on a Sunday, during mass, and the African ceremony that drowns
out with its drums the voice of the priest and steals away his
audience. The final dissolution of order in town takes place during
the Carnival, when after the clash of the two ñáñigo powers
Atilano is arrested and executed as a Communist provocateur by
officials who prefer not to go into further explanations. Calm is
restored and the repetition of the arrival of the train and the
various events that this arrival unchains takes over again. Even
on this level one might begin to discern a synthesis of black and
white history in the fact that Atilano's seizures begin each day with
the arrival of the train. The repetition of events marking off time
in the outside world is conjoined with the recurrence of the
malady that afflicts the black protagonist.

But Carpentier has wrought this narrative with a great deal

more specificity than the novel. Atilano has been the victim of an
embó and fallen under the power of Elegbará or Eshú.[65] The embó
is a spell or curse, but its powers are mixed, benefiting some
and hurting others. This is the case in "Histoire de lunes." Atilano
has been the victim of an embó cast by the rival ñáñigo power
(they have totemic names: here, the Goats and the Bullfrogs).
At the end it is discovered that Atilano raped only women belonging to the opposite power, and that his semen, or so the blacks
believe, cures infertility. The relation with fertility has also been
carefully made. Elegbará is not only the god of vengeance, but
also a phallic deity. The two concrete objects that signify Atilano's
embó have clearly phallic connotations: the eel that acts as his
double, again following Afro-Cuban doctrine to the letter, and the
tree (the tree that grows inside of him, the tree under which he
lies, and the little tree that grows on the head of the eel). The
tree is related to the cult of Elegabará, to whom sacrifices are
made in the forest, or behind a door, perhaps because its wood
is reminiscent of the forest. The phallic powers of Atilano are
stressed in the story. In one sequence he rapes three women in
one night, and it is said that when he emerges in the dark from
the river banks, he does so shining with grease and "holding on
to his sex with both hands" (p. 749).

The significance of Atilano's phallic powers is clear; the incidents of his life, of the story, are predetermined by the relationship between his genital instincts and the phases of the moon.
The text is ordered by this relationship, and not merely on a
thematic level, as in ¡Ecue-Yamba-O!, but in its very composition.
The detail of the train's scheduled arrival at 12:28 is significant
here. Twenty-eight is, of course, the number of days of a lunar
cycle; the text is divided into eight unnumbered sections, the last
being a sort of coda that takes place "the day after," meaning the
day after the action, which was narrated in seven sections, ends.
But the eighth section also announces that in the future the same
events will occur, so eight must stand for Monday (lundi, moonday,

65. For details on all this background, see chap. 3 of Ortiz's Los negros
brujos.

day of the moon). The opposing religious rituals took place on a Sunday, of course, the seventh day, closing a cycle, and it is in the seventh section of the story that Atilano is executed, closing the cycle. Carpentier has attempted to close the gap between writing and belief, between writing and liturgy, by subjecting his text to the numerology of liturgy. History and moons are no longer two disparate forces, but appear united in the same all-encompassing metaphor of order. Writing too will be subject to the vast harmony of forces. Even descriptions are no longer merely settings, but objects with symbolic meaning that attempt to merge into the overall network of relationships that the text establishes. Perhaps by the distancing that writing in French afforded, Carpentier was able to obliterate himself and make writing the simulacrum of a closed system that would bring together the white and black worlds—the liturgical year and black liturgy—as if in a continuum. In this respect, Carpentier anticipates in "Histoire de lunes" solutions to the dilemmas of Latin American writing that he will exploit more fully in the forties. The elements brought together by this story, symbolized by history and moons, are the ingredients of that future fiction.

"Histoire de lunes" does not, of course, provide answers to all the questions arising from the various ideological trends of the avant-garde, the concrete sociopolitical problems of Cuba, and the crisis of the novel. But it is a more organized attempt to answer such questions than Carpentier's essayistic efforts, where Hegel, Marx, Spengler, and Ortega, in addition to the contingencies of Carpentier's own life and the history of Latin America, mingle to produce extremely confused statements. Basically, his answer to the problems posed by the narrative is a theological one, whose basis is mostly Spenglerian. The lack of continuity brought about by the crisis of the novel Carpentier solves with an all-encompassing metaphor of order, where the linear development of the plot is not the sole unifying force; rather, order is created by a complex web of symbolic relations outside the action—a sort of symbolic plenum. It is not an order based on an assumed temporal continuity, but an atemporal system of symbolic relationships, akin to Spengler's model of culture where all modes of expression are linked by a central symbol derived from the observation of landscape. This allows Carpentier to integrate description and action in "Histoire de lunes" in a way that he had not been able to do in ¡Ecue-Yamba-O! and had been able to circumvent in "El milagro de Anaquillé."

One problem remained, however, to make the solution viable. The history that Carpentier offers in "Histoire de lunes" is fictional and abstract: it is a series of events taking place in an imaginary Cuban town at an indeterminate moment (even if the epoch is clearly the thirties). In order for that faith that he proclaims the new artists have to be consistent, and also to make his commitment to a real and distinct Latin American consciousness, the history that is caught in the web of symbolic relationships of the text will have to be actual history. As long as it is not, his answer will remain at an aesthetic level, perhaps satisfying his allegiance to the avant-garde but not his desire to produce a truly transcendental art.

Carpentier's return to Cuba in 1939 became for him The Return. By 1945, when he was interviewed by Liscano upon arriving in Caracas, the year 1939 had already become a turning point for Carpentier, and in his column for El Nacional during the fifties he will often refer to Gómez Carrillo and Augusto de Armas, two Latin Americans who never returned, as well as to the notorious Parisian obsession of others such as Darío and Huidobro.[66] The Carteles articles on the decline of Europe were a kind of account of Carpentier's career and life up to that point. It was a modest career, as far as literary production was concerned, but it had been touched by all the significant trends of the twenties and thirties. Afro-Cubanism was largely dead now, Surrealism had become fragmented, the Cuban revolution of the thirties lost. It was a time for a new beginning. The Return gave Carpentier an

66. See "Un divertido texto," El Nacional, May 27, 1954, p. 32; "Horizontes de ayer y de hoy," ibid., January 28, 1954, p. 32; "Fin del exotismo americano," ibid., September 7, 1952, p. 16.

imprint of legitimacy; he was not going to be one of those hybrid products that he mentions in his conversation with Liscano, nor remain in that "curious indefinition" mentioned by Marinello. Like Menegildo Cué, Carpentier had returned and been reborn, thus closing the cycle of one life. If in Paris he had been a marginal figure, in Havana he could find anew his true center and begin to write from it.

But the metaphysics of returning are not that simple. In the theological world of ¡Ecue-Yamba-O! Menegildo's son is born blind to the wanderings of his father, ready to begin a fresh cycle of which he is not conscious. Not so in the case of Carpentier, who returns to Havana to re-discover and to re-search time past. The problematics of The Return, which will mark Carpentier's work in the forties, are present in another series of articles that he wrote for Carteles shortly after settling in Havana in 1939.[67] The title of the series is, significantly, "Havana Seen by a Cuban Tourist." In the first installment, Carpentier speaks of his new vision of the city:

An eleven-year absence indisputably confers upon anyone returning to his country the soul of a tourist. . . . One places oneself before one's own things—those that were the setting of childhood and a complement to adolescent dreams—with new eyes and a spirit free from prejudice. Besides, wanderings through other lands bring to mind more than one point of reference and comparison. . . . And spurred by a new curiosity, the spectator in his own home feels impelled to revise values, to revitalize old conceptions, to visit carefully the neighborhood that long ago appeared uninteresting, to explore the street that he never crossed before.[68]

With such a double vision, in terms of time and of his own dédoublement, Carpentier takes the reader through many of the prominent places of Havana. He is now able to discover the heretofore hidden charms of the city, not only because of the perspective afforded by time and memory, but also because Surrealism has taught him how to look at things in a different way. What

67. See n. 5 above.
68. Carteles, October 8, 1939, p. 16.

once seemed incongruous, and even vulgar, now offers contrasts that constitute the genesis of every poetic vision. Lottery numbers unveil kabbalas and Freudian symbols, the names of cafés— *Memories of the Future, The Second Luke-Warm Water*—are avant-garde images secreted by a reality that must be explored in all its details. Returning has turned into a rereading of his own memory and of the America that he had conjured in Paris through Surrealism and the many hours of study devoted to texts of and about the New World.

The double vision of The Return, the sign of the permanent traveler, is the point of departure for Carpentier's mature work, which was to begin in the forties. With the major exponents of Afro-Cubanism having joined political parties or moved on to new artistic trends and with the war in Europe, a more broadly conceived notion of American autonomy was needed. This autonomy could not be predicated on a present demographic or political state but had to have roots in a past from which a harmonious and coherent Latin American history would develop toward a better future—a future in which the two images in the double vision could merge into one. This search, this re-search would be the foundation of Carpentier's work in the forties.

3. Fugitive Island

Homecoming is the return into the proximity of the source
Heidegger, "Remembrance of the Poet"

ni isla hoy a su vuelo fugitiva
Góngora, "Soledad primera"

After his return from Paris in 1939, Carpentier was to remain in Havana only until 1945, and his years in Cuba, before he left again to take residence in Caracas, were interrupted by two trips: one to Haiti in 1943 and another to Mexico in 1944.[1] In the forties, Carpentier's places of residence—Havana, Caracas—would not leave as much of an imprint on his works as did his travels. Of these, four should be emphasized: the two already mentioned and the trips to the Venezuelan jungle in the summers of 1947 and 1948.[2] (There were other trips within Cuba, mainly to Santiago.) From these last two trips would emerge, first, the unfinished *Libro de la Gran Sabana* and later *The Lost Steps*, texts that mark the first and perhaps only radical break in the course of Carpentier's work. It seems appropriate, therefore, to think of the period from 1939, when Carpentier returns to Havana, to 1948, when he returns to Caracas after his second voyage to the jungle, as a unit. It must be emphasized, however, that the difference between Carpentier's works of the thirties and those of the forties, through significant, is not radical.[3]

1. Carpentier went to Caracas to take a job in Publicidad Ars, an advertising agency founded by Carlos Frías, a friend from the Paris years. Few details on this move are available in biographical accounts and interviews. According to Rafael Pineda, who also worked in Publicidad Ars, Carpentier worked in public relations; see "Alejo Carpentier en la ciudad de las maquetas," *Imagen,* March 14, 1972, p. 2.
2. We shall deal with these in the next chapter.
3. I agree with Luis Quesada in thinking that the period from ¡Ecue-Yamba-

In the forties Carpentier wrote two books, *La música en Cuba* and *The Kingdom of This World*, published in 1946 and 1949, respectively; three stories, which he collected years later, in 1958, in the first edition of *War of Time*: "Journey Back to the Source," "The Highroad of Saint James," and "Like the Night"; and two other stories never collected in a volume, "Los fugitivos" and "Oficio de tinieblas." With these texts Carpentier became recognized in Latin America and abroad, not simply as another of the many authors of one obscure book, but as an important writer. Carpentier came into his own in the forties, his most prolific and in more than one sense his most important decade of literary activity.

If the five stories and *The Kingdom of This World* hold the most interest from a purely literary point of view, the book that defines this period in Carpentier's career and distinguishes it from the years of the avant-garde and Afro-Cubanism is *La música en Cuba*, a book that traces in scholarly detail the historical evolution of Cuban music from the colonial period to the present. The forties also encompass Carpentier's most sustained and significant experiments with fantastic literature—a kind of literature that critics have commonly associated with the concept of "magical realism." Carpentier's travels through the Venezuelan jungle in 1947 and 1948 and his frustrated effort to write a travel journal stemming from the first trip—*El libro de la Gran Sabana*—will bring this period to a close.

The Latin America to which Carpentier returned in 1939 was, for intellectuals and artists who like himself had experienced the

O! to *The Kingdom of This World* may be thought of as a unity, within which differences may be found; but the differences are sharper than Quesada maintains. See "Desarrollo evolutivo del elemento negro en tres de las primeras narraciones de Alejo Carpentier," in *Literatura de la emancipación y otros ensayos: Memoria del XV Congreso del Instituto de Literatura Iberoamericana* (Lima, 1972), pp. 217–23. On the other hand, I do not consider the difference between the portrayal of blacks in the early novel and in *The Kingdom of This World* as radical as Pedro M. Barreda-Tomás maintains in "Alejo Carpentier: dos visiones del negro, dos conceptos de la novela," *Hispania*, 55 (1972), 34–44.

European avant-garde, a place for rebirth and reimmersion. After the fall of the Spanish Republic and with the beginning of World War II, great numbers of Latin Americans came back from Paris and Madrid, and with them, as Carpentier points out in his *Carteles* articles on the decline of Europe, came many Europeans. The consequences of this return and the emigration of European artists and intellectuals to America (mainly exiled Spanish Republicans) have been analyzed by Emir Rodríguez Monegal: publishing houses were created, magazines founded, new groups of artists formed in the great capitals of the New Continent.[4] In Cuba, for example, an important group gathered around the magazine *Orígenes* (founded in 1944), with which Carpentier became associated, if only marginally. The phenomenon was one of the most significant in modern Latin American cultural history. Rodríguez Monegal writes: "A growth of national consciousness [took] place—which had had its most notable manifestations in Mexico after the Revolution, to give but one well-known example —stimulating the work of essayists, who became ever more committed to an intense investigation of their being Latin American."[5] The cutting of ties with Europe brought about by World War II gave way to a desire on the part of Latin Americans to chart the historical route that had been traveled in the past and to plot the path to be followed in the future. Carpentier's essays on the decline of Europe were but one manifestation of what came to be a renewed *mundonovista* movement; a movement that with greater or lesser militancy and with the combined effort of figures with varying ideologies set out to define Latin America on its own terms and which actively endeavored to recover its past. The forties was a period of search for Latin American consciousness and for the foundations of a literature of its own, distinct from that of Europe. Now, however, the future would not be regarded as the patrimony of a single race whose primitive spontaneity gave it special powers (the thesis of "El milagro de Anaquillé" and *¡Ecue-Yamba-O!*);

4. "La nueva novela latinoamericana," in *Actas del Tercer Congreso Internacional de Hispanistas* (Mexico City, 1970), pp. 47–48.
5. Ibid., p. 48.

instead, all races and cultures in the New Continent would finally be fused into a new historical entity.

The forties were the years of Fernando Ortiz's *Cuban Counterpoint: Tobacco and Sugar* (1940), a book offering a structural interpretation of Cuban history, accompanied by a mosaic of colonial texts gathered from hither and yon; of *Ultima Tule*, in which Alfonso Reyes reinterprets, in another key, the work initiated by Vasconcelos and Ramos; of two fundamental books by Pedro Henríquez Ureña, *Historia de la cultura en la América Hispánica* (1947) and *Las corrientes literarias en la América Hispánica* (1949), which attempt to demonstrate the historical and cultural unity of Latin America; of Leopoldo Zea's *Hacia una filosofía americana* (1945), which explores the possibility of a particular mode of thought emerging from the Latin American experience; of Mariano Picón Salas's *De la conquista a la independencia* (1944), in which the learned Venezuelan attempts to present a coherent panorama of the history of the arts and letters of Latin America in the period before the foundation of the republics.[6] Although the majority of these books are written in the style of *Kulturgeschichte*, the decade closes (and prepares the way for other investigations of the same orientation) with *The Labyrinth of Solitude* (1950), in which Octavio Paz, having read Heidegger's *Being and Time* (which had just been translated by José Gaos, a Spanish emigré and disciple of Ortega), interprets Mexican history and culture as products of rootlessness and alienation. Perhaps the exordium of Henríquez Ureña's *Literary Currents in Hispanic America* can be taken as programmatic for the decade:

In a time of doubt and hope, when political independence had not yet been fully achieved, the peoples of Hispanic America declared themselves intellectually of age, made their own life their "proper study," and set out on the quest for self-expression. Our poetry, our literature, was to be a genuine expression of ourselves. Europe was old; here was a new life, a new world for freedom and enterprise and song. Such was the intent and the meaning of the great Ode, the first of the *Silvas americanas*, published by Andrés Bello in 1823. Bello was not an improviser, not a romantic upstart; he was a scholar, a great grammarian,

6. See my bibliography for details on all these books.

a translator of Horace and Plautus, a pioneer explorer in the still virgin forests of medieval literature. His program of independence was the outcome of careful thought and assiduous labor. Since then, our poets and writers have persisted in the quest; in recent years, musicians, architects, and painters have joined in it. How such a duty has been fulfilled, how far such hopes have been attained, is to be the subject of these papers.[7]

Both of Henríquez Ureña's books, as well as those by Picón Salas, Zea, and Paz (in its second edition), were published by the Fondo de Cultura Económica in Mexico. Zea's work was part of a collection of monographs (Jornadas) distributed by that publishing house, in which, during the decade of the forties, numerous works of political, economic, and social exegesis appeared. Both *Historia de la cultura en la América Hispánica* and Carpentier's *La música en Cuba*, a book that is quite representative of the tendency outlined, were published in the collection Tierra Firme.[8]

Carpentier was commissioned to write *La música en Cuba* in 1944, while he was in Mexico on a vacation, by Daniel Cosío Villegas, the director of Tierra Firme.[9] But he had begun to research the history of Cuban music about the time he arrived in Havana, and had been stimulated by his trip to Haiti in 1943.[10] The re-

---

7. *Literary Currents in Hispanic America* (1945; reprint ed., New York, 1963), pp. 3–4. The book contains the Charles Eliot Norton Lectures delivered at Harvard, 1940–41. The first Spanish edition was published in Mexico City by Fondo de Cultura Económica in 1949.

8. All quotations from *La música en Cuba* are from this edition.

9. This was told to the author by Carpentier in Paris, in May 1973.

10. Carpentier has said in many interviews that he traveled to Haiti in the company of the French actor Louis Jouvet and his troupe. In Port-au-Prince, Carpentier, who is identified by the *Haïti-Journal* as "Délégué Culturel du Gouvernement de la Havane," gave a lecture at the Paramount Theater (see P.R., "La conférence de Alejo Carpentier," *Haïti-Journal*, December 21, 1943, p. 4). The lecture, "L'évolution culturelle de l'Amérique Latine" appeared in the *Haïti-Journal* on December 23 and 28, 1943. In the lecture Carpentier insists on the passionate nature of the Latin American people and their anti-Cartesian method of thinking and acting. He also refers to the Haitian revolution as the first popular uprising in the New World. Carpentier's interest in Haiti and voodoo goes as far back as 1931, when he mentioned in *Carteles* a book that he will later include in his bibliography of *La música en Cuba*: "William B. Seabrook, admirable American writer and traveler,

search and the resulting book grew out of the desire to discover and preserve Latin American—specifically Cuban—tradition and determine its particularities: "Devoid of an indigenous artistic tradition, very poor in popular plastic arts, little favored by the architects of the colonial period—if we compare her in this respect to other nations of Latin America—the island of Cuba has had the power to create nevertheless a music with a physiognomy of its own, which from the very beginning enjoyed an extraordinary diffusion" (p. 9). Carpentier was forced to recover that history from old chronicles, compendia, forgotten manuscripts and papers: "We embarked upon a patient examination of cathedral archives (mainly in Santiago and Havana), documents in churches and municipal governments, of parish cupboards (with brilliant success in Santiago, for example, and none in Santa María del Rosario), of manuscripts, documents, private libraries and collections, shelves in bookstores specializing in old books, totally exhausting newspapers, gazettes and colonial magazines" (p. 11). Carpentier also returned to Bartolomé de las Casas's *Historia de las Indias*, Fernández de Oviedo's *Historia general y natural de las Indias Occidentales*, Bernal Díaz's *Verdadera historia*. He also read the two colonial Cuban chronicles: Morell de Santa Cruz's *Historia de la Isla y Catedral de Cuba* and de Arrate's *Llave del Nuevo Mundo*. He pored over more recent works such as Bacardí's *Crónica de Santiago de Cuba*, Saco's *Memoria sobre la vagancia en Cuba*, and Roig de Leuchsenring's *Historia de La Habana*, not to mention the work of Ramiro Guerra and Fernando Ortiz. He also read histories of Haiti, such as Moreau de Saint-Méry's *Description de L'Isle de Saint-Domingue*, and others from which would come Monsieur Lenormand de Mézy and other characters of *The Kingdom of This World*. It would be difficult to exaggerate the importance of all this research to Carpentier's fiction.

History breaks into Carpenterian fiction as a result of the work done in writing *La música en Cuba*. ¡*Ecue-Yamba-O!*, "Histoire

author of *The Magic Island*, one of the most beautiful books written during recent times" ("Leyes de Africa," *Carteles*, December 27, 1931, p. 46).

de lunes," and "El milagro de Anaquillé" reflect, without historical precision, events that are contemporaneous, or nearly so, with their author. The research and the writing of *La música en Cuba* furnish Carpentier with a new working method, which consists of minute historical investigation, and creation from within a tradition that the author remakes himself with the aid of texts of different sorts. More specifically, *La música en Cuba* channels Carpentier's fiction into a new course, a search for those forgotten texts which will allow him to "finish" the incomplete biographies of obscure historical figures with the aid of rigorous documentation and almost verifiable chronology. All of Carpentier's stories from the forties stem from historical research carried out while writing *La música en Cuba*, and from this time on Carpenterian fiction will revolve around pseudo-historical biographies of figures whom Carpentier rescues from oblivion (with the notable exception of *The Lost Steps*, in which significantly, Carpentier himself is the object of the biography). In a sense, these novelistic biographies will be like notes written by Carpentier on the margins of innumerable volumes handled in many different places.

A brief glance at the stories written in the forties and at *La música en Cuba* reveals how closely the fictional texts follow the scholarly book. In "Oficio de tinieblas," for instance, one reads: "Such was the state of affairs in Santiago de Cuba when, with cross-bearing procession, frilled shirts, and gold-fringed uniforms, General Enna's funeral rites were observed."[11] In *La música en Cuba*, we find reference to the same event: "In 1851, owing to the funeral rites for General Enna, a mass of one hundred musicians gathered [in Santiago de Cuba] to play Mozart's Requiem" (p. 197). "Journey Back to the Source" tells of the youthful escapades of Marcial: "the young men went to the dance hall, where alluring *mulatas* in heavy bracelets were strutting about without ever losing their high-heeled shoes, even in the frenzy of the guaracha."[12] Carpentier had commented in *La música en Cuba* on the impor-

11. *Orígenes*, 1, no. 4 (1944), 34.
12. *War of Time*, trans. Frances Partridge (New York: Alfred A. Knopf, Inc., 1970), p. 117.

tance of the dance halls (casas de baile) in the development of
some forms of Cuban music: "the son of a good family sought
satisfaction for his [sexual] desires in the world of the daughters
and granddaughters of the slaves who had built the foundations of
his wealth, forgetting for a few hours the 'inferiority' of colored
people. This detail . . . explains the cross-breeding of certain
ballroom dances by habits brought from the lower to the upper
classes—from the dance hall to the manor house" (p. 111). Since
"Los fugitivos" shares with "Journey Back to the Source" the same
setting and the character Marcial, its dependency on the research
done for the writing of La música en Cuba is clear. "Like the
Night" not only contains references to Haitian history that obviously derive from the same line of investigation, but also makes
direct mention of musical activities related to the mingling of
popular forms from African and European sources, and includes a
character whose historicity is bound to be factual: "The sailors
from La Gallarda were dancing the zarambeque with enfranchised
Negresses, and singing familiar coplas—like the song of the Moza
del Retoño, wherein groping hands supplied the blanks left in the
words. . . . Our future chaplain was on his way to the harbor,
driving before him two mules with the bellows and pipes of a
wooden organ."[13] The Kingdom of This World reflects in even
greater detail Carpentier's research on the fusion of French,
African, and Spanish musical forms in Santiago de Cuba as a
result of the Haitian revolt of 1791: "A great pastoral ball—a
fashion now outmoded in Paris—was being planned, and for its
costuming all the trunks salvaged from Negro rapine were being
pooled. The palm-frond dressing-rooms were scenes of pleasant
encounters while some baritone husband, carried away by his role,
was immobilized on the stage by the bravura aria of Monsigny's
Le Déserteur. For the first time Santiago de Cuba heard the music
of passepieds and contredanses."[14] Carpentier goes as far as to in-

13. Ibid., p. 139. Further details may be found in my " 'Semejante a la
noche,' de Alejo Carpentier: historia/ficción," Modern Language Notes, 87
(1972), 272–85.

14. The Kingdom of This World, trans. Harriet de Onís (New York:

clude among his characters his most notable find in *La música en Cuba*, the composer Esteban Salas, a man completely forgotten by history but to whom Carpentier attaches a great deal of significance in the evolution of Cuban and even Latin American music.[15]

"The Highroad of Saint James," as Carpentier's publishers noted in a prologue to the first edition of *War of Time*, stems from the discovery of the name Juan de Amberes in an old census of Havana.[16] This discovery was obviously made while Carpentier was doing research for *La música en Cuba*. The story, in addition, offers an unusually revealing glimpse into Carpentier's working methods, because of what he himself stated about its composition in a note published with its initial printing in *Papel Literario de El Nacional*: "Upon finding, in an old list of residents of Havana in the sixteenth century, the name of Juan de Amberes, 'who played the drum when a ship was sighted,' it occurred to me that it would be amusing to write an imaginary biography of this character who left no further trace of his existence."[17] That the writing of imaginary biographies, based on as much solid historical documentation as possible, is a method of composition developed by Carpentier in writing *La música en Cuba*, there can be no doubt. This book is itself full of those marginal historical figures, always traveling from place to place in search of better fortune and caught in the entanglements of history. The best example of this is to be found in the account of the life of Juan Nepomuceno Goetz, an adventurous musician of whom Carpentier says: "Who was Juan Nepomuceno Goetz? . . . A very solid musician with a great deal of novelistic character in him" (p. 88).

Alfred A. Knopf, Inc., 1957), p. 63. All quotations, hereafter indicated in the text, come from this edition, except those from the prologue (not included in it), which are translated from the Mexican edition (Cía. General de Ediciones) of 1969.

15. See *La música en Cuba*, p. 60, and *The Kingdom of This World*, p. 65.

16. See "Nota de los editores," *Guerra del tiempo*, 2d ed. (Mexico City, 1966), p. 10. The first edition, of which the second is merely a reprint, is from 1958.

17. July 22, 1954, p. 1.

Another significant change takes place in Carpentier's writing during the forties, on which his research for *La música en Cuba* had a direct bearing: style. In *¡Ecue-Yamba-O!*, "Histoire de lunes," and even the scenario for "El milagro de Anaquillé," Carpentier's prose is laden with the stylistic tics of the extreme avantgarde: daring metaphors, oxymoronic adjectives, onomatopoeia, syncopated syntax. In the forties, Carpentier's prose begins to rid itself of these (although it will never lose them all) and to become the archaic, textured, and baroque prose for which he is known. The evolution is gradual and allows us to date approximately the composition of these stories.[18] It is evident, for example, that both "Los fugitivos" and "Oficio de tinieblas" still retain many traits that were found in the early works. But the Carpentier who writes the following in "Like the Night" is not the same one who wrote *¡Ecue-Yamba-O!*: "Con bordoneos de vihuela y repique de tejoletas, festejábanse, en todas partes, la próxima partida de las naves. Los marinos de La Gallarda andaban ya en zarambeques de negras horras, alternando el baile con coplas de sobado."[19] *Bordoneos, tejoletas, vihuelas, negras horras, coplas de sabado* are all archaic terms fallen into disuse today, archaisms that most modern readers would have to look up in a dictionary, or simply content themselves with the general antiquarian atmosphere the words evoke. The stylistic transformation could not be more telling, nor its relation to the reading of so many colonial texts more evident. From now on Carpenterian fiction will not be a mere evoking of the past, a fictionalized act of recovery of origins buried by time,

18. It is obvious that "Los fugitivos" and "Oficio de tinieblas" are the first stories written during the period, and Carpentier's decision not to include them in *War of Time* is a fairly good indication that he considered them somewhat dated. It seems to me that "Journey Back to the Source," "Like the Night," and "The Highroad of Saint James" were written, in that order, between 1944 and 1947 or 1948, though perhaps the last of these was touched up before its initial publication in *Papel Literario de El Nacional* in 1954. "Journey Back to the Source" first appeared as a pamphlet in 1944; "Like the Night" in *Orígenes*, 9, no. 31 (1952), 3–11.

19. *Guerra del tiempo*, p. 114. The English translation of this passage appears on p. 104 above.

but will become instead a pastiche of those texts within which Latin American memory is enclosed—a repetition and a textual reelaboration in the most tangible and concrete sense possible.

Carpentier's artistic enterprise in the forties became a search for origins, the recovery of history and tradition, the foundation of an autonomous American consciousness serving as the basis for a literature faithful to the New World. Like an American Ulysses, Carpentier sets forth in search of this goal through the winding roads and the turbulent rivers of the continent, but also through the labyrinthine filigrees of worm-eaten texts eroded by time and oblivion. The décalage in the itineraries of those two routes would eventually lead to a new kind of writing, but it is from their clash that Carpenterian literature of the forties is forged. What remains of all those travels is the texts, with their contradictions and ambiguities, their enigmatic repetitions and concealments. But in those texts the fate of Latin American literature was at stake, suspended between lost origins and history, between fable and chronicle, between the true presence of man in the kingdom of this world and the inscription of that presence in a writing that tenaciously resists all simplification. For in recovering history by in a sense allowing the texts that contain it to repeat themselves in his writing, Carpentier is reaching for that elusive Golden Age when fable and history were one.

A theoretical text remains from those years, one that absorbs other minor pronouncements published during the decade and that has attained unusual notoriety. Before passing on to an analysis of the works of the forties, it is necessary to examine in all of its problematic ramifications the prologue to The Kingdom of This World.

2

If one were to be persuaded by the facts that literary history offers at first glance, one would simply have to declare that since the publication of the prologue to The Kingdom of This World, Carpentier's work answers to what has been indistinctly called "magical realism" or "marvelous American reality."[20] But the facts that link Carpentier to that concept do not display the coherence and continuity that historical accounts of literary or critical movements demand. For example, when in 1955 Angel Flores published the article that disseminated the concept of magical realism throughout the academic world, Carpentier's name was not mentioned.[21] Only after the reprinting of the prologue in *Tientos y diferencias* (1964) and the uproar caused by the "boom" of the Latin American novel in the sixties did Carpentier begin to be considered as a precursor, a theoretician, and a practitioner of magical realism. Such deferred recognition is somewhat ironic, for by the sixties, when *Explosion in a Cathedral* appeared, Carpentier had not written any texts that could be associated with magical realism for many years, unless one were to lump together under that term all fictions which cannot be reduced to the strictest canons of nineteenth-century realism. It should be remembered that all the fantastic stories that Carpentier included in *War of Time* were written in the forties, and it is principally in those stories that critics find magical realism, taking 1958 as their date of original publication.[22]

The confusion, however, was not due entirely to the lack of knowledge of details such as these; a general absence of historical bearings in the formulation of magical realism itself was partly responsible. The theoretical import of the concept does not deserve to be recounted here, because, as shall be seen, magical realism lies in a theoretical vacuum; rather we can delineate the history of its attempts to become a viable theoretical foundation. The widespread use of the concept stems from its being part of a question that goes beyond literature: the question about the place

20. Although the first edition of *The Kingdom of This World* appeared in 1949 (Mexico City, EDIAPSA), the prologue was first published in *El Nacional*, April 8, 1948. The term "marvelous American reality" was first used by Carpentier in this essay,

21. "Magical Realism in Spanish American Fiction," *Hispania*, 38 (1955), 187–92. Many articles on this subject have appeared since 1955.

22. Carlos Santander (see bibliography), for example, is one of many who fall into this trap.

of the New World in the scheme of universal history, stemming from the dissemination of the works of Hegel and Spengler in Spanish. As applied to literature, however, the concept refers specifically to narrative fiction. It is an effort to account for a narrative that could simply be considered fantastic; that is to say, one that does not depend either on natural or physical laws or on the usual conception of the real in Western culture—a narrative, in other words, in which the relation between incidents, characters, and setting could not be based upon or justified by their status within the physical world or their normal acceptance by bourgeois mentality.

Magical realism appears at three different moments, the first in Europe and the last two in Latin America (I simplify, of course, for there are brief flourishings of the concept in Italy and the United States).

Magical realism first appears during the avant-garde years in Europe, when the term is used by Franz Roh in his *Nach-Expressionismus* (*Magischer Realismus*) (1925), and when the Surrealists, especially Breton in the first *Manifesto* (1924), proclaim the "marvelous" (*le merveilleux*) an aesthetic category and even a way of life. Only Borges's brilliant formulation in "El arte narrativo y la magia" (1932) appeared in those years in Latin America.

The concept appears again in Latin America in the forties, when it had already been forgotten in Europe. This new outbreak occurs around 1948, when Uslar Pietri and Carpentier, almost at the same time, dust off the old tag from the avant-garde years. (The two had been in Paris at the same time during the twenties and in Venezuela toward the end of the forties; Uslar, however, spent some time at Columbia University and it is conceivable that he renewed his contact with the term in New York, where it had been picked up by some art critics.)[23] Uslar Pietri adopts Roh's

---

23. See Alfred H. Barr, *Painting and Sculpture in the Museum of Modern Art* (New York, 1942) and *American Realists and Magic Realists*, ed. Dorothy C. Miller and Alfred H. Barr (1943; reprint ed., New York, 1969). Angel Valbuena Briones, "Una cala en el realismo mágico," *Cuadernos*

110   Alejo Carpentier

formula, but just in passing, in an essay that could only be of interest today to scholars concerned with the history of the Venezuelan short story.[24] Carpentier, on the other hand, adopts the Surrealist version and creates the term "marvelous American reality." What provokes the resurrection of these venerable oxymora in the forties is, on the one hand, the emergence of *mundonovismo* and its attempt to formulate the basis of a uniquely American literature, and, on the other, the desire on the part of writers who were associated with the avant-garde and the political left to preserve the legacy of Modernity from the attacks of another school—Socialist Realism (which, though created in the thirties, had sprung up again after World War II fueled by Existentialism and the renewed movement toward committed literature). José Antonio Portuondo, an advocate of Socialist Realism himself, deserves the credit for having shown the opposition between magical realism and Socialist Realism in a 1952 article rarely quoted today.[25]

---

americanos, 28, no. 5 (1969), 233–41, mentions the work of Massimo Bontempelli in Italy. For more information see Emir Rodríguez Monegal's "Realismo mágico vs. literatura fantástica: un diálogo de sordos," *Otros mundos otros fuegos: fantasía y realismo mágico en Iberoamérica. Memoria del XVI Congreso Internacional de Literatura Iberoamericana*, ed. Donald A. Yates (Pittsburgh, 1975), pp. 25–37, and his "Alejo Carpentier: lo real y lo maravilloso en *El reino de este mundo*," *Revista Iberoamericana*, 37 (1971), 619–49.

24. "What came to predominate in the story and to leave an enduring mark was the consideration of man as a mystery in the midst of realistic data. A poetic divination or negation of reality. Something that for lack of a better name could be termed magical realism" (*Letras y hombres de Venezuela*, Colección Tierra Firme, no. 42 [Mexico City, 1948], p. 161).

25. "La realidad americana y la literatura," in *El heroísmo intelectual* (Mexico City, 1955), esp. pp. 135–36 (under the heading "Realismo mágico"). Rodríguez Monegal, in "Lo real y lo maravilloso," has already noted the negative allusion to Sartre and his disciples in the prologue to *The Kingdom of This World*: "Nor are we going to say that certain partisans of a return to the real, of course, are right—the real takes on, then, a gregariously political meaning—when they do nothing but substitute for the tricks of the magician the commonplaces of the 'committed' intellectual or the eschatological delights of certain existentialists" (*El reino de este mundo*, p. 12).

The third moment of magical realism's appearance is more academically inspired; it begins with the 1955 article by Flores and continues during the sixties, when criticism searches for the Latin American roots of some of the novels produced during the "boom" and attempts to justify their experimental nature. Since Flores, these efforts, which frequently purported to be descriptions of literary phenomena indigenous to Latin America, have rarely gone beyond "discovering" the most salient characteristics of avant-garde literature in general. As a critical concept, the magical realism outlined by Flores has neither the specificity nor the theoretical foundation needed to be convincing or useful. How can Flores state, for instance, that "the practitioners of magical realism cling to reality as if to prevent 'literature' from getting in their way, as if to prevent their myth from flying off, as in fairy tales, to supernatural realms," and include Borges among them?[26] But it is perhaps unjust to ask such questions of an article that more than anything celebrates—belatedly—the coming of the avant-garde to Latin American literature. Critics after Flores, however, no longer attempted to celebrate Latin America's claim to such a legacy, but began to appropriate it. Carpentier's contribution was taken up. The results continue to be confusing and unsatisfactory. Luis Leal, for example, maintains that magical realism "cannot be identified with fantastic literature, just as it cannot be identified with either Surrealism or the hermetic literature of which Ortega spoke. Magical realism does not avail itself of oneiric motifs, as does Surrealism; nor does it disfigure reality or create imaginary worlds, as do those who write either fantastic literature or science fiction."[27] Such negations, though, seem somewhat hasty if one considers that Leal includes Juan Rulfo among the magical realists. If a character's ability to speak after death is not supernatural or fantastic, then a more rigorous definition than those offered by Leal is needed. And are there no oneiric sequences in Pedro Páramo or The Kingdom of This World? For Leal it is

26. "Magical Realism," p. 191.
27. Luis Leal, "El realismo mágico en la literatura hispanoamericana," Cuadernos Americanos, 25, no. 4 (1967), p. 231.

not only a question of marvelous reality existing in Latin America, but also that writers present that reality without doubting it, from the perspective of peasants or *llaneros* who steadfastly believe that the dead speak. But what could possibly be specifically Latin American in that?[28] Angel Valbuena Briones, in a more recent article with a somewhat broader documentary foundation than Leal's, also attempts to make Latin America the legacy of the avant-garde. Like Flores, Valbuena Briones includes in his roster Borges and Cortázar, without pausing to consider the critical difference between their literature and that of a primitivistic orientation in Asturias and Carpentier.[29] The dissemination of the concept after this third moment, as could be expected, has gone beyond the confines of the academic community, and some current writers have added to the confusion by invoking it in journalistic pronouncements.[30] Gabriel García Márquez, for instance, seems to allude to magical realism (one will never know with what degree of seriousness) in an interview, when he cites—among other "typical" events in the New World—the story of some Argentine fishermen who hauled in, in their nets, lions and elephants that a hurricane had yanked the day before from a circus in Comodoro Rivadavia.[31]

The relationship between the three moments when magical realism appears is not continuous enough for it to be considered a literary or even a critical concept with historical validity. The third moment is not directly related to the second, since Flores, in 1955, is evidently not aware of the formulations of Uslar Pietri, Carpentier, and Portuondo. Nor is the third moment related to the first, since Flores and his followers scarcely take notice of Roh's theories and usually deny Surrealism without evincing too

28. In Tzevetan Todorov's *Introduction à la littérature fantastique* (Paris, 1970), p. 59, one of the categories of the fantastic, the "marvelous," is defined precisely by the character's acceptance of the supernatural.

29. "Una cala en el realismo mágico."

30. José Donoso, for example, makes a passing reference to the concept in his *Historia personal del "boom"* (Barcelona, 1972), p. 86.

31. Armando Durán, "Conversaciones con Gabriel García Márquez," *Revista Nacional de Cultura* (Caracas), 39 (1968), 31.

much familiarity with it. Moreover, no one seems to have considered the existence of "El arte narrativo y la magia," nor to have
taken into account the theory of fantastic literature that Borges
offers in that essay and all of his works. But if historical continuity
is lacking in the manifestations of magical realism, there is an
underlying foundation which can at least account for its sporadic
appearance in Latin America during the twentieth century. It is
only by analyzing this common denominator in its various functions that the prolegomenon of Carpentier's theories may be
understood.

There are two versions of magical realism, sometimes distinguishable by the two terms mentioned: "magical realism" and
"marvelous American reality." The first, stemming from Roh's
book, is phenomenological; the second is ontological and of Surrealist background. Although in recent critical statements the two
are confused, it is worth differentiating between them.

Roh's book rests on one of those binary oppositions that
crystallize in historical criticism as overall theories of the evolution
of Western art (the best known are Classicism-Baroque and Ro-
manticism-Classicism). The two poles that constitute Roh's all-
encompassing opposition are Impressionism, which respects the
real world and faithfully reproduces its forms, and Expressionism,
in which the forms of the real world are submitted to the categories
of the spirit. In the first, the object imposes itself on the observer,
on the artist; in the second, the artist imposes his subjectivity on
the object. For Roh the history of art consists in a pendular movement between these two tendencies. But with the arrival of Post-
Expressionism, which is the period that interests Roh and that he
describes as magical realist, the dialectical opposition results in a
synthesis.[32] For Roh, magic resides in the wonder felt at the
perception of an object simultaneously in the process of becoming
and withdrawn from that process: "in Post-Expressionism we have
the miracle that the vibration of molecules—eternal mobility—the

---

32. See *Revista de Occidente*, no. 48 (June 1927), p. 281, or *Nach-
Expressionismus (Magischer Realismus): Probleme der neuesten Europäischen
Malerei* (Leipzig, 1925), pp. 29–30.

constant appearance and disappearance of the real, should secrete permanent objects. This miracle, of apparent persistence and duration, in the midst of general becoming, of universal dissolution, is what Post-Expressionism wishes to admire and bring out."[33] This Franciscan worldview that Roh attributes to Post-Expressionism is more reminiscent of Jorge Guillén's poetry than of fantastic literature.

> The balcony, the window-panes,
> A few books, the table.
> Only this? Yes.
> Concrete marvels,
> Joyous material that
> turns into tangible
> surface its forever sad
> and invisible atoms.[34]

The minute describing of the real to undermine the familiarity of habitual perception is characteristic of aesthetics at the turn of the century, from Azorín and Borges to the Russian Formalists, who maintained that the shocking metaphor of the Futurist poet forced the reader to perceive with a fresher and clearer vision the disparate objects that it approximates.[35] What varies in all these cases is perception and the stance or the perspective assumed before phenomena, a perception which, by the unusual nature bestowed upon it by such a stance, casts both the gesture of

33. *Revista de Occidente*, p. 281.

34. *Cántico*, 1st complete ed. (Buenos Aires, 1950), p. 21.

35. "Art is understood to be a means of destroying perceptive automatism, the image does not attempt to facilitate the comprehension of its meaning, but seeks to create a particular perception of the object, the creation of its vision, not of its recognizance" (Boris Eikhenbaum, "La théorie de la 'méthode formelle,'" in *Théorie de la littérature: Textes des formalistes russes*, ed. and trans. Tzvetan Todorov [Paris, 1965], p. 45). Ortega called this tendency "Infrarealism": "The simplest [metaphor] may be described as a change of perspective. From the standpoint of ordinary human life things appear in a natural order, a definite hierarchy. Some seem very important, some less so, and some altogether negligible. To satisfy the desire for dehumanization one need not alter the inherent nature of things. It is enough to upset the value pattern and to produce an art in which the small events of life appear in the foreground with monumental dimensions" (*The Dehumanization of Art, and Other Essays on Art, Culture, and Literature* [Princeton, 1968], p. 35).

perceiving as well as its object into the realm of the miraculous and the devotional—the "concrete marvels" of Guillén, the "magic of being" to which Roh sometimes appeals. It is the interaction of these two elements, subjectivity and reality, mediated by the act of perception, which generates the alchemy, the magic. According to Roh, however, reality remains unaltered.

Although Roh is to be credited for having coined the term "magical realism" and for having isolated a salient characteristic of avant-garde aesthetics—the aesthetics of the minuscule—and notwithstanding the fact that his book was read avidly in Latin America in a translation disseminated by the Revista de Occidente, his version of the concept is not the one that received the most attention among writers of the New World. Carpentier perhaps remembered Roh's book in creating the oxymoron "marvelous reality" (the "marvelous," however, derived from Surrealism) and in some marginal details. In Uslar Pietri, aside from the use of the term itself, there is hardly a visible trace of Roh.

In a review following the publication of Roh's book in Spanish, Antonio Espina makes some observations that may help to account for the German's lack of popularity among the Latin American writers (leaving aside the fact that Roh's theories referred specifically to the plastic arts, painting in particular). Espina notes that the aesthetics defined by Roh is "a halfway aesthetics, resolutely installed between shapeless sensualism and superstructured schematism. It is an idealist realism, . . . magical insofar as it creates a new spirit whose form is contained in the supernatural, the super-real. And it is called magical precisely so as to avoid its falling into and being confused with religious realism."[36] Roh himself, upon recalling years later the genesis of the term, stresses this point: "In an article written in 1924 I coined the phrase Magischer Realismus (magic realism)—magic of course not in the religious-psychological sense of ethnology."[37] Roh's flaw, from a Latin American point of view, lies in his attempt to subtract from the phenomenon he describes a transcendental and religious im-

36. Revista de Occidente, no. 49 (July 1927), pp. 112–13.
37. German Art in the 20th Century, trans. Catherine Hutter (Greenwich, Conn., 1968), p. 112.

pulse that appears inherent to it, in order to preserve the phenomenological and formalistic purity of his theory. But Guillén's
poem is titled "Beyond," and Roh's terminology speaks of devo-
tions and miracles. Roh's formulations do not have a greater impact
in Latin America because the miracle that Latin American writers
seek is not a neutral one but one through which they can fuse
with a transcendental order—an order, however, that is no longer
provided by Western tradition. Because Roh does not consider a
transcendental order other than the one offered by Western
tradition, he must opt for his neutralism and phenomenology; that
is, for differences in the act of perception, not for changes in the
observer. This is clearly the reason for his also calling his magical
realism *Neue Sachlichkeit*, new objectivity. It is also the reason
for his using the term "magic," whereby he covers with a veil of
neutrality the transcendental element of what he describes, and in
the last analysis preserves the separation between the world and
the artist. For, in spite of the distinction that Roh attempts to
establish between his magic and that of ethnology, the fact remains
that "magic" is the term used by the pioneers of ethnology at the
end of the nineteenth century and early in our own to describe
religious rituals and certain beliefs which the researcher did not
share. The term "magic" serves as an instrument by means of
which the observer takes distance from the "supernatural" that he
describes from a European perspective and for the understanding
of Europeans.[38]

The Latin American writer preferred to place himself on the
far side of that borderline aesthetics described by Roh—on the
side of the savage, of the believer, not on the ambiguous ground
where miracles are justified by means of a reflexive act of perception, in which the consciousness of distance between the observer
and the object, between the subject and that exotic other, generates estrangement and wonder. Carpentier states in the prologue

38. See Nur Yalman, "Magic," *International Encyclopedia of the Social
Sciences* (New York, 1968), IX, 521. For a detailed criticobibliographical
introduction to magic, see the first chapter of Marcel Mauss's *Sociologie et
anthropologie* 4th ed. (Paris, 1968), pp. 3–9. Lévi-Strauss's critical introduction to this volume is basic for a theoretical understanding of the problem in
more modern terms.

to *The Kingdom of This World:* "To begin with, the sensation of the marvelous presupposes a faith" (p. 11). The tendency toward that faith, toward that transcendental element that Roh attempted to avoid with the adjective "magical," is found in the other version of magical realism: the ontological one, which is the one to have enjoyed the most favor in Latin America.

As we saw in Chapter 2, European Modernism, since the period Roger Shattuck called "the banquet years," constituted a search for a vision of the world different from, if not opposed to, that provided by Western culture. The products of that search are well known: primitivism, interest in the unconscious, a reaction against positivism and Neo-Kantism, the apogee of Bergsonian vitalism, irrationalism (Unamuno, for example), the popularity of Nietzsche. All of these manifestations are accompanied by a highly significant phenomenon: the unusual development of ethnology, which tends to decenter European thought, history, and art by describing in rich detail cultures hitherto considered barbarous (the work of Tylor, McLennan, Spencer, Lang, Lévy-Bruhl, Frazer, Frobenius). These tendencies were widely disseminated throughout the Hispanic world from 1923 on, owing to the editorial policies of the *Revista de Occidente* and the work of Ortega y Gasset. In *Las Atlántidas* (1924), Ortega made the following observations and predictions:

In the past twenty-five years, the horizons of history have been expanded enormously—so much that Europe's old pupil, accustomed to the circumference of her traditional horizon, of which she was the center, cannot manage now to fit within one perspective the huge territories suddenly added. If up to the present "universal history" has suffered from an excessive concentration on a single gravitational point, toward which all processes of human existence converged—the European point of view—at least for one generation, a polycentric universal history will be elaborated, the totality of the horizon will be obtained by a simple juxtaposition of partial horizons, with heterogeneous radii, which, held as in a bunch, will yield a panorama of human destinies quite similar to a cubist painting.[39]

39. *Las Atlántidas* (Madrid, 1924), p. 31. Note Ortega's obvious anti-Hegelianism in those years. For details on this see Ciriaco Morón Arroyo, *El sistema de Ortega y Gasset* (Madrid, 1968), esp. pp. 299–303.

The impact of ethnological investigations in Europe was enormous. The European artist began to see the possibility of fulfilling his desire to be another and to observe the world from a perspective other than his own. Latin Americans, who since Romanticism, as was seen in Henríquez Ureña, wanted to establish the autonomy and uniqueness of their culture, immediately took up this tendency (Asturias wrote in Paris his *Leyendas de Guatemala*, which derived from his ethnological studies with Georges Raynaud and were published in 1930 with a prologue by Paul Valéry). Afro-Cubanism and *indigenismo*, as we saw before, were the immediate reaction to this movement. While in painting and sculpture there was a break with what is considered to be the European tradition by means of a reduction to primary colors and forms, in the narrative the decentering took place at the level of causality—the cause and the effect relation by which the plot is organized that had been the cornerstone of all narrative since Aristotle. In *¡Ecue-Yamba-O!*, for instance, we saw how Carpentier shuffled scenes, rather than organizing them, although the plot of the novel itself remains fairly linear. Consideration of how Borges approached this problem might be illustrative.

In "El arte narrativo y la magia" Borges states that every narrative process is magical, and alludes to Frazer's popular book *The Golden Bough:* "That procedure or ambition of ancient men has been held together by Frazer in a convenient general law, that of sympathy, which stipulates an inevitable link between distant things, whether because their shape is similar—mimetic or homeopathic magic—or because of an anterior proximity—contagious magic. Kenelm Digby's ointment was an illustration of the second, for it was applied not to the bandaged wound, but to the guilty steel that inflicted it—while the wound, without suffering the rigors of barbaric cures, healed" (p. 88).[40] Narrative fiction, states

40. All quotations from this essay are translated from *Discusión* (Buenos Aires, 1966), pp. 81–92. For an introduction to the problems raised by this essay, see Emir Rodríguez Monegal, "Borges and *la nouvelle critique,*" *Diacritics*, 2, no. 2 (1972), 27–40, and my "With Borges in Macondo," *Diacritics*, 2, no. 1 (1972), 57–60. It is significant that Frazer is included in the *Antología de la literatura fantástica* (Buenos Aires, 1971), by Borges, Silvina Ocampo, and Adolfo Bioy Casares.

Borges, is governed by an analogous law: "That dangerous harmony, that frenzied and precise causality, also rules in the novel. . . . The fear that a frightful event will be beckoned by its mention is not pertinent or useful in the chaotic disorder of the real world, but this is not true of a novel, which should be a precise game of observances, echoes, and affinities" (pp. 89–90). Borges does not deny causality, nor does he offer a new and exotic causality, as would many European and Latin American writers at odds with what they took to be European trends of art and thought. He underlines, instead, the similarity between narrative procedure and the primitive's homeopathic cure. Causality in fiction is not determined by a natural law, nor by its reflection of the order of the physical world, since for Borges it is the real world that lacks accord and congruence.

Aristotle had formulated in his *Poetics* the basis for a narrative teleology analogous to that of Borges: the plot is a coherent whole, with beginning, middle, and end; nothing can precede the beginning nor exceed the end; and every incident issues from a previous one by a law of necessity. The key to that basic concept of the *Poetics*, however, is not merely aesthetic but the very foundation of Aristotelian philosophy: the cosmological argument. Just as the cosmos is ruled in its movement by a series of potential actions that remit to an immovable prime mover—an indifferent and hieratic god—the structure of poetry, which is an imitation of action, should reflect the same principle of composition.[41] In one way or another, with variations in the mode of presentation of that reflection, all versions of realism assume such a specular relation between art and the world. The whole avant-garde was pitted against that realistic bias. But instead of breaking the mirror to create a series of discontinuous images, Borges polishes it to make it reflect more keenly a complete and ordered image—an image, however, which is not a reflection of a real order, but a whole in itself. The magic defined by Borges in his essay does not depend, as in Roh, on the privileged observation of a concordant world, organized down to

41. Georg Lukács has noted this magical aspect of Aristotelian theory, see his *Estética I, vol. II, La peculiaridad de lo estético* (Barcelona–Mexico City, 1966), p. 54.

its most minute particles and for which we feel wonder or devotion. Borges's marvels are not concrete and static, but dynamic functions of the self, of the being that emerges from his fictions, a sort of minor Aristotelian god who thinks himself and invents a world. The term "magic" no longer neutralizes the transcendental element implicit in such a vision, but underlines it, not without an irony very characteristic of Borges. We accept causality in the narrative without objections, with blind faith, in the same way that the primitive accepts the efficacy of the homeopathic cure. In both there is a leap over the chasm of chaos and arbitrariness by an act of faith. This is why Borges considers theology a form of fantastic literature, perhaps the highest, since in it there is assumed the existence of an ordering principle that lends coherence to the universe:

I compiled at one time an anthology of fantastic literature. I have to admit that the book is one of the few that a second Noah should save from a second flood, but I denounce the guilty omission of the major and unexpected masters of the genre: Parmenides, Plato, John Scotus Erigena, Albertus Magnus, Spinoza, Leibniz, Kant, Francis Bradley. In fact, to what do the prodigies of Wells or Edgar Allan Poe amount —a flower that comes to us from the future, a corpse subjected to hypnosis—confronted with the creation of God, with the laborious theory of a being that in some way can be three and solitarily endures everlastingly *without time?* What is the bezoar compared to the notion of a pre-established harmony? What is the unicorn before the Trinity? Who is Lucius Apuleius before the Great Vehicle's proliferators of Buddhas? What are all the Arabian nights of Scheherazade paired with a Berkeley argument? I have venerated the gradual invention of God; also of Heaven and Hell (an immortal remuneration, an immortal punishment). They are admirable and curious designs of man's imagination.[42]

In the Borgesian universe, fantastic literature and theology are reflections of the same fictitious pattern. But, for Borges the creators of order in the universe of writing are not perfect beings but creatures of dubious motivation. In "Death and the Compass" it is Scharlach, the criminal, who has contrived the false order that

42. *Discusión*, pp. 172–73.

entraps his own specular reflection, that other writer, the vain and pompous detective Lönnrot. In "The Garden of Forking Paths" the Chinese spy is the one to have wrought an order, and who by the death of Stephen Albert manages to communicate to the enemy the fatal message. In "The Secret Miracle" the reader never knows if a higher being has allowed the condemned writer a year in which to finish his play, or if the playwright himself glimpses the entire plot a second before he dies. In Borges's fraudulent theology the minor gods are the detective, the criminal, the spy, and, of course, the writer. They all confirm and at the same time deny the existence of a superior being, perhaps more perfect than they, but also more perverse. They confirm it in the arduous labor of construction and deny it in the fact that they all die the moment they are able to contemplate the totality of that order that they contrive in all its tenuous and labyrinthine complexity. As in the tragedy, vision precedes death; final conjunction brings about definitive disjunction—the irrevocable crossing to the other shore, the king dead in his labyrinth.

Though Borges's essay is clearly related to the upsurge in ethnological studies, it does not lead to the kind of polycentrism forecast by Ortega, but to the absence of a center. If the magic of primitive man is homologous in its functioning to narrative process in Western culture, then a common structure underlying all cultures must be posited. Another conclusion to be drawn is that the visible order of European culture conceals another order, one which neither differs from nor is superior to any other. In Borges, therefore, there is not only an absence of primitivism, but a denial of the very possibility of any sort of primitivism. In that respect, Borges's essay is more akin to Surrealism than to ethnology, since the Surrealists presupposed the existence of a subconscious order which could crop up in dreams or in the flow of automatic writing.[43] Surrealists maintained, in other words, that

43. Although here the relationship between Surrealism and Freud is obvious (and the contacts between the Viennese doctor and Breton well known), it is not as simple as that. The fundamental difference between Freud and Breton stems from the materialism of the latter, who does not accept the

free association was not free, in the same way that Borges proclaims that causality in the narrative, although arbitrary with
respect to the real world, is systematic and rigorous within itself.
From such a tightly sealed perspective there is no possible break
through which the component elements of fiction may be questioned: in the case of Borges, because for him all literature is
fantastic; in the case of the Surrealists, because the new order revealed is one with the universe. All vessels are communicating.
What Borges and Surrealism seem to suggest is the existence of
a kind of supralogic, or universal superlogic. Magic, dreams, hal-
lucinations, the narrative, are not the exclusive domain of this or
that culture, but superficially dissimilar although homologous
manifestations of being. Breton and Borges seem to propose the
existence of a sort of onto-theology.

One must hasten to add, however, that the distance between
Borges and Surrealism is significant and sets him quite apart from
Carpentier. Surrealism, as Octavio Paz explains, aspired to a form
of monism that would erase all mediations between man and the
universe.[44] In Borges, whose philosophical roots are sunk in a
transparent idealism, there persists a duality between the smooth
order of the spirit and the murky chaos of the world. What is
pertinent here, nevertheless, is that Borges's work, like Surrealism,
posits defining qualities of man and history in a universal sense,
against a centralized vision of history of Hegelian orientation, or
a polycentric history of Spenglerian design.

For Carpentier, as well as for the majority of Latin American
artists and intellectuals, it was not so. They opted for the polycentrism announced by Ortega, which was supported by books

---

separation that psychoanalysis established between the "work of dreams" and
reality: "As a consistent materialist, Breton tries to show that space, time
and the principle of causality are identical in dreams to what they are in
reality, i.e., laws of objective forms of existence, and not properties of our
mind" (Jean-Pierre Morel, "Breton and Freud," *Diacritics*, 2, no. 2 [1972],
19). Jean Starobinski speaks of a "magical materialism" in Breton in "Freud,
Breton, Myers," *L'Arc*, 34 (1968), 95.

44. *The Bow and the Lyre*, trans. Ruth L. C. Simms (Austin, 1973), esp.
p. 153.

with persuasive theories like *The Decline of the West* and which produced a different version of magical realism, though sharing the same ontological thrust.

In spite of his fascination with Surrealism at one time in his life, Carpentier never completely succumbs to Breton and his theories. On the contrary, Carpentier endeavors to isolate in his concept of the "marvelous" something which would be exclusively Latin American. If Borges and Breton define a mode of being in which the savage and civilized man strip themselves of their differences, Carpentier searches for the marvelous buried beneath the surface of Latin American consciousness, where African drums still beat and Indian amulets rule; in depths where Europe is only a vague memory of a future still to come. As he says in the prologue to *The Kingdom of This World*, "because of its virginal landscape, its gestation, its ontology, the Faustic presence of Indians and blacks, because of the Revelation constituted by its recent discovery, by the fruitful racial mixtures that it favored, Latin America is far from having exhausted its wealth of mythologies" (pp. 15–16). Besides his attacks against certain Surrealists, which are echoes of skirmishes in the thirties, Carpentier's essay affirms that the marvelous *still* exists in Latin America, and *reveals* itself to those who believe in it, not to those who would apprehend it by a reflexive, self-conscious act.[45] The appeal to faith and to history ("still"), cast Carpentier's formulations in a Spenglerian mold. Even Carpentier's attacks on the Surrealists are based on Spengler, and it is only by returning to *The Decline of the West* that we can understand the meaning that Carpentier assigns to the marvelous and his definition of the faith that sustains it.

As we noted in Chapter 2, Spengler posited that cultures were

45. Emir Rodríguez Monegal, in "Lo real y lo maravilloso," and Klaus Muller-Bergh, in "Corrientes vanguardistas y surrealismo en la obra de Alejo Carpentier," *Revista Hispánica Moderna*, 35 (1969), 323–40, have studied in detail Carpentier's break with the Surrealists. Rodríguez Monegal is right when he speaks of the political tensions that emerged within the group, but in my view, as was explained in Chapter 2, Carpentier can never accept Surrealist doctrine because it clashed with the Spenglerian conception of man and history he had absorbed through the *Revista de Occidente*.

like organisms that underwent homologous evolutions until they disappeared (the world as history). While this idea, the most popularized one of the German philosopher's, is pertinent to Carpentier, the point here is that, contrary to Hegel, Spengler maintained that the decline of a culture began to manifest itself when self-reflexiveness occurred:

The feeling of strangeness in these forms [of culture], the idea that they are a burden from which creative freedom requires to be relieved, the impulse to overhaul the stock in order by the light of reason to turn it to better account, the fatal imposition of thought upon the inscrutable quality of creativeness, are all symptoms of a soul that is beginning to tire. Only the sick man feels his limbs. When men construct an unmetaphysical religion in opposition to cults and dogmas; when a "natural law" is set up against historical law; when, in art, styles are invented in place of the style that can no longer be borne or mastered; when men conceive of the State as an "order of society" which not only can be but must be altered—then it is evident that something has definitely broken down.[46]

For Spengler, as for Carpentier and other Latin American intellectuals who fell under his spell, the New World found itself in a moment of its historical evolution—a moment of faith—prior to the moment of reflexivity, while Europe felt estranged from the forms of its own culture and searched in laws and codes of universal pretensions, like Surrealism, the mystery of creation irretrievably lost. The polarity between the European and the primitive established by Spengler, and its correlative polarity, incredulity/faith, is the same that he established between civilized man and the man of culture: "The essence of every Culture is religion, so—and consequently—the essence of every Civilization is irreligion. . . . And, correspondingly, the ethical sentiments belonging to the form-language of the megalopolis are irreligious and soulless also."[47] Here we have, precisely, the arguments used by Carpentier to attack Surrealism, since, according to him, the movement had become a "code of the fantastic," attempting to

46. *The Decline of the West*, vol. I, *Form and Actuality*, trans. Charles Francis Atkinson (New York, 1926), p. 353.
47. Ibid., p. 358.

rule as a universal ethic and aesthetic; here, too, the basis for his opposing the vibrant rural world of Latin America to the limp and inanimate urban constructs of Surrealism. Spengler is the common ground of Carpentier's works of the thirties and forties; the differences are only a matter of narrative strategy. Whereas in ¡Ecue-Yamba-O! and "Histoire de lunes" he attempts to situate the narrative focus or source within an unreachable African world of beliefs to which his own consciousness has no access, now he will attempt to clear a space from within which he can lay claim to a more broadly conceived faith. The works of the forties are also grounded on a theological view of history and the narrative process except that such theology has become better refined and its contradictions more skillfully concealed. Magical realism, or "marvelous American reality," is but a new theology of fiction bent on bridging the gap between source and product, between maker and cosmos. If in ¡Ecue-Yamba-O! the dissolution of such theology was visible in the fissures and cracks apparent in the product, in "magical realism" its dissolution is more intimate, and fictional—and, from a literary point of view, clearly more successful, even if it is doomed to give way, because of its irreconcilable contraditions to a new formulation in the fifties.

In one of the few analytical studies devoted to magical realism, Fernando Alegría noted the onto-theological import of Carpentier's theories in the prologue to The Kingdom of This World: "The magic of Carpentier and Asturias can be a genuine metaphysical experience, that is to say, a personal commitment not only to the kingdom of this world, but also to the other world."[48] Carpentier's concept of the marvelous or of magic rests on an onto-theological assumption: the existence of a peculiar Latin American con-sciousness devoid of self-reflexiveness and inclined to faith; a con-sciousness that allows Latin Americans to live immersed in culture and to feel history not as a causal process that can be analyzed rationally and intellectually, but as destiny. From the perspective to which that mode of being aspires, fantasy ceases to be incongru-

48. "Alejo Carpentier: realismo mágico," Humanitas, no. 1 (1960), 356.

ous with reality in order for both of them to turn into a closed and spherical world without cracks or ironic detachment, glimpsed, as Carpentier says in the prologue to The Kingdom of This World, "by virtue of an exaltation of the spirit that leads it to a mode of borderline state" (p. 11).

In Borges, as has been seen, the religious nature of the narrative process is underlined, since it demands a transcendental principle to give it order, and engenders the existence of a specific being to elaborate it. But the irony in Borges's prose always leaves unconnected and godless his rigorously fortuitous universe of writing. That being and that god which demand to be posited refract and disperse like a ray of light—the multiple and always elusive Borges of his fiction (the plural "I" of the "Poem of the Gifts"), the minor gods mentioned before. Carpentier, on the contrary, seeks to ground the transcendental principle that narrative demands on the faith offered by the culture and history of Latin America, in the wealth of mythologies and beliefs that he considers still to be in force in the New World. But Carpentier's essay, at least in the terms in which he posits the problems, is fraught with contradictions that are made evident by the very writing of the essay. For, if we carry to its ultimate consequences the Spenglerian system within which Carpentier maneuvers, a discursive analysis of "marvelous American reality" excludes all possibility of spontaneity stemming from faith and lack of self-consciousness. If marvelous reality only reveals itself to the believer, what hope can Carpentier have of elevating himself to the state required in order to perceive it? The question of reflexivity and dualism remains open: miracles stay on the other side, the side of the Afro-Antillians whom Carpentier supposes to be believers and who populate his fiction. The question is, Where does Carpentier stand? Not only the Carpentier who travels to Haiti in 1943, but the Carpentier implied by his stories. It is only fair to say that Carpentier's efforts reach at this point an impasse common to Latin American writing. Does the Latin American lose his authenticity when he sets pen to paper and allows the ink to flow? Does this essence vanish or dissolve in the process of writing?

As a critical concept, magical realism depends on philosophical questions much broader than literature, though its thoughtless application has also sidestepped literature's own complexity and specificity. Lukács, after many pages of his *Esthetics* devoted to the study of the origins of literature from a Marxist anthropological perspective, comes to the conclusion that "it is essential to aesthetics to conceive the reflected reproduction of reality precisely as a reflection, while magic and religion assign objective reality to its system of reflections and demand the corresponding faith. In their later evolution the consequence of this is the radical opposition arising from the aesthetic reflection's constitution as a closed system (work of art), while all reflection of a magical or religious nature refers to a transcendental reality."[49] On a theoretical level, Carpentier's error, as well as that of the *mundonovistas* and their academic followers, has been to confuse levels: attributing simultaneously to literature an objective reality and a nexus with an assumed transcendental level—Latin American nature, Latin American consciousness, and so forth. It has already been seen that Roh's phenomenological version, and Spenglerian and Surrealist variations of the ontological version (these two united by a Romantic and Naturalistic substratum), offer a clear transcendental side—veiled in the first case by the term "magic," underlined in the second. But the desire to abolish the difference between the self and the other, between observer and the cosmos, is undermined in both cases precisely by the use of terms such as "magic" or "marvelous." All magic, all marvel, supposes an alteration of order, an alterity—assumes the other, the world, looking back at us from the other side. Octavio Paz has explained in this way the ambivalent nature of magic: "On the one hand, it tries to put man in an active relation with the cosmos, and in this sense it is a sort of universal communion; on the other, its practice merely implies the quest for power. 'Why' is a question that magic does not ask and one that it cannot answer without being transformed into something else: religion, philosophy, philanthropy. In short, magic is a conception of the world but it is

49. *Estética*, II, 40.

not an idea of man. That is why the magician is a figure torn between his communication with the cosmic forces and his inability
to reach man, except as one of those forces. Magic affirms the
brotherhood of life—an identical current runs through the universe
—and denies the brotherhood of men."[50] Is the writer's detachment not the same? But this is not the only distancing characteristic of magic that weakens Carpentier's effort; the implica-
tion that the marvelous is found in America and not in Europe
has the same effect. To assume that the marvelous exists only in
America is to adopt a spurious European perspective, since it is
only from the other side that alterity and difference may be discovered—the same seen from within is homogeneous, smooth,
without edges. The best efforts of well-intentioned academic
criticism to use the label "magical realism" fall into this contradiction. The occultist tradition that reaches us from Romanticism
may have some Latin American peculiarities, but not radically
different characteristics. Perhaps one of these is precisely that
writers such as Carpentier and Asturias have felt the need to proclaim magic to be here, attempting to evade the alienation of the
European for whom magic is always there. But in this attempt
there is a double or meta-alienation; it may very well be that
magic is on this side, but we have to see it from the other side
to see it as magic. What is peculiarly Latin American is the
round trip, that utopia suspended between here and there—perpetual voyage, charting a course to that always elusive Antilla. The
error lies in the erring, in the wandering. The question, then, is
not whether the Latin American loses his authenticity as he puts
pen to paper, but the validity of the question itself, its foundation
and its necessity.[51]

Carpentier's erring is, of course, manifest only on a theoretical
level, where his formulations claim a status of provable truth, not
on a literary level. To demand of literature the truthfulness of
such formulations would amount to assigning to it an objective

50. *The Bow and the Lyre*, p. 44.
51. For a detailed analytical history of this prejudice see Jacques Derrida,
De la grammatologie (Paris, 1967), pp. 149–202.

reality, a concrete link with its referent. On the other hand, if we may ask coherence of Carpentier's arguments in his essay, we may not do the same of his stories: it is permissible to assume that there is no concrete link, no magical nexus, between literature and the universe, but we cannot deny literature's desire to establish such a relationship, or pretend that it does not exist. What on an essayistic level are losses, on a literary one are gains. This is what Borges appears to be suggesting in his works; that the literary text moves within the space between affirmation and denial—between a foreseen order and an announced dissolution.

Besides, set in the context of the stories to which it alludes, specifically *The Kingdom of This World*, Carpentier's prologue may lose the assertive status that it claims and assume a more strategic position within his writing.

3

Carpentier's stories of the forties are distinguishable from his earlier production and from that which immediately follows them by their historical setting; costumes, objects, known incidents, and other aspects serve to designate a past epoch which in most cases is the late eighteenth and early nineteenth centuries. "Oficio de tinieblas," "Los fugitivos," and "Journey Back to the Source" take place in the Cuba of the early nineteenth-century sugar boom and *nouveau riche* aristocracy it created; *The Kingdom of This World* in Saint-Domingue and Santiago de Cuba at the turn of the century; "Like the Night," which thoroughly problematizes the relationship of narrative and history, in six different moments from Homeric Greece to the present; and "The Highroad of Saint James" in Flanders, France, Spain, and Cuba during the sixteenth century. In "Like the Night," the most radical experiment with history and the narrative, history is fictionalized in spite of and because of the precision with which it is used in the story. All of the incidents and characters in the middle section are historical, but the beginning and ending are taken from *The Iliad*, bringing back all allusions, as it were, to a horizontal textual level and making the historical and the literary texts one uninterrupted continuum. The denial of literature by the sally into historical texts turns into an affirmation of literature through the very circularity of the textual voyage. However, if the problems posited by this story are extended from historical writing to history (the succession of real events), it is soon evident that "Like the Night" represents nothing more than Spenglerian doctrine taken to its ultimate consequences. Lukács has already pointed out, in a recent autocritical prologue to his *Theory of the Novel*, that "by radically historicising all categories and refusing to recognise the existence of any suprahistorical validity, whether aesthetic, ethical or logical, [Spengler] . . . abolished the unity of the historical process: his extreme historical dynamism finally became transformed into a static view, an ultimate abolition of history itself, a succession of completely disconnected cultural cycles which always end and always start again."[52] The plot of "Like the Night," set against the background of six distant historical events, is but a projection of this static view of history. What unites all those apparently disconnected cycles, however, is nature, which is the only permanence or suprahistorical category left standing after Spengler's historical whirlwind. That static history characterizes Carpentier's fiction in the forties. It is not simply that Carpentier offers a decentered anti-Hegelian view of history, but that the historical process appears as a dynamic cycle of repetitions that results in a static and permanent image, like the spokes of a turning wheel which project static images of themselves. This is why the historical world presented by Carpentier in his stories is always one of imposing buildings and ruins, a world of palaces and dismantled mansions, the two poles of a universe in constant construction and demolition. But where is that permanence, that achronic island always seen in a cross-current of time? If the result of historicity in Carpentier is ahistoricity, what of his avowed project to rescue the origins and history of Latin America? And, if in the latter that island is caught in the cross-currents of history, how does it leave a trace on the historical texts that Carpentier recovers and on his own narrative work?

52. *The Theory of the Novel*, trans. Anna Bostock (Cambridge, Mass., 1971), p. 16.

To answer these questions we must return to Carpentier's prologue, particularly to that section where he alludes directly to the composition of *The Kingdom of This World:*

Without my having systematically intended it, the text that follows corresponds to this kind of concern [the concern with "marvelous American reality"]. A succession of extraordinary events is narrated there, which occurred in Saint-Domingue in a specific period that does not reach the span of a lifetime, allowing the marvelous to flow freely from a reality which has been followed in every detail. For it must be kept in mind that the story about to be read is based on extremely rigorous documentation. A documentation that not only respects the true history of the events, the names of characters—including secondary ones—of places and even streets, but that it also conceals, beneath its apparent atemporality, a minute correspondence of dates and chronology. [P. 16]

Anyone who has read Carpentier with some care will not hesitate to take these words quite seriously. And, in fact, even a cursory knowledge of the historical circumstances narrated in *The Kingdom of This World* seems to confirm his statements. The story relates fairly well-known incidents: Macandal's rebellion, Bouckman's uprising, the French colonists' arrival in Santiago de Cuba, General Leclerc's campaigns, Henri Christophe's agitated monarchy. Even a closer preliminary investigation will reveal that M. Lenormand de Mézy was indeed a rich colonist from the northern region of Limbé in Saint-Domingue; that, in fact, it was at his plantation that Macandal's revolt began, as in *The Kingdom of This World;* that Rochambeau succeeded Leclerc on the island; that Labat and Moreau de Saint-Méry were, in fact, contemporary historians of the events; that Cornejo Brelle was actually Corneille Breille; that Esteban Salas, as we saw, was a composer from Santiago whom Carpentier discovered while doing research for *La música en Cuba;* that there was a slave called Ti Noël.[53] Carpentier, however, claims much more. He speaks of

53. Corroboration of many of these details may be found in Moreau de Saint-Méry, *Description topographique, physique, civile, politique et historique de la partie française de l'Isle de Saint-Domingue,* originally published in 1797 (Philadelphia) and now available in Blanche Maurel and Étienne Taillemite's three-volume edition (Paris, 1958); Pierre de Vaissière, *Saint-Domingue: La société et la vie créoles sous l'ancien régime, 1629–1789*

not having sought the marvelous in a systematic way, alleging that it "flows freely from a reality which has been followed in every detail," and he refers to a "minute correspondence of dates and chronology." In other words, what Carpentier claims is perfectly consistent with the rest of his theory—the marvelous that emerges spontaneously from American historical reality is ciphered onto his text.

If we submit Carpentier's accounts of some of the memorable incidents in the story to textual comparison with their historical sources, Carpentier's method in writing The Kingdom of This World quickly emerges—a method that does not vary in the least from the one used in "Like the Night" and other stories of the forties. And this is the collage, the superimposing and collation of historical texts. Let us take two scenes to which we shall later return for other reasons. In chapter 8 of part I, we read the following description of Macandal's execution:

The fire began to rise toward the Mandingue, licking his legs. At that moment Macandal moved the stump of his arm, which they had been unable to tie up, in a threatening gesture which was none the less terrible for being partial, howling unknown spells and violently thrusting his torso forward. The bonds fell off and the body of the Negro rose in the air, flying overhead, until it plunged into the black waves of the sea of slaves. A single cry filled the square:

"Macandal saved."

Pandemonium followed. The guards fell with rifle butts and the howling blacks, who now seemed to overflow the streets, climbing toward the windows. And the noise and screaming and uproar were such that very few saw that Macandal, held by ten soldiers, had been thrust head first into the fire, and that a flame fed by his burning hair had drowned his last cry. When the slaves were restored to order, the fire was burning normally like any fire of good wood, and the breeze blow-

(Paris, 1909), which is particularly useful for its sketch of the life of the colonists, although much of it taken from Moreau de Saint-Méry; and V. Schoelcher, Vie de Toussaint-Louverture (Paris, 1889), which narrates many episodes that Carpentier's story skips and contains several detailed chapters on the period up to 1791. Very useful because it gathers documents that Carpentier could have had access to in Havana is José Luciano Franco, comp., Documentos para la historia de Haití en el Archivo Nacional (Havana, 1954), the introduction to which is also very useful.

ing from the sea was lifting the smoke toward the windows where more than one lady who had fainted had recovered consciousness. There was no longer anything more to see.

That afternoon the slaves returned to their plantations laughing all the way. Macandal had kept his word, remaining in the Kingdom of This World. [Pp. 35–37]

If we turn now to the *Description topographique, physique, civile, politique et historique de la partie française de l'Isle de Saint-Domingue*, published in 1797 in Philadelphia by Moreau de Saint-Méry ("that ruddy, pleasure-loving lawyer of the Cap, Moreau de Saint-Méry," as Carpentier calls him in the novel, p. 58), we find the following paragraph:

Le hasard ayant voulu que le poteau où l'on avait mis la chaîne qui le saisissait fut pourri, les efforts violens que lui faisaient faire les tourments du feu, arrachèrent le piton et il culbuta par-dessus le bucher. Les nègres crièrent: *Macandal sauvé*; la terreur fut extrême; toutes les portes furent fermées. Le detachement de Suisses qui gardait la place de l'exécution la fit évacuer; le geolier Massé voulait le tuer d'un coup d'épée, lorsque d'après l'ordre du Procureur-général, il fut lié sur une planche et lancé dans le feu. Quoique le corps de Macandal ait été incinéré, bien des nègres croyent, même à présent, qu'il n'a pas péri dans le supplice.[54]

It would be just as naive to think that Carpentier simply copies the scene as not to notice that his text is but a careful recasting of it. The narrative text discretely supplements or suppresses details of the historical text, whose integrity is "respected," even in the rational explanation of the Mandingue's actual fate, as opposed to the slaves' beliefs. The same procedure is found in another well-known scene—"The Solemn Pact," chapter 2, part II—when Bouckman summons the slaves to a clearing in the Bois-Caiman to plot his uprising. It is a stormy night ("The claps of thunder were echoing like avalanches over the rocky ridges of Morne Rouge," p. 47):

Suddenly a mighty voice arose in the midst of the congress of shadows, a voice whose ability to pass without intermediate states from a deep to a shrill register gave a strange emphasis to its words. There was

54. Moreau, *Description*, II, 630–31.

much of invocation and much of spell in that speech filled with angry inflections and shouts. It was Bouckman, the Jamaican, who was talking. Although the thunder drowned out whole phrases, Ti Noël managed to grasp that something had happened in France, and that some very powerful gentlemen had declared that the Negroes should be given their freedom, but that the rich landowners of the Cap, who were all monarchist sons of bitches, had refused to obey them. At this point Bouckman let the rain fall on the trees for a few seconds, as though waiting for the lightning that jagged across the sea. Then, when the thunder had died away, he stated that a pact had been sealed between the initiated on this side of the water and the great Loas of Africa to begin the war when the auspices were favorable. And out of the applause that rose about him came this final admonition:

"The white men's God orders the crime. Our gods demand vengeance from us. They will guide our arms and give us help. Destroy the image of the white man's God who thirsts for our tears; let us listen to the cry of freedom within ourselves." [Pp. 47–49]

Turning now to V. Schoelcher's *Vie de Toussaint-Louverture*, published in Paris in 1889, we read:

C'était une nuit de violent orage, les éclairs sillonaient le ciel et les échoes des mornes retentissaient des éclats de la foudre. Boukman, fidèle aux superstitions africaines, fait des invocations magiques, et, comme inspiré du Grand Esprit, il prononce cet oracle au milieu de la tempête:

Bon Dié qui fait soleil, qui clairé nous en haut, qui soulevé la mei, qui fait grondé l'orage.

Bon Dié là, zot tendé, caché dans zon nuage, et là li gardé nous, li vouait tout çà blancs fait.

Bon Dié blancs mandé crime et pa nous vlé benfèts.

Mais Dié la qui si bon ordonnin nous vengeance; li va conduit bras nous, li ba nous assistance.

Jettè potrait Dié blancs qui soif dlo dans zié nous; couté la liberté, qui parlé coeur nous tous.[55]

55. Schoelcher, *Vie*, pp. 30–31. Schoelcher offers the following translation to standard French: "Le bon Dieu, qui fait le soleil qui nous éclaire d'en haut, qui soulève la mer, qui fait gronder l'orage, entendez-vous, vous autres, le bon Dieu est cachè dans un nuage, la il nous regarde et voit tout ce que font les blancs. Le bon Dieu des blancs commande le crime, par nous il veut les bienfaits! Mais Dieu qui est si bon nous ordonne la vengeance. Il va conduire nos bras, nous donner assistance. Brisez l'image du Dieu des blancs qui a soif de l'eau dans nos yeux, écoutez la liberté qui parle au coeur de nous tous" (p. 31).

Examples such as these could be multiplied until the entire text of the story, or very nearly, could be set against some historical text: the scene of the Mass of the Assumption, in which Cornejo Brelle appears before the tormented Christophe; the burial of the black king in the damp cement of his fortress, and so forth. But this is not all that Carpentier claims when he refers to the free flow of the marvelous. The history that he narrates is verifiable, documented, one could even say that it is merely repeated in his text. Yet Carpentier states that history has a marvelous concordance and coherence. But who establishes the link between events, who selects? Here it is not merely a question of aesthetic selection, since Carpentier speaks of a free flow that excludes such a selection for aesthetic purposes. It is a question of *relation*, of the connection between incidents in history and in the text of the story.

The unity of *The Kingdom of This World* has preoccupied critics who have wondered if the story is nothing but a series of extraordinary scenes collected somewhat chaotically, without a unifying plot. A first reading of the story produces this impression, for in fact there is no visible thread between its different parts. There is an overall movement, but its force is not clearly discerned.[56] What does the first part have to do with the third, where M. Lenormand de Mézy does not even appear? Ti Noël unifies the various historical events with his presence, but because of his passivity he hardly qualifies as more than a mere witness; he is certainly not a protagonist in the sense of a maker of events or a character who polarizes the action. Carpentier nonetheless speaks of a "succession of extraordinary events" in the prologue. But what principle, source, or reason determines the succession? If, as Carpentier states, the composition of the story emerges

56. See Emil Volek, "Análisis e interpretación de *El reino de de este mundo* y su lugar en la obra de Alejo Carpentier," *Unión* (Havana), 6, no. 1 (1969), 98–118. This essay is full of interesting suggestions and formulates a contrapuntal structure that I take to be a worthwhile descriptive metaphor. But Volek does not address himself to the question of what rules that counterpoint, simply alluding to a "semantic structure" derived from Wolfgang Kayser that I find unsatisfactory.

from a free flow, then the disposition of history, its concordance, if such exists, cannot be the result of a Borgesian process of selection; there must be, if we are to believe Carpentier, another source of order.

If history is one of the most important components of Carpenterian fiction in the forties, the complicity between history and nature is another. In "Oficio de tinieblas" there are earthquakes and plagues that scourge Santiago de Cuba at significant dates. In "Los fugitivos" Perro and Cimarrón live according to the cycles of nature. In "The Highroad of Saint James" it is the constellation of that name which guides the pilgrim. In "Journey Back to the Source" the Marquise drowns in the Almendares River in spite of the warning of the black sorceress to beware of "anything green and flowing" (p. 112). In "Like the Night" it is suggested that history consists of rhythmical repetitions such as those of darkness and light. In *The Kingdom of This World* the complicity of history and nature pervades the whole story. The night of "The Solemn Pact," as we just saw, is stormy, premonitory, and Bouckman's words seem to come out of the claps of thunder that echoed through the hills. Macandal avails himself of poisoned herbs and mushrooms to kill animals and colonists, thus instigating the first slave revolt. On this level we can speak of a sort of symphonic concordance, in the style of Romantic or Renaissance poetry, between events and nature. There is yet another level on which this complicity is manifested: Ti Noël's prophecies. Recalling the African folk tales told to him by Macandal, Ti Noël states: "One day he [Macandal] would give the sign for the great uprising, and the Lords of Back There, headed by Damballah, the Master of the Roads, and Ogoun, Master of the Swords, would bring the thunder and lightning and unleash the cyclone that would round out the work of men's hands. In that great hour—said Ti Noël—the blood of the whites would run into the brooks, and the Loas, drunk with joy, would bury their faces in it and drink until their lungs were full" (pp. 28–29). These prophecies are fulfilled first in the "The Solemn Pact," when thunder accompanies the propitiatory ritual announcing the revolt, and later in "The Call of the Conch Shells," when the slaves massacre the colonists and the blood literally runs, and at the finish, when a "green wind" does wipe everything off the face of the earth to "round out the work of men's hands."

The unity of the work is not given by a causal process, but, as Volek has suggested, it is a contrapuntal unity, not linear but reiterative. Nature, summoned by the powers of Macandal and Bouckman, rules history and the disposition of the story. The same is suggested in "Journey Back to the Source," where Melchor, the sorcerer, by waving his magic wand puts in motion the regressive vision of the Marquis's life. At this level, the complicity between nature, history, and Carpentier's text is clear. But this is a thematic level, or an exclusively textual and fictional one, suggested from within the story. On the other hand, when analyzing the relationship between historical texts and *The Kingdom of This World*, we saw that the night of "The Solemn Pact" was indeed a stormy one, and research will verify that in fact Macandal began his revolt by using poisons. These events seem not to be merely the result of a textual need, but real historical facts: "[Macandal] became notorious during his desertion for poisonings that spread terror among the blacks and subjected all of them to his will. He openly taught this despicable art, had his agents in all points of the Colony, and death spread its wings at his slightest command."[57] Are the correspondences with history in the text fictional or factual?

Although the story does not say so explicitly, the night of the Solemn Pact was August 14, 1791, while that of the Call of the Conch Shells, eight days later, as the story does say, was August 22, 1791. The dates are verifiable: "A priest of the Voodoo cult, Bouckman, a black native of Jamaica, mysteriously called together a large number of the slaves, since he exercised enormous power over all who came near him, for the night of August 14, 1791, at a clearing of the Bois-Caiman. . . . The uprising broke out eight days after the ceremony."[58] Carpentier himself relates the incident

57. Moreau, *Description*, II, p. 630.
58. Franco, *Documentos*, pp. 22–23.

138   Alejo Carpentier

and gives the dates in *La música en Cuba*: "On the night of August 14, 1791, a grave event takes place in Saint-Domingue. Voodoo drums beat in the Bois-Caiman. Under a torrential downpour, two hundred delegates from the slave garrisons of the Northern Plain, called by the inspired Bouckman, drink the luke-warm blood of a black pig, thereby pledging allegiance for the coming rebellion. Eight days later the hoarse voice of the conch shells flew over the mountains" (p. 100). To be even more precise, August 14, 1791, was a Sunday; August 22, a Monday.[59]

There is nothing startling about the rigorous historical precision of these dates until it is realized that the only date specifically mentioned in the story is August 15 (chapter 5 of part III, "Chronicle of August 15"). This is the Ascension Sunday when Henri Christophe, tormented by his conscience, falls thunder-struck before the vision of Cornejo Brelle. The recurrence of the days is suggestive, and even more so when it is realized that the next chapter (6 of part III, "Ultima Ratio Regum"), when the king commits suicide, also takes place on a Sunday—"At sunset the following Sunday" (p. 110)—August 22, of course. It can be substantiated, in fact, that Henri Christophe suffered a sort of stroke on August 15, 1820: "One Sunday, a few weeks later [after the execution of Brelle; the footnote indicates here that 'August 15 is the date usually given'], the king suddenly presented himself at the little parish church at Limonade and sent word to the priest that he desired to hear mass. The astonished curate made ready, but as he entered the chancel he was horrified to see the king rise, clutching his prie-Dieu, mutter the name of Corneille Brelle and fall forward in a faint, opening a deep gash in his forehead as it struck the pavement."[60] Indeed, the story appears to follow a rigorous chronological scheme, revealing here quite a coincidence provided by history:

59. I have determined days of the week by consulting the "Easy Reference Calendar" in *Whitaker 1973* (London, 1972), pp. 194–95.

60. Charles Moran, *Black Triumvirate: A Study of Louverture, Dessalines, Christophe—The Men Who Made Haiti* (New York, 1957), pp. 145–46.

1791	Sunday	Sunday	Monday
	August 14 ("The Solemn Pact")		August 22 ("The Call of the Conch Shells")
1820	August 15 ("Chronicle of August 15")	August 22 ("Ultima Ratio Regum")	

The coincidence lies in the fact that the ceremony or ritual announcing the downfall of the white regime happens on a Sunday, August 14, while the uprising that sets off the revolt occurs on a Monday, August 22; and the ceremony including the incident that foretells the downfall of the black regime happens on a Sunday, August 15, and the death of the king occurs the night of the following Sunday, August 22. The coincidence is startling and links in a rhythm of cyclical repetitions the events of the story; but it is not completely historical, since Henri Christophe did not die on Sunday, August 22, but on Sunday, October 8, 1820.[61] Besides, on the one hand we have a Sunday and a Monday and on the other two Sundays. A fissure, a divergence between history and fiction begins to open. But there is more.

The suggestion of an order lurking beneath the chronology of the novel becomes stronger when we realize that "The Solemn Pact," which is chapter 2 of part II, is the tenth chapter in the novel if one counts consecutively, and thus "The Call of the Conch Shells" is the eleventh, the "Chronicle of August 15" is the twentieth, and "Ultima Ratio Regum" is the twenty-first. The symmetry is alluring, and if we return to part I of the story with this suspicion of order, we soon realize that the execution of Macandal, who initiates the sequence of historical events, happened according to the text, "one Monday in January" (p. 33)— that is to say, the first day of the week of the first month of the year. On the other hand, if we appeal to history we shall see that Macandal was executed on January 20, 1758, a Friday.[62] We may also note that the chapter relating Macandal's execution, "The

61. Hubert Cole, *Christophe, King of Haiti* (New York, 1967), p. 286.
62. Moreau, *Description*, II, 630.

Great Flight," is the eighth of the first part of the story, while the events of the preceding chapter, when Macandal suddenly appears to the slaves during a voodoo rite, have to fall, unless chronology fails us, on December 25 (Christmas), 1757—a Sunday.[63] Chapter 8, a Monday in January 1758; Bouckman's uprising is planned for eight days later, a Monday, while all the propitiatory rituals occur on Sunday: 8 will always have to be a Monday, beginning of the cycle and of the week. The 7 will be a Sunday; chapter 7 of part I, December 25 (2 + 5 = 7), 1757. Being twelfth, December, like Sunday, seventh, will be the month of rituals; January will be thirteenth, like Monday, eighth, the day of events. In an excellent article on *The Lost Steps*, Eduardo G. González has shown how the week functions as an ordering principle in that novel, and how Sunday is "Ending and Beginning, opening toward the realm of creativity."[64] In *The Kingdom of This World*, Sunday will be the day of great propitiatory rituals; Monday, the day of events and beginnings. The missing Sunday in the previous chart is the one when Macandal appears on a Christmas day during the voodoo ceremony, a scene whose parallel with the one in which Brelle appears could not be more clear. The missing Monday is then (although it is not narrated) the one when the Cap is taken by Christophe's opponents in 1820—the morning after the Sunday night of his death. The great event, then, is the occupation of the Cap and Sans-Souci by the rebels, who would later be defeated by Boyer.

Let us summarize:

Sundays

Ti Noël's visit to Macandal's cave, where the Mandingue prepares his poisons; death of the first animals ("That very same Sunday," p. 21).

---

63. Historically, it did not, in fact, happen on December 25, although it is true that a *calenda* was organized to celebrate the birth of a male heir at the Dufresne plantation (Dufrené in the story), as may be verified in Moreau. The story does not say that it was a Christmas day, but the suggestions are so strong that it must be taken as such.

64. "*Los pasos perdidos*, el azar y la aventura," *Revista Iberoamericana*, 38 (1972), 612.

Death of M. Lenormand de Mézy's first wife, on a Pentecost Sunday (p. 24).

December 25, 1757, Macandal's appearance in the middle of a voodoo ritual; birth of M. Lenormand de Mézy's first male son.

August 14, 1791, "The Solemn Pact."

August 15, 1820, Mass of the Ascension; appearance of Brelle; Christophe's stroke.

August 22, 1820, drumbeats and revolts at the Cap calling for the death of Christophe.

Mondays

Macandal's execution on a "Monday in January"; "The Great Flight."

August 22, 1791, Bouckman's uprising.

August 23, 1820 (not narrated directly), rebellion against Christophe; taking of Le Cap and Sans Souci; fall of Christophe's government.[65]

The significance of this pendular movement between Sundays and Mondays, as well as that between December and January (Macandal's metamorphosis also takes place in January, p. 26) is the ritualistic repetition to which Carpentier has submitted history and his text. The correspondences multiply as one investigates further. For example, the novel has a total of twenty-six chapters. The numerical center, then, would be the thirteenth, "Santiago de Cuba," when M. Lenormand de Mézy and Ti Noël arrive at the Cuban city sometime (probably December) in 1791. The symbolical importance of Santiago will be seen shortly, but at this

65. The insistence on that month of August is not gratuitous. August is the month when the danger of hurricanes is greatest in Haiti, so it could be conjectured that the story also ends in August (the eighth month); see Ivan Ray Tannehill, *Hurricanes*, 2d ed. (Princeton, 1943), p. 63. Carpentier, as we saw, has a hurricane destroy the San Lucio *batey* in ¡Ecue-Yamba-O!, and the same thing happens in other stories, most notably in *Explosion in a Cathedral*. In 1947, Fernando Ortiz published a detailed book on the mythology of the hurricane, with numerous pages devoted to the Antilles, that Carpentier most probably knew; see *El huracán: su mitología y sus símbolos* (Mexico City, 1947).

point we need only note the strong suggestion that Santiago is not merely the center in the formal sense just seen, but also the chronological center of the events. If we review the chronology outlined, the following may perhaps be conjectured: we know that Macandal was executed in January 1758, and further, that chapter 7 takes place in December 1757. So, since chapter 6 states that four years have elapsed since the first adventures of the Mandingue (p. 29) the narrative must then have started in 1753 (I would never discount here that $5 + 3 = 8$; $8 =$ beginnings). This being the case, thirty-seven years pass before 1791 (which would be the thirty-eighth year in the story); it seems quite plausible to infer from this that thirty-seven years elapse between this chapter and the end of the story, making the conclusion occur in 1828, during Boyer's presidency (it does end during his presidency, but it has been impossible to determine the year, although it must have been sometime after 1824, when the princesses arrive in Italy).[66] The action, then, would have lasted seventy-five years (a "period that does not reach the span of a lifetime," Carpentier says in the prologue). The rondure and symbolic suggestions of these numbers are too strong not to provoke conjectures about their correspondences: $3 + 7 = 10$; $2 + 8 = 10$; $7 + 5 = 12$. All of them suggest completion, the completion of cycles—order.

There are more numerical correspondences that tend to corroborate these conjectures and are in themselves quite revealing. For instance, if the four-part division is abandoned and chapters are numbered consecutively, several possibilities arise. If Chapter 13 is the mathematical center, then the story is divided into two unequal parts, of twelve and thirteen chapters respectively. Upon

66. Cole, *Christophe*, p. 276. The princesses arrive at Pisa, not Rome, as the story has it. The end of the story has to occur after 1826, when Boyer's Rural Code is issued. Its effects in *The Kingdom of This World* are seen in the arrival of the surveyors, and other details outlining the conduct of the mulattoes. It is conceivable, however, that since the government's seat is now in the south, in Port-au-Prince, implementation of the Code was delayed until 1828. I have not been able to corroborate this suspicion. For more details on this period, see James G. Leyburn, *The Haitian People* (New Haven, 1966), pp. 66 ff.

closer observation, though, the following emerges: chapters 12 (II, 4) and 25 (IV, 3) round off cycles. In chapter 12, after the insurrection of August 22, 1791, in which his house was destroyed, M. Lenormand de Mézy appears hidden in a dry well; in chapter 25, after the surveyors plunder the remains of the house and its furnishings, Ti Noël appears, taking refuge first in the chimney and then under a table amid the debris. Chapter 13 (II, 5) is the last in which M. Lenormand de Mézy appears alive; chapter 26 (IV, 4) marks both the death of Ti Noël and the end of the narrative. In chapter 13, M. Lenormand de Mézy is seen, after the destruction of the house, in a storeship, a kind of Noah's Ark (the word in Spanish for this kind of vessel, urca, is significantly close to arca), which takes him and other colonists to Santiago de Cuba. In this same chapter, in Santiago, a city famous for its carnivals, there is a series of carnivallike scenes, theatrical performances, the surrender to the summons of the flesh on the part of M. Lenormand de Mézy and his fellow colonists. In chapter 26 we have the apocalypse, the "green wind" that razes everything after a series of omens that are taken directly from the Apocalypse in the Bible. Is it not significant then that chapter 13 is the fifth of part II $(5 + 2 = 7)$ and that chapter 26 $(2 + 6 = 8)$ is the fourth of part IV $(4 + 4 = 8)$? That 7 and that 8, that Sunday and that Monday—Carnival and Apocalypse—are the two poles between which the action of the story stands suspended. It is an action divided into two perfect cycles of twelve chapters each:

1 2 3 4 5 6 7 8 9 10 11 12 13 14 15 16 17 18 19 20 21 22 23 24 25 26

       1st cycle   2d cycle

And in view of this, could it be dismissed as purely accidental that, counting consecutively, the Sunday of Macandal's apparition occurs in the seventh chapter of the first cycle; while Brelle's apparition on Ascension Sunday happens in the seventh chapter of the second cycle? And also that Macandal's and Christophe's deaths occur in parallel chapters?

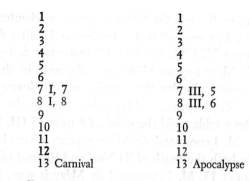

1		1	
2		2	
3		3	
4		4	
5		5	
6		6	
7	I, 7	7	III, 5
8	I, 8	8	III, 6
9		9	
10		10	
11		11	
12		12	
13	Carnival	13	Apocalypse

The overall significance of the numerological and symbolic system on which the action of *The Kingdom of This World* is based could not be clearer. To begin with, it is evident that Carpentier presents history as a series of cyclical repetitions. In the next-to-last chapter of the novel, Ti Noël becomes aware of these repetitions when, already demented and senile, he wishes to escape into a world of ants: "He made the mistake of becoming an ant, only to find himself carrying heavy loads over interminable paths under the vigilance of big-headed ants who reminded him unpleasantly of Lenormand de Mézy's overseers, Henri Christophe's guards, and the mulattoes of today" (p. 144). There are, moreover, networks of "echoes and affinities," to use Borgesian terminology, some of which have already been pointed out, that transcend the arithmological system,[67] and a complex system of Biblical and liturgical resonances that begin with the very title of the story and encompass the numerical concordances. The name Ti Noël suggests that the slave was born on Christmas Day, and if to this is added his having fathered twelve children, he appears as a sort of *figura Christi*; Macandal appears on Christmas Day; M. Lenormand de Mézy's wife dies on Pentecost Sunday; Brelle appears on Ascension Sunday; and Palm Sunday is mentioned near the end of the story. All of the repetitions and Christian rituals are an attempt to make the action fit into a cycle like that of the liturgical year—an attempt, in other words, to fuse the dynamics of the cosmos and writing. It must be kept in mind that Carpentier

67. See Volek, "Análisis," p. 106.

pretends to insert history into this vast mechanism, a history manifested through the rigorous chronology and documentation that he speaks of in his prologue and that has been briefly sketched above. The numerical concordance between history and the cosmos represents—as in medieval literature, as in Dante—a fusion between the latter and nature, between history and the work of an omnipotent divinity who has created the universe perfect in measure, number, and weight:

> Creatori serviunt omnia subjecta,
> Sub mensura, numero, pondere perfecta.
> Ad invisibilia, per haec intellecta,
> Sursum trahit hominem ratio directa.[68]

Magic, the marvelous, would be the relation between the numerical disposition of historical events and the text, a relation between those two orders whose transparent mediator would be Carpentier. By this relation the separation between being and cosmos mentioned by Paz when speaking of Surrealism could be

68. This poem, from the *Praedicatio Goliae*, was probably written by Walter of Châtillon; quoted by Ernst Robert Curtius, *European Literature and the Latin Middle Ages*, trans. Williard R. Trask (New York, 1953), p. 504. In a study devoted to numerical symbolism and concordances in the *Divine Comedy*, Charles S. Singleton asks himself the inevitable question, For whom has the poet intended such a complex and concealed system? His answer deserves to be repeated here: "One may perhaps suggest the answer to such a question by turning it another way, by directing it, say, to Chartres Cathedral, to some sculptured and finely finished detail in the stone work on the roof of that great edifice, a detail as carefully wrought as any on the façade itself, but which, being where it is, might never be seen again by human eye, once the roof was finished and the workmen had withdrawn—unless someone should climb up to repair that roof and happen to take notice of it. But may we think that any such consideration even occurred to the master who designed that detail or to the stonemason who fashioned it with loving care? We may not, for we know that such an edifice was not addressed to human sight alone, indeed not primarily to human sight at all. He who sees all things and so marvelously created the world in number, weight, and measure, would see that design, no matter where its place in the structure; and would surely see it as a sign that the human architect had indeed imitated that created Universe which the Divine architect had wrought for His own contemplation, first of all, and for that of angels and of men" ("The Poet's Number at the Center," *Modern Language Notes*, 80 [1965], 10).

transcended and the relation itself could constitute the credible, documentable miracle sustaining the faith that Carpentier speaks about in his prologue. The presence of such a relation could also allow one to speak of the marvelous as being inscribed in the text without the benefit of a systematic effort on the part of a reflexive consciousness to do so—the revelation of a sort of automatic writing through which a Pythagorean and Platonic cosmos left the harmonious figures of the luminous wakes of its gyrations. Carpentier's text would constitute only a fragment of that immense book which would include in its dense and complex concordance the total design of the universe. But Carpentier's hand has already been shown in the act of violating that assumed harmony between history and nature in order to force history into the design of its own text, into the itinerary of his own writing. In the case of Henri Christophe's death, for instance, which did not occur on Sunday, August 22; or Macandal's death, which occurred not on a Monday in January, but on a Friday. Moreover, how far can the coherence of Carpentier's numerology be taken? If one accepts that chapter 13 signifies the Carnival, which would be in accord with the liturgy, since 13 would mean January, the month of the Carnival's beginning, how can it be that Macandal dies in January? Should his immolation not have taken place in December? One could always argue, of course, that Macandal's death, which marks a beginning, is a victory for the slaves who believe that he was not killed, that his death is a Resurrection. The problem, however, is that once the signifying resonances of events and their assigned places in the system expand and disseminate, the very order of the system begins to crumble into chaos: "To perceive the distance between the human and the divine," Borges says, "one need but compare these coarse, trembling symbols that my fallible hand scribbles on the cover of a book, with the organic letters inside—punctual, delicate, extremely black, inimitably symmetrical."[69] The numerical disposition in Carpentier's text does not lead ultimately to faith, but rather to positing the existence of one of Borges's minor gods who assemble a complex and precise game of affinities only to perish in the kingdom of this world on

69. *Ficciones* (Buenos Aires, 1956), p. 87.

completing their work. Both Borges's and Carpentier's fictional worlds are those of man after the fall in search of reintegration and unity. And in fact, the one who metaphorically rules *The Kingdom of This World* is Satan, the Fallen Angel who speaks in the story's epigraph through the lines of a Lope de Vega play; the Satan who appears at the end of "The Highroad of Saint James"; the same one who obviously governs the dissipated life of M. Lenormand de Mézy and is worshiped by the sensuous Pauline Bonaparte and the arrogant and ambitious Christophe, the Satan who within the text—in the web of its history—attempts to exert control over all destinies. But all these systems are simulacra, semblances of order, like those created by the Devil in Calderón's *The Wonder-Working Magician*—schemes that fail or are revealed as lies and imposture. The text is the creation of an ornate order with pretensions of permanence, but constituted with the bad faith of its ultimate and imminent dissolution, as when its system is pressed to the limit of meaning and dissolves into chaos and formlessness. Its creation involves in the end a faith in the tangible and ephemeral, an abandonment to the letter in its concrete manifestation. Liturgical and grave—Calderonian—Carpentier erects discrete monuments only to find himself trapped in them, like Henri Christophe dead and turned to stone within his labyrinth (baroque writing will always be an epitaph chiseled on ruins, for all those thirteens announce nothing but annihilation and disillusionment). The prologue-epilogue to *The Kingdom of This World* is also part of the fiction, of the baroque masquerade. It is Carpentier's first/last mask in the text. The affirmation of a presence which simultaneously denies and affirms itself, it is the Carnival. His prologue is the false formulation of an American ontology, of the apocryphal presence of a marvelous reality.

4

It might be convenient at this point to ask if the disposition found in *The Kingdom of This World* is characteristic of that story only and to analyze in greater detail that axis-scene that divides the text into two parts.

The Carnival, in all its surrender to the desires of the flesh, the theatrical, and the joyous inversion of hierarchies, is what characterizes that central scene, that axis on which the story pivots. The scene is a baroque moment of frenzy and unrestrained sensualism before the forebodings of death—the affirmation of the most tangible aspects of life as reaction to the threat of imminent annihilation:

While others more foresighted than they had got their money out of Santo Domingo and had gone to New Orleans, or were starting new coffee plantations in Cuba, those who had salvaged nothing reveled in their improvidence, in living from day to day, in freedom from obligations, seeking, for the moment, to suck from everything what pleasure they could find. The widower discovered the advantages of being single; the respectable wife gave herself over to adultery with the enthusiasm of an inventor; the soldiers rejoiced in the absence of reveilles; young Protestant ladies came to know the flattery of the boards, appearing before the public in make-up and beauty spots. All the bourgeois norms had come tumbling down. What mattered now was to play the trumpet, give a brilliant performance in a minuet trio, or even strike a triangle for the greater glory of the Tívoli orchestra. [Pp. 61–62]

The saturnalia is accompanied by pompous religious devotion. *Horror vacui* thrusts the colonists toward the most tangible aspects of the cult, to the theatrical rituals and the ornate temples—the signs and symbols of the ecclesiastical baroque: "Once a Mason, he [M. Lenormand de Mézy] now began to distrust the triangle. And so, accompanied by Ti Noël, he took to spending long hours groaning and rasping out ejaculatories in the Santiago Cathedral" (p. 64); "The baroque golds the human hair of the Christs, the mystery of the richly carved confessionals, the guardian dog of the Dominicans, the dragons crushed under saintly feet, the pig of Saint Anthony, the dubious color of St. Benedict, the black Virgins, the St. Georges with buskins and corselets . . ." (p. 65). The detail that all this occurs in *Santiago* de Cuba cannot be overlooked. For the colonists, the city is like the end of the high-road of Saint James—the arrival in Paradise, the ceasing of desire and motion toward a specific goal and the reveling in atemporality and dissolution. If, as analyzed before, history appears as a cycle of inexorable repetitions, the axis-scene, the center of the story, is the celebration, the joy and the fear, of finishing one cycle and beginning the next; it is a celebration which announces a beginning and marks an end, which momentarily suspends dissolution, hiding it and showing it at the same time—the double sign of the baroque.

If it were only in *The Kingdom of This World* that such a liturgical structure appeared, and only in that story that the Carnival axis-scene constituted the center, one could perhaps doubt the validity of the design found in the composition of that text. But other stories of the forties show a similar composition.

Klaus Müller-Bergh has shown that the plot of "Oficio de tinieblas" (as the title itself suggests) was composed by Carpentier "closely paralleling the nine prayers that comprise the first office of Good Friday."[70] Not only that, but the events narrated (based on historical documentation for the most part) encompass a year that is in accordance with the liturgical year. The most salient event, the famous earthquake in Santiago de Cuba, takes on an apocalyptic meaning akin to the "green wind" in *The Kingdom of This World*. And could it be fortuitous then that the two middle chapters deal one with the theater and the other with the Carnival? In "Journey Back to the Source," the action of the story, which narrates backwards the biography of Marcial, occurs in twelve hours and is divided into thirteen chapters. Could it be accidental that at the end of chapter 6 it is said that it "was carnival time," and that it should be in this very chapter that Carpentier inserts a favorite scene of his which has overtones of Calderón's *The Great Theater of the World*, the theater or the masquerade?

Then they all [Marcial and his young friends who are at a party] trooped upstairs to the attic, remembering that the liveries and clothes of the Capellanías family had been stored away under its peeling beams. On shelves frosted with camphor lay court dresses, an ambas-

---

70. " 'Oficio de tinieblas,' un cuento escasamente conocido," in *Asedios a Carpentier: once ensayos críticos sobre el novelista cubano* (Santiago, Chile, 1972), pp. 53–62.

sador's sword, several padded military jackets, the vestment of a dignitary of the Church, and some long cassocks with damask buttons and damp stains among their folds. The dark shadows of the attic were variegated with the colors of amaranthine ribbons, yellow crinolines, faded tunics, and velvet flowers. A picaresque *chispero's* costume and hair net trimmed with tassels, once made for a carnival masquerade, was greeted with applause. Señora de Campoflorido swathed her powdered shoulders in a shawl the color of Creole's skin, once worn by a certain ancestress on an evening of important family decisions in hopes of reviving the sleeping ardor of some rich trustee of a convent of Clares.   [P. 116]

Could it be disregarded that in chapter 6 Marcial's coming of legal age is celebrated and that in chapter 12 he completes his *regressus ad uterum?* It is also in chapter 6 that Marcial, in a drunken stupor, "had the strange sensation that all the clocks in the house were striking five, then half past four, then four, then half past three" (p. 115); and also when he muses sleeplessly on how "one may believe that one could walk on the ceiling, with the floor for a ceiling and the furniture firmly fixed between the beams" (p. 115). The action of "Journey Back to the Source" is framed by two voids, the prenatal and the postmortal, with the Carnival at the center—the Carnival in all the senses mentioned in our analysis of *The Kingdom of This World:* surrender to the summons of the flesh (it is in chapter 6 that Marcial and his friends visit the dance house in the scene quoted earlier for other purposes), masquerade, inversion. The emblem of the story is the statue in Marcial's garden of Ceres, goddess of the harvests and of the underground abode of the dead. As Sharon Magnarelli has shown, the Burgos Fair is the axis on which the cycles of that repetitive story "The Highroad of Saint James" hinges, the place where Juan's life changes course and where he meets the double who is about to repeat his journey.[71]

"Los fugitivos," Carpentier's most "primitive" story from the forties (the one most like his work of the thirties), allows us to observe in an even more synoptic manner the structure uncovered

71. " 'El camino de Santiago' de Alejo Carpentier y la picaresca," *Revista Iberoamericana,* 4 (1974), 72.

in *The Kingdom of This World* and other stories of the time. The story is a sort of parable. The maroon (Cimarrón) escapes from the barracks of the sugar mill but succumbs to the temptations of alcohol and women and is captured. Later, when he attempts to escape again, the dog that had been his companion during his first sally (Perro) kills him. What condemns Cimarrón is the superfluity of his desires and actions. While in the bush with Perro, both experience sexual urges at the coming of spring, but Cimarrón's extend beyond the natural cycle, while the dog, "once the crisis of spring had passed . . . , showed himself increasingly unwilling to go near the towns."[72] The cause of Cimarrón's superfluous desires is given in a quasi-allegorical scene: "One day, Perro started to scratch at the foot of one of the walls [of the cave where they have taken refuge]. Soon his teeth brought out a femur and some ribs, so old that they had no flavor left and crumbled on his tongue releasing insipid dust. Later he took to Cimarrón, who was making himself a snake-skin belt, a human skull. Although there were in the hole some pieces of pottery and stone scratchers that could have been useful, Cimarrón, terrified by the presence of dead bodies in his house, left the cave that same afternoon, muttering prayers and not giving a thought to the rain" (p. 30). Before the taino remains, Cimarrón is stricken by the fear of death; others before him have occupied that cave and have left their ruins—his fate is to repeat theirs, to leave his bones as relics. Like a Hamlet with Yorick's skull, Cimarrón takes cognizance of his own mortality and is thrown by it outside natural rhythms and into vices and excess. It could not be fortuitous that on that very same day—the day of Marcial's death, since the priest is taking the viaticum to the sugar mill—the Carnival scene occurs. Perro frightens the horse of the calash in which Gregorio is taking the priest, and both are killed as the carriage overturns. Cimarrón "took possession of the priest's stole and other garments, and of the driver's jacket and high boots. In the many pockets

72. I am translating from *Narrativa cubana de la revolución*, ed. J. M. Caballero Bonald (Madrid, 1968), p. 33. "Los fugitivos" was originally published in *El Nacional*, August 4, 1946, p. 8.

there were almost five duros. There was also the small silver bell.
The thieves returned to the mountains. That night, dressed in the
cassock, Cimarrón dreamed of forgotten pleasures" (p. 31). Overturning, inversion, death, costumes, sensuality, all the elements of
the Carnival scene are here, reduced to a minimum, but in their
assigned places. The action of the story comprises two years and
three springs. In the first spring, Perro appears chasing Cimarrón;
during the second they are united; in the third, Perro kills Cimarrón. It is shortly after the second spring, the middle one, that the
Carnival scene just mentioned occurs. The repetition of the scene
at the end makes the circumvolution of the plot unnecessary,
superfluous. It is as if the story were always at the beginning and
another possible denouement were being offered—unravelings that
have no necessary relation with the center. What remains between
both chase scenes is superfluous, carnivallike, baroque, as are
Cimarrón's actions, which take him, in spite of his efforts, to the
end from which he is always trying to escape: "For many years,"
the last sentence of the story reads, "the hands of the sugar mill
avoided that road, which had been spoiled by bones and chains"
(p. 37). Could the hands be on their way to visit the prostitutes,
like Cimarrón, and thereby be starting a new cycle? The bones
and chains are the relics of Cimarrón's passing through the kingdom of this world—they are his ruins, his Sans-Souci, and are
emblematic of the surplus man imposes on nature: "Men usually
leave their bones and wastes wherever they go. But it is better to
be wary of them because they are the most dangerous animals,
because by walking on their hind legs they can lengthen their
gestures with the aid of sticks and objects" (p. 36). Caught in the
inescapable rhythm of life and death that nature imposes on him—
between Mondays and Sundays—man leaves in his ruins the trace
of his passing. In The Kingdom of This World he leaves not only
the ruins of his excesses—palaces, fortresses, mansions—but his
body, like a stone monument: "Having chosen his own death,
Henri Christophe would never know the corruption of his flesh,
flesh fused with the very stuff of the fortress, inscribed in its
architecture, integrated with its body bristling with flying but-

tresses. Le Bonnet de l'Evêque, the whole mountain, had become the mausoleum of the first King of Haiti" (p. 124). The warm and tremulous flesh of sensuous Pauline becomes the cold marble statue that Soliman strokes at the Borghese Palace; the image of the Magi Melchor is announced in the white corneas of Bouckman and Soliman; the wax heads appearing at the beginning are a forecast of M. Lenormand de Mézy's fate. The baroque echoes of this somatic petrification are too strong not to be taken into account. "Even for the sepulcher there is death," as Quevedo says; but the sepulcher, like the body—"portable tomb," as he calls it in another poem—is the last inscription, the last message encoded on flesh or stone. The coarse materiality of the human enterprise belies the vanity of its effort to transcend itself; the final petrification, as pointed out before, is an allegory of the text itself, and of Carpentier. In his rescue of history, in his pilgrimages in search of the lost origin, Carpentier finds ruins, dismantled monuments, epitaphs. The only presence of the past is the ruins, the petrified texts—hieratic and monumental, archaic and artificial; Carpentier's prose is the erection of another monument, the new epitaph inscribed between a 7 and an 8, between a Sunday and a Monday, on his own mask.

All the devices used by Carpentier to evoke the fantastic during the forties must be seen within the context of this baroque magic: fantasies conjured in the name of a faith that is the greatest artifice, the all-encompassing fiction, the liturgical, sacramental theater where the irreconcilable poles of the contradictions are exchanged, conjugated, where they interplay. Such a faith is the space of literature that does not satisfy the Carpentier of the prologue, but within which all of his gestures are inscribed.

The contradictions seen throughout this study of the works of the forties destroy the theoretical core of the prologue to The Kingdom of This World, for there is no real complicity between the Latin American world and writing. But we owe to them the richness of that story, and also The Lost Steps, the novel of disillusionment that unveils the fallacies of "marvelous American reality" and leads Carpentier away from fantastic literature. *The Lost Steps* is the text through which reflexivity and self-consciousness dissolve the mock faith of *The Kingdom of This World* and points at the void between writer and world, between creative consciousness and a consciousness predicated on nature. In the stories of the forties (Carpentier does not call *The Kingdom of This World* a novel, in spite of its length), the depersonalized, abstract figures of a puppet theater traveled through jungles and seas, caught in the circularity of meaningless journeys, hopping powerlessly from island to island. This is noticeable in the detached stance of the narrator of *The Kingdom of This World*, who reports what "actually" happened during the execution of Macandal and then what the black slaves believe to have happened. But in the novels that immediately follow, the contradictions will be consciously assumed by Carpentier and his characters will at least appear to have more direct control over their destinies. The transition from the theories of "marvelous American reality" to *The Lost Steps* could not be more telling. Faced with the problem, implied by his theory, of being unable to establish a dialogue with his culture that does not at the same time reify that culture, being unable to be autochthonous at the moment of writing, Carpentier's only possibility is to turn himself into the object, unfolding and fragmenting the self of his prologue—interrogating his own mask.[73] Because it is only by objectivizing that self that he can displace it to that other side where culture always remains when it is the object of writing. *El libro de la Gran Sabana*, an unfinished travel journal of Carpentier's pilgrimages through the Venezuelan jungle and *The Lost Steps*, an autobiographical novel, are the answers to the questions opened by *The Kingdom of This World*.

73. This is, of course, the usual movement in subject-object philosophy. Lévi-Strauss works out the problem in anthropological terms in his "Introduction à l'oeuvre de Marcel Mauss," *Sociologie et anthropologie*, pp. ix–liii.

4. The Parting of the Waters

> And God said, Let there be a firmament in the midst of the
> waters, and let it divide the waters from the waters.
>
> *Genesis* 1:6.

> the waterways parted, the brooks ran freely between the
> mountains, and the waters were parted when the high moun-
> tains appeared.
>
> *Popol Vuh,* 1

> since time immemorial when they watched over the separa-
> tion of the waters and the mystery of the first coming to-
> gether of the rivers.
>
> *The Lost Steps,* IV, 20

"I wrote *The Lost Steps* three times," Carpentier said in an interview in 1971. "The first time I didn't like it: the second time I
was disenchanted with it. Then I went through a period of reflection about my work and wrote it for the third time. At that moment I was satisfied."[1] A few years before Carpentier had made a
similar confession: "Three times I rewrote it completely."[2] Though
it is known that Carpentier polishes his prose with Flaubertian intensity and our reading of *The Kingdom of This World* shows the
care with which he composes his fiction, it is still difficult to accept
that those three versions of his most ambitious novel are merely
the result of his striving to achieve stylistic perfection. Besides,
Carpentier speaks not of corrections or revisions, but of rewritings,
and of undergoing a period of reflection (*recapacitación,* taking
stock) about his work in general.

We do not have the two versions that preceded, according to
Carpentier, the final text of *The Lost Steps,* but there are two

---

1. Joaquín G. Santana, "Muertes, resurrecciones, triunfos, agonías" (Interview), *Bohemia* (Havana), March 26, 1971, p. 6.
2. "Autobiografía de urgencia," *Insula* (Madrid), no. 218 (1965), p. 13.

other versions which show that the writing of this novel represents a major break in the course of his work: first, some chapters on an unfinished book of travels (*El libro de la Gran Sabana*), written during the fall of 1947 and published in newspapers and magazines during the same year and the beginning of the next;[3] and, second, Carpentier's own published recollections about the gestation of the novel. Given the first-person, autobiographical form of *The Lost Steps* and Carpentier's repeated suggestions that the novel reflects his own experience, as well as the novel's own speculations about artistic creation, consideration of these texts as versions of the novel seems justified. Besides, such a juxtaposition will afford an unusually clear glimpse into the dynamics of the contradictions at work not only in all forms of autobiographical fiction, but those specific contradictions which inform Carpentier's entire enterprise, particularly as his own work moves beyond the problems posed by *The Lost Steps*.

The entire process of creation and re-creation to which *The Lost Steps* was subjected, mirrored in the text of the novel itself, manifests a point of closure as well as a point of departure—a point from which Carpentier's writing may be viewed advantageously, as he himself seems to have reviewed his previous production in composing this novel. The concern here is not with his writings in the sense of a closed system or a homogeneous whole, but rather with the series of shifts and breaks that we have studied, and those that follow *The Lost Steps*—shifts and breaks that result from his desire to locate Latin America and his own discourse within Western history and writing, or, more often, outside of it.

There are many indications of a new Carpentier in *The Lost Steps*. To begin with, this is the first work of his that he calls a novel since ¡Ecue-Yamba-O! (the title page of the original reads: *Los pasos perdidos. Novela*).[4] *The Kingdom of This World*,

3. The chapters first appeared during the fall of 1947 in the literary page of *El Nacional*, under the general heading "Visión de América," and the subheading "(Fragmentos de una Crónica de Viaje)." They were reprinted in *Carteles* (*Havana*) in the early months of 1948. A note in the first installment of *Carteles* speaks of these articles as part of a book called *El libro de la Gran Sabana*.

4. All references to *The Lost Steps* indicated in the text are from *The Lost*

though commonly referred to as a novel, was subtitled *relato*
(French, *récit*). The distinction is noteworthy. The stories written
during the forties and *The Kingdom of This World* are fragmentary accounts of lives caught up in the swirl of history represented
as a series of repetitions and circularities. The emphasis falls on the
telos of the narrative or on the formal interrelation of the various
scenes, not on the characters' lives or the motivation of their actions; the characters are like hieratic figures in a large historical
tapestry. Marcial, Ti Noël, M. Lenormand de Mézy, appear as
functions within the mechanics of history: their fate is to complete tasks within a preordained network of interrelated events
whose meaning they do not understand. Ti Noël, the most "developed" of these, is merely a passive presence, a witness to a series
of events beyond his comprehension, a kind of zombie who, frayed
by history, starts to grasp what has happened around him only at
the end, when he begins a rudimentary process of stock-taking and
recollection. But his reminiscences are cut short by death. The relation between events and dates, however, is what ultimately gives
coherence to the story, not a synthesis brought about by a consciousness in search of meaning (*relato* is, of course, etymologically
derived from *relacionar*, relating). The ordering presence, the implied authorial and authoritative voice, is masked behind a prologue
that only hints at the composition of the text; it remains concealed
in the numerous intricacies of the very complex system of correspondences that make up *The Kingdom of This World*. All of the
stories written before the fifties, as we saw, are set in the eighteenth and nineteenth centuries (with the exception of parts of
"Like the Night") and within relatively familiar historical episodes
or recognizable past circumstances. The paradigmatic story, "Like
the Night," occurs in six monumental historical events, including
the Crusades, the colonization of America, and D-Day.[5]

Steps, trans. Harriet de Onís, introd. J. B. Priestley, 2d ed. (New York: Alfred
A. Knopf, Inc., 1971). Quotations from the Spanish come from the third
Mexican edition (1966).

5. For historical details see my " 'Semejante a la noche,' de Alejo Carpentier: historia/ficción," *Modern Language Notes*, 87 (1972), 272–85.

Viewed against Carpentier's previous production, The Lost Steps represents an attempt at unification and synthesis, if only because it is centered on a continuous and reflexive narrative presence—a narrator-protagonist who sets before the reader a totality of his life and experience in our times, instead of a series of fragments projected against a background of monumental and dwarfing historical events. Not since ¡Ecue-Yamba-O! had Carpentier placed a narrative in his own time, with the exception of the final two episodes of "Like the Night." And never had he attempted a narrative with a complex relationship between character, setting, and action—a narrative in which the characters appear as active agents within, as well as reflectors of, their own history. Even if in "Like the Night" there is already a first-person narrator (and one can see in the story forebodings of The Lost Steps), the protagonist merely relates his own story, without reflecting upon it or taking cognizance of the obvious tour de force of which he is an object.[6] History, in the form of the six events in which he takes part, parades behind him, like a series of backdrops, without leaving their image on his text.

Whereas Carpentier wove his previous fictions around the biography of an obscure historical figure, in The Lost Steps he himself is the object of the biography, and the writing of the novel becomes a theme of the narrative. The impersonal, even hieratic tone of the earlier works is abandoned in favor of a self-reflexiveness that is connected to the autobiographical nature of the novel. Furthermore, the ideological framework of earlier works (mainly Spenglerian) is set off against a different and conflicting conception of man and history: Sartrean existentialism.[7] In spite of Carpentier's negative comments about Sartre in the prologue to The

6. Writing about Proust, Carpentier refers to the first-person technique as "that tremendously efficient, though anonymous first-person" ("Un acontecimiento literario," El Nacional, October 26, 1951, p. 4).

7. Raúl Silva Cáceres has explored the existentialist implications of the novel, particularly in regard to the actualization of the past through memory and the protagonist's consciousness of the temporal dimension, in "Una novela de Carpentier," Mundo Nuevo, no. 17 (November 1967), pp. 33–37. See also Eduardo G. González, "Los pasos perdidos, el azar y la aventura," Revista Iberoamericana, 38 (1972), 585–614.

Kingdom of This World and in journalistic pieces that precede and follow The Lost Steps, Sartrean concepts like "authenticity," to mention only one, surface in this novel, and the predicament of the protagonist, caught between a search for his essence in the past and a commitment to the present-in-history, is clearly Sartrean.[8] (So are many of the moral dilemmas and choices that the protagonist faces—for example, whether to falsify the instruments that he has been commissioned to find, whether to shoot the leper, and whether to resist Mouche when he returns from the jungle.) If Carpentier's insistence on the presence of past history and tradition is essence-giving in its assumption of origins, the very contemporaneity of The Lost Steps is in a way a negation of such pre-existing, essence-giving historicity.

The clash of Spenglerian and Sartrean concepts in The Lost Steps reveals its recollective, stock-taking quality—as does the title itself, a translation of Breton's Les pas perdus that might allude to Carpentier's Surrealist past (the title of the French translation of the novel had to be rendered as Le partage des eaux). On a purely textual level the novel contains abstracted versions of earlier stories of Carpentier's such as "Journey Back to the Source," as well as echoes and even excerpts of his journalistic work in the forties— particularly the articles written upon his return to Latin America from Europe and the published chapters of El libro de la Gran Sabana.[9] Beyond this, the novel shows a totalizing desire on both the level of personal and world history; as the protagonist moves through the jungle, he believes he is traveling across all of man's history, as if his voyage were not through landscape but through an

8. Throughout Carpentier's columns in El Nacional there are quite a few uncomplimentary remarks about Sartre and the popularity of existentialism. Criticism of Sartre is often directed against the concept of committed literature. In The Lost Steps, there is also a somewhat ironic allusion to existentialism: "Inverting for his own use a philosophical principle we commonly employed, he used to say that anyone who acted 'automatically was essence without existence'" (p. 29).

9. See the quotations from the 1941 articles on pp. 39–41 and compare with pp. 94–95 of The Lost Steps. The negative ideas about Latin America that Carpentier attributed to certain European writers are held by the protagonist's father in the novel.

160   Alejo Carpentier

imaginary museum or through a compendium of world history read backward. His voyage is also through individual memory, across all the stages of his past life, to childhood and ultimately his own birth. The overall movement is toward the moment of plenitude when the end of these journeys will coincide and merge in a true synthesis of the totality of history and the self. It is be- cause of this search for restoration and integration that The Lost Steps assumes such an abstract form. Whereas in his previous work there was a particular history and geography, here we have the Latin American Capital, the Jungle, the River, and an unnamed protagonist who stands for Modern Man—in the sense of Man after the fall, entering into the decay and separation of temporality and history. As such, the novel attempts a Hegelian fusion of Bildungsbiographie and Universalgeschichte. In a completely ab- stract way, the protagonist's journey is a kind of Romantic Bildungsreise, the educational journey of that wayfaring general spirit or collective human consciousness—der allgemeine Indi- viduum or der allgemeine Geist—of Hegel's Phenomenology of the Spirit.[10] In more literary terms, the narrator-protagonist is like Blake's Albion, or Verne's Captain Nemo (no one), in search of the absolute. This, of course, constitutes a recoiling from the Spenglerian system within which Carpentier's fiction operated pre- viously, since it leads to a self-reflexiveness that was denied in the earlier texts, particularly in Carpentier's theory of "marvelous American reality."

The context of that theory was, as we saw, a broad one. The prologue to The Kingdom of This World is but one manifestation of a whole movement in Latin America literature whose central metaphor is the recuperation of the lost origin, that Edenic begin- ning of beginnings destroyed by the violent birth of history with the European invasion, that supreme fiction evoked by Neruda in the opening lines of his "General Song":

10. I am indebted to M. H. Abrams's lucid discussion of Hegel and other Romantic philosophers and authors in "The Circuitous Journey: Through Alienation to Reintegration," in his Natural Supernaturalism: Tradition and Revolution in Romantic Literature (New York, 1971), pp. 199–324.

Before wig and frockcoat
were the rivers, the arterial rivers,
the cordilleras, on whose scraped escarpments
the condor or the snow seemed immobile,
humidity and density, the thunderclap
not-yet-named, the planetary pampas.

Man was earth, a vessel, the eyelid
of the quivering clay, a shape of potter's earth,
Carib spout, Chibcha stone,
Imperial cup or Araucanian silica:
he was gentle and bloody, but on the hilt
of his wetted glass weapon
the earth's initials were
written.
        No one
could later recall them: the wind
forgot, the water's idiom
was buried, the code was lost
or inundated by silence or blood.[11]

The literature, of which Carpentier's famous prologue to *The Kingdom of This World* was a sort of manifesto, was one of re-membrance, of re-call. The reconstitution of the code depended on the fusion of nature, history, and creative consciousness. But given that such a union, as exemplified by *The Kingdom of This World*, was a strategy devised in dusty libraries, Carpentier now sets out to look for that privileged moment where all begins in the sidereal silence of the great savannas. His voyage to the jungle and the at-tempt to write *El libro de la Gran Sabana* constitute a search, on a personal, unmediated, biographical level, for that inscription of the earth's initials—for the writing that precedes writing. That is, since the magic Latin American consciousness that he posits remains alien to him, he chooses to objectivize himself instead, to reverse

11. "Love, America (1400)" from *Selected Poems* by Pablo Neruda, trans. Anthony Kerrigan, ed. Nathaniel Tarn, copyright © 1970 by Anthony Ker-rigan, W. S. Merwin, Alastair Reid, and Nathaniel Tarn; copyright © 1972 by Dell Publishing Co., Inc.; used with the permission of Delacorte Press/ Seymour Lawrence and the Estate of Pablo Neruda and Jonathan Cape Ltd., London.

the process, making himself, not Latin American history, the object of his (re)search. Both the movement away from literature into history in The Kingdom of This World and the shift to biography in The Lost Steps are exemplary of the constant desire of post-Romantic literature to transcend itself. These movements constitute the core of the dynamics of loss and gain that subtends Carpentier's entire enterprise. The persistent inconclusiveness of this process, as exemplified by his earlier fiction and by the attempt to write El libro de la Gran Sabana, is perhaps the reason why Carpentier ultimately elected to fictionalize his life and cast it in The Lost Steps within such grandiose literary myths (Jason, Ulysses, Prometheus), in the middle of his life's journey. Instead of king, slave, wandering musician, or soldier, the protagonist is now the contemporary artist. The war of time is waged in the act of writing, and the only mythic figure that can emerge is that of the modern writer, who is by definition the undoer of myths, including his own. In undertaking self-demystification, Carpentier subjects the bulk of Latin American literary tradition to its most serious challenge. If the steps leading to its origins indeed are lost, the novel presents itself not as a keeper of the tradition, but as a new beginning.

2

The anecdotal parallels between The Lost Steps and Carpentier's own life are numerous and many of them well known, for Carpentier himself has often drawn them, first and foremost by adding a note to the novel suggesting that some of the adventures in the book were experienced by the author.[12] (The function of that note is the same as that of the prologue to The Kingdom of This World, and without it there would be no hint in the text of

12. One of the reasons Carpentier offers for the popularity of the autobiographical novel after World War II is that "many writers were trapped by necessity in an intractable modern city, having to perform the professions most at variance with their vocations" ("La novela autobiográfica," El Nacional, October 18, 1956, p. 24). In "Médico y poeta," Carpentier gives many examples of artists who "have to lead a 'double life'" (ibid., October 27, 1953, p. 24).

the autobiographical nature of the novel, unless the reader were to surmise it by the confessional mode of the narrative.) In 1945, Carpentier moved from Havana to Caracas to take a position similar to that of his protagonist in an advertising agency; like his protagonist, Carpentier is a composer and musicologist.[13] Carpentier barely had time to settle in the Venezuelan capital when, in October 1945, a military coup toppled the government. For several days Carpentier and his wife were trapped in a hotel as shooting went on around them, much as the protagonist and Mouche during the Revolution in the Latin American Capital.[14] Chronicles by Márquez Rodríguez and Müller-Bergh, based largely on Carpentier's own accounts, as well as statements by Carpentier himself, indicate that while he was in Venezuela in 1947 he traveled to the jungle and that, during his trip, he conceived the idea of writing *The Lost Steps*, much as his composer-protagonist begins to work anew in the jungle on his piece based on Shelley's *Prometheus Unbound*.[15] Further details attest to more significant autobiographical elements in *The Lost Steps*—notably, the parallel between the protagonist's Latin American childhood, which he attempts to recover upon his return after many years abroad, and Carpentier's own return to Cuba in 1939 after more than ten years

13. One interesting detail furnished by Salvador Bueno is that Carpentier's great-grandfather, Alfred Clerec Carpentier "was one of the first explorers of Guiana way back in 1840" ("Alejo Carpentier, novelista antillano y universal," in Bueno's *La letra como testigo* [Santa Clara, Cuba, 1957], p. 154). Rafael A. Pineda has given further details, though changing the great-grandfather to grandfather: "Alejo Carpentier was always tied to the desire to come to Venezuela because of a pair of cuff-links made of Manaos gold, for they could have had no other origin, having been molded in 1842 according to the date engraved on them, and that I saw him wear for the first time in 1949. It was a bequest of his grandfather Alfred Clerec Carpentier, French explorer who traveled through Guiana to the High Orinoco" ("Alejo Carpentier en la ciudad de las maquetas," *Imagen* [Caracas], March 14, 1972, p. 2).

14. See Alexis Márquez Rodríguez, *La obra narrativa de Alejo Carpentier* (Caracas, 1970), p. 62.

15. Ibid., and Klaus Müller-Bergh, *Alejo Carpentier: estudio biográfico-crítico* (Long Island City, N.Y., 1972), pp. 76–77. Carpentier's own testimonies appear later in this chapter.

in France, and the parallel between the protagonist's European father and Carpentier's.

However, if the novel were autobiographical in the direct and almost literal way in which critics (and recently Carpentier himself) would have us believe, what can be made of the ending? The protogonist's quest ends in failure. When he is able to organize a return to Santa Mónica de los Venados (a name that alludes to Augustine's *Confessions* and is associated with the progression, or regression, from Mouche to Rosario to María del Carmen),[16] he learns that Rosario has married Marcos, and that it is impossible to find the village because the inscription on a tree marking the secret passageway has been obliterated by the rising waters of the river. He has to return, dejected, to the Latin American Capital, and, like a sane Don Quixote on his deathbed, realize that his journey is impossible, that the return in time is an illusion, for he has a consciousness of history that Rosario and the others, who live in an unmediated present, do without. If the protagonist's journey is a *Bildungsreise* in the Romantic tradition, the culmination of his education is recognizing the necessity of subverting that tradition; restitution, reintegration is impossible, only a plurality-in-the-present. His only success is writing the text that we are reading, but that in itself is a plunge back into the ambiguities of literature and can only be considered an achievement outside the fiction of the novel; in the novel he was unable to finish his Threnody, thereby foreclosing the imaginative accession to the absolute through art devised by some of the Romantics. Thus the novel ends with the protagonist's realization that only the present-in-history is given to him, that he must assume historicity and temporality as the conditions of his existence (the history he did not

16. There is direct mention of Augustine and a quotation from the *Confessions* in *The Lost Steps*: " 'It is called Santa Mónica de los Venados,' Fray Pedro explained, 'because this is the land of the red deer, and Mónica was the name of the founder's mother, Monica, who bore St. Augustine, *herself a saint who had been the wife of one man and herself had brought up her children*' " (p. 190). Carpentier devotes a few paragraphs to Augustine and the *Confessions* ("one of the best written books that may be found in a library") in "La Biblia y el estilo," *El Nacional*, April 1, 1953, p. 26.

want to assume by killing the leper, the time that forces him to record his music on paper). Such self-denying realization at the end would entail, paradoxically, a liberation, a Romantic shedding of disguises. But it is precisely because of that liberation, denying the teleological validity of the quest that it simultaneously affirms, that the progression toward such a moment—the text of the novel— must be seen as shattered, the picture of man as a "many-sided mirror" (*Prometheus Unbound*, Act IV), rather than the harmonious record of a presence that has gained entrance to a privileged world lacking temporal dimensions. The end, in other words, is not a synthesis attesting to the unity of the text. It is from that last moment of self-denial that the various selves of the narrator-protagonist should be considered as nothing more than a succession of predicates attached by linguistic convention to the unassertive "I" of the narrative.[17]

The "predicativeness" of the narrating "I," its unassertiveness, is more poignant in the Spanish original because in Spanish it is possible to omit the personal pronoun, and the verb forms of the first- and third-person singular imperfect are identical. In the first sentence, particularly, it is impossible to ascertain whether the narrative is first- or third-person, a confusion that is further emphasized by the use of *hacer*, which in its imperfect can also be taken for an impersonal use: "*Hacía* cuatro años y siete meses que no había vuelto a ver la casa de columnas blancas, con su frontón de ceñudas molduras que le daban una severidad de palacio de justicia, y ahora, ante muebles y trastos colocados en su lugar invariable, *tenía* la casi penosa sensación de que el tiempo se hubiera revertido."[18] The impersonal third person (*hacía*) and the identical forms of *tener* in the first and third persons (*tenía*) make it impossible to determine whether someone is speaking about himself or about another person. In a sense the thread of the whole novel runs through this

17. For a detailed discussion of this, see Jean Starobinsky, "Le style de l'autobiographie," *Poétique*, 3 (1970), 261–62. The categories of "discourse" and "history" used by Starobinski in this essay are drawn from Emile Benveniste, *Problèmes de linguistique générale* (Paris, 1966), p. 242.

18. *Los pasos perdidos*, p. 9.

sentence, which encompasses the circulation of the narrating self between first and third person and the displacement between an indeterminate past (hacía) and the present (ahora), all in one syntactical period. In the novel this lack of identity of the narrator-protagonist is indicated, of course, by his remaining nameless, and the shifting temporality of the text by the fact that the reader (as we shall see) never knows just when the narrator has set down what he is reading. These unknowns also preclude the possibility of considering the text "finished." The narrator is that space between the "I" and the "he" and between then and now; he is the stylistic écart (gap, spread, lapse) of which Starobinski speaks. This lack of center generates the baroqueness of Carpentier's style —the excessive accumulation of predicates attempting to define an ever fleeting subject—and the repetitiveness and open-ended nature of the text. As in Proust, the ending is the announcement of a new beginning, but this in itself, of course, makes the autobiographical status of the novel problematic.

Bewildering discrepancies as well as insights into the more complex autobiographical nature of the novel arise if we shift our focus to Carpentier's reminiscences about the composition of The Lost Steps. In 1964 he said the following to César Leante in an interview:

Knowing Venezuela completed my vision of America. There one can find the great rivers, the endless plains, the gigantic mountains, the jungle. The Venezuelan landscape was for me a way of coming into contact with the soil of America, and to penetrate its jungles was to come to know the fourth day of creation. I made a trip to the Upper Orinoco and lived there for a month with the most primitive tribes in the New World. Then, the first idea of writing The Lost Steps was born in me [nació en mí]. Going up the Orinoco is like going back in time. My character in The Lost Steps travels to the roots of life, but when he wants to find them again he is unable to, for he has lost the door that leads to authentic life.[19]

19. "Confesiones sencillas de un escritor barroco," Cuba, 3, no. 24 (1964), 30. The same appears in "Autobiografía de urgencia," which is an adaptation of this interview.

A year later, Carpentier said much the same thing in a radio program recorded by Müller-Bergh: "In 1947, finding myself in Venezuela, I had the desire to go into the virgin jungle, that is to say, to the landscape of the fourth day of creation. For that purpose I left Caracas, crossed an important region of the country, and arrived at Ciudad Bolívar, on the banks of the Orinoco. [As] I journeyed up the Orinoco I realized that there is an American space-time. [As] we moved forward during that twenty-day navigation . . . civilization disappeared and one entered into a life that seemed like the European middle ages."[20]

Carpentier's statements, even his choice of words (to complete a vision), reveal a totalizing desire whose satisfaction can only be possible from a privileged position in time; Venezuela is given as a spatial and temporal model of the whole of Latin America, a construct similar to the one attributed to that diabolical "author" of The Kingdom of This World. Such a desire harks back to notions that The Lost Steps seemed to have debunked by its ending and echoes the protagonist's belief that his journey takes him through all the stages of man's history. Carpentier's placing of the birth of the novel ("born in me") in the midst of the jungle is also part of the Romantic mystification that the protagonist of The Lost Steps sheds. In the novel the protagonist never finishes his musical composition, just as Carpentier left unfinished El libro de la Gran Sabana. There are, in fact, no geneses in the novel, only repetitions, rediscoveries, and falsifications. When the protagonist begins to compose music in Santa Mónica, it is suggested that Rosario has become pregnant, but he never knows for sure, and then she marries Marcos. Ruth, his own wife, only feigns a pregnancy, and Mouche, his mistress, turns out to be a lesbian. Natural conceptions are fictional or nonexistent. The failure of the protagonist's intended marriage with Rosario, her inability to unite with him once he had reached the Valley Where Time Had Stopped, is the most clear formulation of the protagonist's failure at reintegration

20. Estudio biográfico-crítico, pp. 77–78.

within the Romantic symbolism that the novel mobilizes. For it was precisely in this sort of marriage that the Romantic poets saw the final reconciliation of all contraries, the cosmic fusion of all warring forces, as the union of Asia and Prometheus in Shelley's *Prometheus Unbound*.[21] Carpentier's statements equating his experiences in writing the novel with those of his fictional character also reveal that no true synthesis occurred outside the text. In those statements he is not so much betraying his novel as in a sense repeating it.

Carpentier's insistence on identifying his own voyage with that of the protagonist of *The Lost Steps* has helped to create further fictions by critics, which are quite revealing in themselves. Luis Harss, for example, says, contradicting elementary notions of South American geography, that *The Lost Steps* "describes a trip the author took up the Orinoco river to the Great Savannas, the old terrestrial paradise of the conquistadors."[22] It would be difficult to reach the Great Savanna traveling up (westward) the Orinoco, since that region is found southeast of the Orinoco Valley, in the region of Venezuela bordering British Guiana, while the river flows from sources around the southwest regions of Venezuela, near the Colombian and Brazilian borders, to the Atlantic. But Carpentier had already confused the issue. In the note at the end of the novel he had pointed out that "the landscape [in the novel] changes from the Upper Orinoco to the Great Savanna, the vision of which is offered in various passages of chapters III and IV."[23] This is my own translation: the English translation of the "Author's Note" (inserted at the beginning of the novel) makes the matter even more confusing. It reads: "From this point on, the landscape becomes that of the Great Savanna, a vision of which . . . " (p. vi). "Becomes" indicates a progression only possible in the fiction.

A way of accounting for this discrepancy would be to remember

21. See Abrahms, "Romantic Love," in *Natural Supernaturalism*, pp. 292–99.

22. Luis Harss and Barbara Dohmann, *Into the Mainstream: Conversations with Latin American Writers* (New York, 1967), p. 52.

23. *Los pasos perdidos*, pp. 287–88.

that the myth of El Dorado placed the golden lake on whose shores Manaos was found in the area of the Great Savanna. Significantly, then, in order to make the region coincide with the sources of the Orinoco, as the myth usually did, the river had to have a circular course. As Alexander von Humboldt put it: "It is not possible to move [the sources] east indefinitely without having the Upper Orinoco, which runs from East to West, cross the bed of the Rio Branco, which runs from North to South."[24] By making the action of the novel take this geographically impossible detour, Carpentier may be underscoring the fictionality of the text and the relationship between the narrator-protagonist's quest and those of the many explorers who set out to find the lake with the golden sands and the king whose body was painted gold. The opposition river/lake, flowing waters/still waters, and the naming of the region in which the fictional Santa Mónica de los Venados is found, the Valley Where Time Had Stopped, certainly encourage this supposition. Not so, of course, if Carpentier's own voyage and that of the protagonist are to be equated, unless Carpentier were very subtly pointing at the fictionality of his own trip or bringing out its literary nature. As in the relation between prologue and fictional text in The Kingdom of This World, the "Author's Note" and The Lost Steps can only be coherent if read as fiction, and even then, their coherence depends upon the claim to reality that one or the other makes. Otherwise questions arise. For example, why did Carpentier choose to model Santa Mónica de los Venados after Santa Elena de Uairén, and not after San Fernando de Atabapo, San Carlos, San Francisco Solano, or any of the other missions in the Upper Orinoco that he might have seen and that were described by Humboldt? And why, when evoking years later

24. Viaje a las regiones equinocciales del Nuevo Continente . . . (Caracas, 1942), IV 536. Humboldt's account of the explorations made to reach El Dorado up to his own time (pp. 532–99) is an extremely important text, obviously known to Carpentier. In "Una página de Humboldt" (El Nacional, July 31, 1956, p. 16), Carpentier speaks of having an 1826 edition of Humboldt's book, and in "El mito paradisíaco" (ibid., October 14, 1955, p. 16) he discusses the persistence of the paradisaical myth in some detail while referring to Mircea Eliade's work.

the trip and the composition of the novel, did he omit the savannas, reminiscing instead about the more richly symbolic voyage up the river? Why, in other words, instead of finishing *El libro de la Gran Sabana*, did he write *The Lost Steps*?

Although in interviews and other public statements Carpentier speaks of only one trip to the backlands of Venezuela, there were in fact two such trips, during his summer vacation in July 1947 and in September 1948. We have the evidence of the first in *El libro de la Gran Sabana*; of the second (other than the novel itself) there is only a brief account given in a highly ironic article by the Venezuelan writer Guillermo Meneses ("Carpentier Returned from the Jungle" is the title of this mock-heroic piece): "He [Carpentier] brought back curare, arrows. . . . Like Buffalo Bill he bartered powder and trinkets for arrows and quiver. He was able to look at the signs of the plumed serpent in the petroglyphs of the Amazon Territory. For three long days he was detained on a desert island, waiting for the repair of a serious break-down in the sloop in which he traveled. He ate tapioca and drank chicha among the Mariquitares. He was the personal friend of an Araguato and agreed to write to a perfectly multicolored and brilliant family of macaws. . . . Carpentier has returned to Venezuela from that other Venezuela worthy of a Scandinavian wanderer... The sign of the plumed serpent marks today the activities of Alejo Carpentier."[25]

Carpentier insists on 1947 as the year when the idea of the novel first came to him, and even a cursory reading of *El libro de la Gran Sabana* reveals that this is the primitive text of the novel: paragraphs, scenes, images, characters have been incorporated almost unretouched from the travel journal into the novelistic text: Fray Diego de Valdearenas, a Franciscan monk Carpentier meets in Santa Elena, becomes Fray Pedro Henesterosa; Santa Elena becomes Santa Mónica de los Venados; Lucas Fernández Peña, the true founder of the village, becomes the Adelantado, and many essayistic passages on the history of Latin America are incorporated into the novelistic text, particularly those describing the landscape

25. *El Nacional*, September 12, 1948, p. 4.

of the area. Furthermore the perspective of Carpentier in writing
his journal parallels that of the narrator-protagonist: there is a
sense of discovery and astonishment, of wonder before the majesty
of the landscape. More importantly, there is a contradictory desire
simultaneously, on the one hand, to describe the landscape in terms
of metaphors and similes which domesticate the newly discovered
realities through allusions to Western tradition, while on the other
to preserve their originality and uniqueness. The tension is that of
a language in search of the "proper" though ever elusive forms of
expression in a movement that clearly parallels the novel's plot—
a return to a moment of original innocence before the duplicities
and ambiguities of language that metaphor and simile attempt un-
successfully to obliterate. It is the desire to name for the first time
that Modernity inherited from the Romantics—the wish, in Shelley's words, to make language "a perpetual Orphic song, / Which
rules with Daedal harmony a throng / Of thoughts and forms,
which else senseless and shapeless were." Just as the narrating
voice in the novel is a void, the space between "I" and "he," so is
the text of the descriptions in *El libro de la Gran Sabana* the locus
between those poles that metaphor cannot bind together.

The editorial note that accompanies the first installment of the
Libro de la Gran Sabana in *Carteles* reveals much about the
1947 trip and the book Carpentier thought of writing: "In the past
month of July, our contributor, Alejo Carpentier, made one of the
most extraordinary voyages that can be undertaken in South
America. Departing from Ciudad Bolívar, he flew . . . to the
Great Savanna, over the peaks of the Caroní, in a special plane
furnished by the Ministry of Communications of Venezuela. After
a stay at the Franciscan Mission of Santa Elena de Uairén, the
writer returned to Ciudad Bolívar, traveling later up the Orinoco
River to Puerto Ayacucho, whence he proceeded by launch to the
Atures Falls, covering, therefore, a great portion of von Humboldt's
route."[26] The anonymous note goes on to explain, in what sounds
now very much like Carpentier's own prose, the gestation and

26. *Carteles*, January 25, 1948, p. 35.

nature of the book: "Profoundly impressed by the revelation of a virginal world, inhabited by men who continue living as in the days of the Conquest and are still motivated by the same forces, Alejo Carpentier wrote a book entitled *El libro de la Gran Sabana*, in which the description of nature, beings, and things is accompanied by a series of reflections about the history, myths, and realities of America."[27] The *Libro* was going to be, then, very much like *The Lost Steps* (critics have often objected to the "essays" that appear in the course of the narrative), except that the narrator-protagonist was going to be Carpentier.

Other things in that note may begin to answer some of the questions raised above, or at least to cast them in a different context. The most startling is that the region to which the action of the novel is displaced as the characters approach the innermost recesses of the jungle was seen by Carpentier from the air; it was not directly observed and experienced, as the minute descriptions of the novel and Carpentier's more recent statements would lead one to assume. This is not an empiricist's quibble, for there is more here than the question of recording "real" events or describing "actual" landscapes. It is a matter of conflicting reports. The note goes on to explain that, in spite of the proverbial inaccessibility of the region, the Great Savanna had been the object of explorations dating back at least to the nineteenth century, as well as the subject of various written accounts by explorers, not to mention that Conan Doyle placed there the action of his *Lost World*. The same contradictory gestures found in the language of both the *Libro* and the novel are at work here: the region is untouched and inaccessible, yet it has been the object of literary as well as real explorations.

Carpentier speaks of the 1947 trip as the genetic one; yet it was in 1948 that he made a voyage up river that could conceivably be compared to that of the narrator-protagonist in *The Lost Steps*.[28]

27. Ibid.
28. In reply to a query by the author, Carpentier sent (August 19, 1972) the following addendum in a letter:
"Added:

Meneses corroborates this: "He crossed a mysterious duct. He came to know a secret river. He discovered obscure signals that mark the way to the Guahiba villages. He crossed silvery waterways hidden under the trees. He brought back rare experiences of his life with the Cuibas."[29] Of this marvelous voyage Carpentier did not write

---

With respect to the trip (or trips):
1) Great Savanna, by plane, in a craft of the Department of Cartography—that is to say, it went through narrow passages and canyons, flying over *unexplored places*.
2) Same trip—Two days in Santa Elena, with journey to Icaburu.
3) Same trip—Flight over the Orinoco, at very low altitude, to Puerto Ayacucho.
[Written in margin] 1947:
1) By land to Ciudad Bolívar (by bus). I pass through 'El Tigre' ('the-Valley-of-the-Flames')—
2) Attempt to board 'El Meta', immobilized by an engine breakdown. Trip, finally, in a cattle launch carrying breeding bulls, to the Upper Orinoco (nine days)—
3) I continue the trip to Samariapo, in a small launch, up to San Fernando de [sic] Atabapo—
4) Entrance to the jungle (through the Guacharaca channel) by the spot where the sign **v** is engraved (the three **V**'s one inside the other).
5) Return to Caracas at the end of the trip—Study of Schomburgk, of Koch-Grunberg, etc.—(National Library, Caracas). I have about three hundred photographs (that I took myself with a bad camera, where all the places where the action [of the novel] takes place appear)— . . . I believe that I have little to add—"
[Written in margin] 1948

[Signed] AC

Carpentier does allude in passing to his second trip in several of his "Letra y Solfa" columns for *El Nacional*—for example, in "Poesía del Orinoco," January 26, 1952, p. 4, and "Recuerdo de Salinas," December 12, 1951, p. 4. A list of the travels and travel journals relating to the Great Savanna may be found in S. E. Aguerrevere, Víctor M. López, C. Delgado O., and C. A. Freeman, "Exploración de la Gran Sabana" (Informe que presenta al ciudadano doctor Manuel R. Egaña, Ministro de Fomento, la Comisión Exploradora de la Gran Sabana), *Revista de Fomento* (Caracas), no. 63 (1946), pp. 183–84. This article also states that "beginning with the same year, 1936, the Línea Aereopostal Venezolana established air traffic with the Great Savanna, touching down in Luepa and Santa Elena once a month" (p. 186). Carpentier quotes from this article, which is an account of the 1938 expedition, in the second installment of *El libro de la Gran Sabana*.
    29. *El Nacional*, September 12, 1948, p. 4.

much, except for the novel; why was *El libro de la Gran Sabana* abandoned in favor of *The Lost Steps* between 1947 and 1948? And why is the landscape in *The Lost Steps* that of 1947?

The first page of *El libro de la Gran Sabana* contains the following passage which sets in motion the aforementioned dynamics of metaphor. Carpentier is describing the Caroní:

The routines of my Western imagination make me evoke, immediately, Macbeth's castle. But no. When one is in the entrails of virginal America these images are too limiting and inadmissible. These towers of steely rock, just barely translucent, are too tall to constitute a stage décor: they are too inaccessible, too husky, under this dramatically turbulent sky... Never would [the Indians] commit the sin of reducing the vision [of this landscape], following a train of thought, to the scale of the scenery of a theater, as I was about to do, I, a man shackled to the printed letter. . . . Here the man of the Sixth Day of Creation contemplates the landscape that is given him as his own home. No literary evocation. No myths framed by the Alexandrian line...[30]

In spite of the self-admonition and the struggle to escape from the routines of the imagination, *El libro de la Gran Sabana* is full of allusions to the vast literature of paradise and utopia, from Pedro Mártir de Anglería to Milton, from the Bible to Alexander von Humboldt, from Lope de Vega to the Schomburgk brothers and Sir Walter Raleigh. Instead of the unmediated presence that Carpentier seeks in his voyage to the source of time and history, he finds that road to paradise littered with texts that form an unpliable and dense memory from which he can find no release. He is caught in the paradox of being "in the entrails of virginal America," the fruit of a fatherless, unmediated conception; the product of an originality which denies anteriority while affirming at every step that his own text is a repetition—a new version, perhaps, but one whose lineage can be traced. His attempt to inscribe his autobiographical "I" within a present-past without history turns into a sifting of the endless variations of the myth of origins. It may well be for this paradox that *El libro de la Gran Sabana* was never finished and gave way instead to *The Lost Steps*, where the auto-

30. *Ibid.*, November 9, 1947, p. 8.

biographical "I" who suffers defeat gives way to a fictionalized "I" who must attempt the futile quest for the one inscription on the bark of the mythical tree in the garden of Eden.

Only within this process of discovery and concealment can the swerve in the action of the novel from the Upper Orinoco to the Great Savanna be explained. In the first and third installments of *El libro de la Gran Sabana* there are long paragraphs devoted to two German explorers, Richard and Robert Schomburgk, who traveled in the area of the border between British Guiana and Venezuela in the mid-nineteenth century, and a series of quotations from the extraordinary book that Richard wrote recounting their experiences in the Great Savanna.[31] In the first installment Carpentier quotes from *Travels in British Guiana* to support his statement that words cannot convey an image of the savage beauty of Mount Roraima; in the third he tells the story of the Schomburgk brothers, quotes again from the book, and relates several bizarre incidents from it, such as the conferral of the name "Hamlet" upon one of the blacks in their retinue, the twenty-one-gun salute and three hurrahs given in the midst of the jungle to celebrate the birthday of Queen Victoria, the two bottles of Rhine wine carried by the explorers to celebrate the birthday of the King of Prussia.[32] Here is the most immediate source of the language and problematics of *El libro de la Gran Sabana* and *The Lost Steps*—the text that supplies Carpentier with an appropriate setting for the third and fourth chapters of the novel.[33] Schomburgk's Romantic ver-

31. *Travels in British Guiana, 1840–1844*, trans. Walter E. Roth, 2 vols. (Georgetown, B. G., 1922). Carpentier also mentions Schomburgk's book in "El mundo del tiempo detenido," *El Nacional*, January 16, 1952, p. 4, and in "Julio Verne y el Orinoco," ibid., April 23, 1952, p. 16.

32. Of all the scientific books on the region, Schomburgk's is by far the most self-consciously "literary." *Travels in British Guiana* is one of the unknown classics of the genre devoted to Latin America.

33. Silva Cáceres, "Una novela de Carpentier," p. 35, notes the presence of Joseph Gumilla's *El Orinoco ilustrado* (1745), to which the narrator-protagonist alludes indirectly in the text, in certain descriptions of the jungle. While it is not disputable that Gumilla's book has left some traces in *The Lost Steps*, the fact that the landscape of the novel changes to the Great Savanna, instead of continuing up the river, makes the presence of

sion of the Great Savanna, his constant though futile effort to resist describing the landscape in Western terms, his struggle to preserve its newness and uniqueness, is analogous to the stylistic tensions of Carpentier's books. *Travels in British Guiana* is the secret source, the element which is suppressed when Carpentier reminisces about the gestation of the novel; it is the veiled father of the unmediated conception—and also, to be sure, one of the "thousand books" (p. 107) that separate the narrator-protagonist from Rosario, the mother/lover, the true, inaccessible source.[34]

El Orinoco ilustrado a tenuous one in Carpentier's text and accounts for descriptions before the characters enter the jungle. Moreover, for reasons that shall be seen in brief, the style of Gumilla, pre-Romantic as it is, does not correspond to that of *The Lost Steps*.

34. The scope of Carpentier's readings of anthropological accounts and journals of travels in the Orinoco Valley cannot be limited to the classical books such as von Humboldt's, Schomburgk's, Koch-Grunberg's, or Gumilla's, and in this respect the "topicality" of the Orinoco at the time the novel was being written cannot be discounted. The Schomburgk brothers had drawn the famous, and in Venezuela infamous, Schomburgk line, dividing the territories of Venezuela and British Guiana. Their expedition was undertaken at the urging of von Humboldt but carried out under the auspices of the English Crown (see Manuel Segundo Sánchez, *Obras, vol. I, Bibliografía venezolana* [Caracas, 1964], pp. 343–45). The sources of the Orinoco had been discovered in 1951, creating a great deal of interest in the region; a review of periodicals of the time shows that in 1950 all Venezuela was speculating on the success of the expedition (see the account by its commander, Col. Dem. Franz A. Risquez-Iribarren, *Donde nace el Orinoco* [Caracas, 1962]). Two of the publications issuing from a 1948–1950 Franco-Venezuelan expedition bear particular relevance to *The Lost Steps*: Pierre Gaisseau's recordings of native instruments (see Carpentier's commentary in *El Nacional*, May 23, 1954), and Alain Gheerbrant's account and photographs of paintings and petroglyphs found in the Guaviare region (Carpentier wrote about this book in *El Nacional* on May 14 and 24, 1952). During this time Carpentier also devoted an article to Lévi-Strauss: "Luz del Páramo irá a Venecia en Junio," *El Nacional*, April 18, 1952, p. 12; and again some years later he wrote about Lévi-Strauss in "El Kodachrome y la etnografía," ibid., October 30, 1956, p. 12. In the latter he alludes to *Tristes tropiques* ("magnificent and undeceived book"), whose remarkable parallels with *The Lost Steps* were first noted by John Freccero ("Reader's Report," Cornell University, John M. Olin Library Bookmark Series, no. 36 [April 1968]) and developed more fully in Eduardo G. González's unpublished doctoral dissertation, "El tiempo del hombre: huella y labor de origen en cuatro obras de Alejo Carpentier" (Indiana University, 1974).

Schomburgk's book is not a source in the trivial sense of Carpentier's having taken from it the plot of the novel, for if anything is beyond question it is that the source of The Lost Steps does not exist as such. The novel falls within such a vast literary and para-literary tradition of travel journals and novels that listing one or many books is as futile as the protagonist's quest. The point is that Travels in British Guiana embodies, as it describes the landscape of Latin America, the Romantic and Spenglerian problematics within and against which the text of the novel is working.

The broad outline of Schomburgk's book is, of course, similar to that of The Lost Steps (voyage into untamed nature, return, and written account), but the more visible traces of Travels in British Guiana appear in chapter 4 of the novel, when the characters enter into the deepest part of the jungle. The traces are, above all, of a linguistic nature—images, adjectives, similes; but there are broader resemblances between particular descriptions of natural phenomena. The unifying theme of these coinciding descriptions is the constant transformation of nature: the manifestation of nature's moods and inner forces through spectacular events in which the elements clash in a sudden apocalyptic struggle of contraries.

The echoes of Schomburgk's book in Carpentier's novel are too many to cite: the Sturm und Drang of The Lost Steps derives from Travels in British Guiana, as do the descriptions of the heart of the jungle. Schomburgk sees the jungle as a chaos of constant transformations. His prose conveys this sense of continuous movement and change by its appeal to simile and metaphor: the thuds of breaking tree-trunks become "cannonades," repeated lightning becomes "sheets of lightning," huge trees are "ships." Nature is a code, akin to that of writing, in which meanings are always changing and signs serve only to engender other signs in perpetual multiplication. The narrator-protagonist of The Lost Steps becomes aware of the impossibility of "reading" the jungle properly as he is on the launch: "The jungle is the world of deceit, subterfuge, duplicity; everything there is disguise, stratagem, artifice, metamorphosis. The world of the lizard-cucumber, the chestnut-hedgehog, the cocoon-centipede, the carrot-larva, the electric fish that electrocutes from the slime" (p. 166). It is not fortuitous, of course, that most of these descriptions occur in the novel as the narrator-protagonist floats on a launch in the arms of Rosario. Schomburgk's Romantic descriptions of the jungle represent here the maternal world, the moment of immersion into the formlessness and form-giving prenatal existence, which is anterior to a fixed, historical past, one in which signs have yet to acquire a set meaning. Here the jungle is the world of the waters before their parting, the formless world of primeval slime. Aside from the undeniable charm of Schomburgk's prose (much more "literary" than Humboldt's), there is a much more compelling reason for the textual grafting evident in Carpentier's novel.

The repeated allusions to "forms" in *El libro de la Gran Sabana, The Lost Steps,* and *Travels in British Guiana* are no mere coincidence, but rather the key to the familial relationship between these texts. A comparison of the same scene in the three books should reveal the correspondence. In the novel we find the following scene:

Beyond the gigantic trees rose masses of black rock, enormous, thick, plummet-sheer, which were the presence and testimony of fabulous monuments. My memory had to recall the world of Bosch, the imaginary Babels of painters of the fantastic, the most hallucinated illustrators of the temptations of saints, to find anything like what I was seeing. And even when I hit upon a similarity, I had to discount it immediately because of the proportions. What I was gazing upon was a Titans' city—a city of multiple and spaced constructions—with Cyclopean stairways, mausoleums touching the clouds, vast terraces guarded by strange fortresses of obsidian without battlements or loopholes whose role seemed to be to guard the entrance of some forbidden kingdom against man. There, against a background of light clouds towered the Capital of Forms: an incredible mile-high Gothic cathedral, its two towers, nave, apse, and buttresses situated on a conical rock of rare composition touched with dark iridescences of coal. The belfries were swept by thick mists that swirled as they broke against the granite edges.

In the proportions of these Forms, ending in dizzying terraces, flanked by organ pipes, there was something so not of this world—the mansion of gods, thrones, and stairs designed for some Last Judgment

—that the bewildered mind sought no interpretation of that discon-
certing telluric architecture, accepting, without reasoning, its vertical,
inexorable beauty. The sun was casting quicksilver reflections on that
impossible temple suspended from heaven rather than resting on the
earth. On different planes, defined by the light or shadow, other Forms
could be distinguished, belonging to the same geological family, from
whose edges hung cascades of a hundred falls that finally dissolved in
spray before they reached the treetops. [Pp. 171–72]

In *El libro de la Gran Sabana*, Carpentier had written:

We are entering now the dominion of the Great Monuments. On the
left, over the sea of trees two gigantic mausoleums, of such barbarous
architecture that they remind one of certain pyramids with angles worn
out by the work of centuries, rise up. . . . Those masses, situated
parallel to each other but separated by a great distance, offer a grandiose and funereal appearance. It is as if under shrouds of stone,
sculpted and polished by millennia of storms and rains, the corpses of
titans lay, with their profiles turned toward the rising sun. . . . But
our astonishment is far from vanishing. Since we are new before such
a new landscape, as little used as could have been to the first man the
landscape of Genesis, the Revelation of Forms continues in front of
us. What has arisen to our right has nothing to do with the mausoleums. Imagine a cluster of organ pipes about four hundred meters
high, tied together, soldered and planted vertically on a foundation of
pebbles, like an isolated monument, a lunar fortress, in the center of
the first plain to appear after so much jungle... [*El Nacional*, October
19, 1947, p. 10]

Schomburgk had rendered his vision of this landscape in the same
terms (notice the coincidence in the mention of the plummet, a
metaphor that appears several times in *Travels in British Guiana*):

I have never since met with more bizarre rocky masses, nor again
with valleys and hills that could in the slightest degree compare with
those included in our journey today. Though on previous occasions I
had perforce smiled at the wealth of imagination displayed by the
Indians, and bewailed my northern materialism, when they pointed
out a human being in this rock here, and some animal or other in that
one over there. I nevertheless now fancied that I had been trans-
ported to a veritable fairyland where the world now turned into stone
was passionately awaiting the wizard's wand for deliverance so as to
resume undisturbed once more the active life that a mysterious spell

had brought to a sudden stop. The summit of the collective circle of hills ran out into black masses of granite, gneiss, and quartz, of the most peculiar shapes, whilst the quartz, on account of the reflected solar rays over the dark foliage of the valley, shed a lustre that only increased the illusion still further. It was not long before the thought of losing oneself in this rocky labyrinth gave me an uncanny shudder. [II, 52–53]

In a real labyrinth of mountains, wrestling with, and towering over one another, there suddenly spread out before us the picturesque mountain-chain from the base of which the 2 to 300 foot high Piatzang Rock, bare of all vegetation, raised itself and its two giant granite watchtowers: a stone wall some 50 to 60 feet in height, resembling the crumbling masonry of an old feudal castle, had built itself around it. My first glimpse at this wonderful picture called to mind a hundred memories of the homeland, such as Sachsenburg (Thuringia) with its two old towers, of the narrow Pass where the River Unstrut fights its way to the golden meadows . . . for its hoary granite towers became so transformed with each stroke of the paddle that sometimes the ruins just referred to, or the crumbling and cracked tower of Kyffhäuser, or again one of the old castles along the Rhine, stood before my enraptured gaze.   [II, 144]

The mountains in our immediate vicinity rose in mighty terraces that could not have been laid more skillfully by human hands and here and there even jutted out into the most regular bastions of which the mathematical precision of the slope and sharply corresponding angles could hardly upset the belief that the square and plummet have been used in their construction.   [II, 175]

With eyes continually directed on Roraima and taking but scanty notice on anything else in form and close by, we finally reached the base of the mountain itself and started to climb it, over one of the flats devoid of forest, between huge sandstone boulders of the most fantastic shapes.   [II, 206–7]

Although variously rendered in English as "shapes" or "forms," these are echoes of Goethe's theory of *Urformen* (Shelley's "thoughts and *forms*, which else senseless and *shapeless* were," Neruda's "*shape* of potter's earth") and ultimately of Romantic monism—the emergence of master forms from the desired communion of Mind and Nature. Spengler's theory of the materialization of master cultural symbols in man derived from the observation of landscape is a part of this Romantic doctrine, as is

Surrealism. This is also at the basis of Carpentier's "marvelous American reality" and the narrator-protagonist's mimetic theory of the origins of music in *The Lost Steps* (the field of allusions in the novel—Schiller, Shelley, and Beethoven—is decidedly Romantic).

But the composite (maternal-paternal) nature of such monism remains manifest in the opposition between the vegetal world of the jungle and the rocky masses of the mountains. As the gigantic tree turns to granite with the passage of time, the master forms appear as stony structures with sharply defined edges and lines: "Sometimes, after centuries of existence, the leaves dropped from one of these trees, its lichens dried up, its orchids were extinguished. Its wood aged, acquiring the texture of pink granite, and it stood erect, its monumental skeleton in silent nakedness revealing the laws of an almost mineral architecture, with symmetries, rhythms, balances of crystallized forms" (p. 165). The indefinition and perpetual transformation of signs in nature turns into a stony text that hardens in an ever repeated code of unchanging forms. The living shapes of the jungle become petrified shrouds and the sculptured bodies of fossilized titans. The maternal, watery mansion of the womb turns into the rocky temple of the father; the unpliable memory of previous texts is revealed as the stony tablet upon which the new text can only follow a chiseled message. Accompanied by Fray Pedro, the narrator-protagonist has a vision of this stony text in the cliff of the petroglyphs:

I raised my eyes and found myself at the foot of the gray wall with the rock carvings attributed to the demiurge who, in a tradition that had reached the ears of the primitive inhabitants of the jungle below, triumphed over the Flood and repopulated the world. We were standing on the Mount Ararat of this vast world. This was where the ark had come to rest when the waters began to withdraw and the rat had returned with an ear of corn between its paws. We were where the demiurge threw the stones over his shoulder, like Deucalion, to call into being a new race of men. But neither Deucalion, nor Noah, nor the Chaldean Unapishtim, nor the Chinese or Egyptian Noahs left their signature scrawled for the ages at the point of their arrival. Whereas here there were huge figures of insects, serpents, creatures of the air, beasts of the water and the land, designs of the moon, sun, and stars which someone had cut here with a Cyclopean chisel, employing a method we could not divine. Even today it would be impossible to rig up the gigantic scaffolding that would be needed to raise an army of stonecutters to a height at which they could attack the stone wall with their tools and leave it so clearly inscribed... [Pp. 204–5]

The signature of the father remains fixed, carved into stone; the negation of anteriority, of the father, menaces an originality that can only be achieved through somatic petrification.[35] The jungle turned into a labyrinth of architectural forms announces the city to which the protagonist will have to return and casts the fear of death in its monumental and stony silence. This danger of petrification had been forecast in the novel by the image of the frozen expeditionaries, evoked by the characters as they make their way to the jungle over mountain ridges: "Some stated that near the mouth of that volcano disappearing from sight behind the lower peaks eight members of a scientific expedition lay encrusted in ice as in a show window; they had succumbed half a century before. They sat in a circle, in a state of suspended animation, just as death had transfixed them, gazing from the crystal that covered their faces like a transparent death mask" (p. 80). The closing of

35. A similar evocation of masculinity in stone is seen in the description of the island that the Adelantado calls St. Priapus: "A blind geometry had taken a hand in the scattering of these perpendicular or horizontal stones, which descended in series toward the river, rectangular series, series like congealed pourings of metal, combinations of both joined by flagged paths set at intervals with broken obelisks. In the middle of the stream islands were like piles of haphazard stones, handfuls of unimaginable pebbles tossed here and there by some fantastic leveler of mountains" (p. 138). Also, as a mass of thanksgiving is celebrated after the storm, the trees become a Gothic cathedral at the mention of the Father: "Those ancient, unchanging words took on a portentous solemnity in the midst of the jungle, as though coming from the hidden galleries of primitive Christianity, from the brotherhood of its beginnings, taking on anew, beneath these trees which had never known the ax, a heroic meaning antedating the hymns intoned in the naves of the triumphant cathedrals, antedating the belfries towering aloft in the light of day. *Sanctus, Sanctus, Sanctus, Dominus Deus Sabaoth* . . . The pillars here were tree trunks. Over our heads hung leaves that hid dangers. And around us were the Gentiles, the idol-worshippers, gazing upon the mystery from a narthex of lianas" (p. 176).

the gap between "I" and "he," between the disparate elements that simile and metaphor approximate—the accession to textuality—evokes the fear of somatic petrification.

The addition of Schomburgk's account of his own lost steps creates yet another version and begins to produce a Cervantian kind of composition en abîme—a series of infinitely repeated and receding sequences, evoked in the text by the V's set within each other that mark the entrance to the Valley Where Time had Stopped. This is the kind of infinite regression that is found within the novel itself—a novel which is, ostensibly, in parts that have dates, the travel journal written by the narrator-protagonist, but which could also be the newspaper accounts that he plans to write for profit, or even the novel that he also says he is writing ("and this gave an air of reality to the setting of the novel I was forging," p. 159). One is inclined to believe the latter when, upon close examination, an "error" and concordances are found in the dating of the journal. They uncover a complex numerological system which, barring the wild workings of chance, bespeaks the presence of a creative consciousness that shapes the account of the protagonist's life. Although the first chapter of the novel does not carry a date, the reader knows that the action begins on a Sunday, June 4, because the narrator says: "I was seized by an unwonted curiosity to know which saint was being honored that day. 'June 4, St. Francis of Carraciolo,' said the Vatican edition of the volume in which I once studied the Gregorian chants" (p. 11). That most of the action of the first chapter takes place during Sunday is evident because of Ruth's special performance in the theater, and the various allusions to their weekly coitus, which always occurred on the seventh day (p. 13). Toward the end of the chapter we are told what happens on the next day, Monday June 5: "In the morning, while she [Mouche] was visiting the various consulates, I went to the university" (p. 34). Chapter 2, which begins the dated travel journal, is headed "(Wednesday, June 7)" (p. 37). Each of the four subchapters in chapter 2 is correctly dated: "(Thursday the 8th)" (p. 42), heads subchapter V; "(Friday, the 9th)" (p. 53), subchapter VI; and "(Saturday, the 10th)" (p. 65), subchapter VII. The "error" occurs in chapter 3, where the first subchapter (VIII) is headed "(June 11)" (p. 76), without indication of the day of the week; the second one (IX) simply by "(Later)" (p. 84) and the third (X), by "(Tuesday, the 12th)" (p. 97), when it should have said, Monday, the 12th. The meaning that days of the week acquire throughout the novel bars considering the "error" to be of the Cervantian type. Chapter 5, subchapter XXVI, contains an allusion to the missing Monday: "Today I had made the great decision not to return there. I would try to learn the simple crafts followed here in Santa Mónica de los Venados, beginning by watching the building of the church. I would liberate myself from the fate of Sisyphus, which was laid upon me by the world I came from. I would flee the empty callings, the spinning of a squirrel in a cage, the measured time, the trades of darkness. Mondays to me would no longer be Ash Mondays, nor would I need to remember that Monday is Monday, and the stone I had borne would be for whoever wanted to bow beneath its useless weight" (p. 198). Eduardo G. González has shown further concordances in the dating of the novel. The action, which takes six months, oscillates between Mondays and Sundays —the former being the day of work, of beginning, and of history, the latter being the day of freedom and of magic. Furthermore, the novel begins in June of a year that, taking into account the dates given, can only be 1950, i.e., in the middle month of the year that divides the century. Finally, the last two dates given in the journal are Saturdays, which, like the V's set within each other, announce that magic Sunday to which the protagonist cannot return. As González writes: "The distance of writing is that which mediates between desire and its object, between Saturday and Sunday. Such distance makes possible, in addition, the fiction of today and of the future. Weeks and years will follow one another and a Saturday will always dissolve into a Sunday, but in fiction, the Week and the Year will always remain open. Fiction is the persisting illusion of attempting to close them."[36]

36. Eduardo G. González, "Los pasos perdidos, el azar y la aventura," Revista Iberoamericana, 38 (1972), 614. The configuration of the narrative

The lack of closure in the text (except on a level where the "error" were accepted as correct) indicates, as does the erroneous geography of the landscape, the fictionality of the novel. This inner or self-referential fictionality is underscored precisely by the fact that the novel ends on a Saturday and that it contains six chapters. Saturday is the day of fiction, of Saturnalia and Carnival. Saturn's day is the feast where the king is ritualistically killed to give way to a new epoch: "A characteristic of ancient mythology is the idea that each reign must give way to another, even on the plane of the divine; it was an idea which was inextricably bound up with the notion of life as a continuity and succession, and of sacrifice as the sole source of re-creation. The successive cosmic reigns of Uranus, Saturn and Jupiter provided a model for earthly government, for the 'ritual assassination of the king' at certain astral conjunctions or at the end of certain periods, and later for the displacement of this bloody ceremony by its simulacra."[37] Whereas in *The King-dom of This World* the Carnival is at the center of the text, in *The Lost Steps* it is at the end, the temporal throne of the narrator, who must occupy that temporal space to survey what has happened before. The bogus king ritualistically killed at the end is the narrator-protagonist, the author, encased in that fictional no-time where, like the frozen explorers, he presides over the time of transformations.

The missing Monday suggests that the novel is "discordant," an "unfinished" text. The fact that some sections are dated while others are not, the presence of unassimilated essayistic passages, and the blatant contradictions in what the narrator-protagonist says about others and what he says about himself (his scorn of Mouche for faults that he shares with her, for example) reinforce this suggestion of incompleteness. Is the text a travel journal in the process

---

according to the week, traces of which we saw in *The Kingdom of This World*, derives from the well-known Hebraic and Christian tradition. See Frank E. and Fritzie P. Manuel, "Sketch for a Natural History of Paradise," *Daedalus* (Winter 1972), "Myth, Symbol and Culture," pp. 103–4.

37. J. E. Cirlot, *A Dictionary of Symbols*, trans. Jack Sage (New York, 1962), pp. 266–67.

of becoming a novel, or is it an unfinished novel that will imitate a travel journal? This reading, accepting the fictional identification of narrator and author, would have to lead to the conclusion that *The Lost Steps* is an unfinished work, in the same way that *El libro de la Gran Sabana* and the protagonist's musical piece were left unfinished. Such a reading would of course corroborate the inconclusiveness signaled by the recurring Saturday. If, on the other hand, one takes into account the symbolic order that emerges from the error and the dating of the text, including the Monday, one would have to accept the presence of a higher authorial source—Carpentier—responsible for contriving the interconnectedness of the text. But, as we have seen, if we take Carpentier's voice as being the authorial one—the one that identifies itself in the "Author's Note"—we still encounter further duplicities and "errors." Either reading leads to a lack of completion, to an absent synthesis and unachieved wholeness.

As with the search for the fusion of self and history in *The Kingdom of This World*, only the order of writing emerges—a simulacrum. The fusion of self and history in the Valley Where Time Had Stopped proves illusory, both in the process that led to the composition of *The Lost Steps* and within the novel itself: the error in the dating of the journal, which can be unveiled by means of a careful reading of the text itself (not as in *The Kingdom of This World*, where anachronisms are concealed almost irretrievably), may very well be a sign of this incongruousness. The self-reflexive emblem of these multiple refractions within the novel could be that often-mentioned Baroque mirror in which the protagonist sees himself in the Curator's office: "In the familiar mirror with its heavy rococo frame crowned by the Esterházy coat of arms, I saw myself sitting stiffly like a child taken visiting" (p. 16).

The autobiographical nature of *The Lost Steps*, in all its complexity, is both cause and effect of the strategic position that this novel occupies in the totality of Carpentier's production. Its recollective synthesizing attempt, at both a biographical and a literary level, bear the mark of the conversion. John Freccero has this to say in a remarkable paragraph about what he calls the "novel of the self" (the pattern of which was established by Augustine's *Confessions*):

Conversion in Pauline terms was a burial of the "old man" and a putting on of the new. Similarly, this detachment of the self that *was* from the self that *is* constitutes the first requirement of any literature of the self that pretends to sincerity. This is most apparent in some of the modern forms of the literature of the self which end not in synthesis, but in infinite regression—a series of attempts to grasp the truth about oneself which are constantly being replaced by fresh attempts: the novel, the journal on the novel, the journal on the journal. In such cases there is no real detachment, no gap between *persona* who was and author who is. Because of the essential continuity of subject and object, of observer and the self which is observed, there is no place to stand from which the flow of consciousness can be measured, let alone judged, because both subject and object are swept along by the flow of time. Only death can close the series, lock the door of the self so that inventory may be taken. Death being what it is, however, it is impossible for the self to "take stock" of itself. It is the anguish of the novelist that he can know himself with sufficient detachment only when he is all that he can ever be, at which point he ceases to know anything at all. For this very simple reason bad faith and self-deception seem built into the genre, and modern "confessions" usually wind up in protestations of innocence.[38]

Such is clearly the case in *The Lost Steps* and in the process of its composition, though the last version (his statements about the genesis of the novel), when Carpentier appears to revert to the mystifications of 1947, may show that the continuity between subject and object is not a given, but that the positing of such a continuity *is* essential in order to write—that one must give in to what Paul de Man has called "this persistent temptation of literature to fulfill itself in a single moment. The temptation of immediacy is constitutive of a literary consciousness and has to be included in a definition of the specificity of literature."[39] But if every attempt at self-examination turns into a new version multiplying the lost steps into infinity, where then is the conversion?

38. "Introduction" to *Dante: A Collection of Critical Essays* (Englewood Cliffs, N.J., 1965), p. 5.
39. "Literary History and Literary Modernity," in *Blindness and Insight: Essays in the Rhetoric of Contemporary Criticism* (New York, 1971), p. 152.

As we have noticed by examining Carpentier's statements about the composition of *The Lost Steps*, the conversion is not to be found outside the fictional texts. For example, in 1952, when he was either finishing *The Lost Steps* or had already finished it, Carpentier said the following in a panel discussion printed in *Cruz del Sur*: "I have many times maintained (and it is an old hobby-horse of mine) that our truth is not to be found necessarily in Europe. It should not be sought by the facile solutions of Darío's generation, which consisted mainly in falling in step with the latest Parisian movement and attempting to adapt to it the spirit of our poetry and even our language. Our truth is not at the existentialist café in Paris, nor in some avant-garde clique which may be very interesting, very amusing, whose existence it is useful to be made aware of. No, our goals are different."[40] Carpentier goes on to say, in terms that are very familiar, that the goal of the American artist is to find an American "accent": "That American accent comes from the adaptation of the European conqueror to the life that he is forced to lead in a continent subject to different telluric forces, that offers him new scales of distance, a new table of proportions between man and the landscape—a continent where one of the most extraordinary cultural events of history took place, since it became the crossroads in which, for the first time, races that had never met found each other."[41] The Spenglerian accent of those remarks becomes even stronger when Carpentier alludes to Heitor Villa-Lobos as the model Latin American artist: "But there is in that quartet [by Villa-Lobos], a kind of assimilation of landscape, of songs, of nature, of popular music, of such a nature—being so total—that when Villa-Lobos makes the instruments of his quartet perform, they make a music that can only be Brazilian."[42] There can be no question that the Carpentier reflected by this text is in perfect consonance with the one who wrote in 1941 the essays on

40. Antonio Estévez, Alejo Carpentier, Inocente Palacios, Pedro A. Ríos Reyna, and Vicente Emilio Rojo, "Problemas de la música en América Latina," *Cruz del Sur* (Caracas), 1, no. 4 (June 1952), 53.
    41. Ibid., p. 56.
    42. Ibid.

the decline of Europe but not with the multi-faceted one who emerges from his fictions. To seek unity on this level would amount to falling prey to the desire for reconciliation and congruity present and frustrated in *The Lost Steps*. "Manhunt" (1956), Carpentier's next published work, is a better guide to the transformations undergone by Carpentier's fictions.

3

Because readers have most often encountered "Manhunt" in *War of Time* (1958), where it was reprinted along with "Journey Back to the Source," "Like the Night," and "The Highroad of Saint James," the novella has been associated with magical realism and Carpentier's experiments with fantastic literature in the forties.[43] Carpentier's statement that the idea for the novel occurred to him in the forties, while he was in Havana, has made this association even more plausible.[44] The return in "Manhunt" to a consideration of the theology of narrative also seems to confirm it. But, while it is not entirely erroneous to see "Manhunt" in

43. "Manhunt" was published in 1956 (Buenos Aires: Losada), although several fragments appeared in *Orígenes*, 11, no. 36 (1954), 6–16. In 1954 Carpentier stated that the novel was finished and the manuscript already at the printer's (C. D. [Carlos Dorante] "Contrapunto entre selva y ciudad establece la nueva novela de Alejo Carpentier," *El Nacional*, December 18, 1954, p. 44). All quotations here are from Harriet de Onís's translation in *Noonday*, 2 (1950), 109–180, which differs from the original in three ways: (1) an explanatory note signed by Carpentier was inserted at the beginning informing the reader of the presence of two narrators who live near each other; (2) the interior monologue of the ticket seller was italiziced to distinguish it from those of the fugitive; (3) the subchapter divisions were eliminated.

44. "Carpentier stated that 'Manhunt' is based on a true incident that happened in the Havana of the period scoured by bands of terrorists following the downfall of Machado. In the first years of Fulgencio Batista's regime [the first regime, 1940 to 1944] the author was installing and synchronizing the sound effects for Aeschylus' *Coeforas* at the University of Havana. In the midst of the dramatic scene of Clytemnestra's death a shot rang out. Carpentier interrupted his work with various pieces of sound equipment and saw a gangster fall assassinated in the Boreas courtyard" (Klaus Müller-Bergh, "Entrevista con Alejo Carpentier," *Cuadernos Americanos*, 28, no. 4 [1969], p. 144).

the light of *War of Time*, a reading of the novella must take into
account *The Lost Steps*. Such a reading would indicate that, although preserving some features of the works of the forties, the
transition from *El libro de la Gran Sabana* to *The Lost Steps* has
radically altered those features and eliminated others. Yet it must
be also borne in mind that there are characteristics of Carpentier's
works after *La música en Cuba* that remain until the present—
namely, the historical research involved in the composition of his
fictions and their reconstruction of an obscure historical figure.[45]
But aside from this, what remains of the forties in "Manhunt" is
above all the prominent role played by the old black woman, who
suggests the presence of magic, and the intricate technical display,
which suggests the fantastic. From *The Lost Steps* on, Afro-
Americans cease to occupy a central position in Carpentier's work,
and the fantastic as stemming from the fusion of nature and creative consciousness is unveiled as a literary conceit.

But in spite of the presence of the black woman and the daz-
zling technical experiments, there are no fantastic elements in
"Manhunt." The black woman, significantly, is dead, or nearly
dead, throughout the story, as if the mother had been annihilated
after *The Lost Steps*. And not only is "Manhunt," like *The Lost
Steps*, a first-person narrative (for the most part), but Carpentier
has subtitled it "novel," indicating an organic relationship between
character and setting, and a "development" of the characters only
conceivable after that novel. Both the protagonists in "Manhunt,"
like the narrator-protagonist in the previous novel, remain nameless. Moreover, even if more obliquely than *The Lost Steps*, "Manhunt" is made up of many autobiographical elements: one character studies architecture and the other music, and both are led to
betray their vocations. In addition, the novel is set in a precise
historical period that not only is contemporaneous with Carpentier

45. Here the "biography" is that of José Soler, a student-activist of the
thirties. For details on these and all other matters pertaining to the historical
background of the novel, see Modesto G. Sánchez, "La elaboración artística
de *El acoso*" (M. A. thesis Trinity College, Hartford, Conn., 1972). Part of
this thesis has appeared in print as "El fondo histórico de *El acoso*: 'Epoca
Heroica y Epoca del Botín,' " *Revista Iberoamericana*, 41 (1975), 399–422.

but also constitutes the historicopolitical context of his youthful life—the aborted revolution of the thirties in Cuba.

The fact that it reconstructs a history closely related to the author, the fact that both protagonists are artists of sorts, and the fact that commitment to the present-in-history leads them away from their vocations justify considering "Manhunt" in relation to *The Lost Steps*. These and other elements indicate that "Manhunt" is, as it were, a postscript to *The Lost Steps*. If the narrator-protagonist of that novel realizes at the end that he must return to the city, to present history, the drama lived by the two protagonists of "Manhunt" in the city is the future that their predecessor did not narrate, but acted out by writing the text of the novel. If *The Lost Steps* was generated by the questions about history and the artist raised by *The Kingdom of This World*, "Manhunt" centers on the problems of writing that *The Lost Steps*, in turn, opened. Like an *auto sacramental* in its intense and self-reflexive symbolism, "Manhunt" is Carpentier's allegory of writing. What the novel dramatizes is the generation of the text: a liturgical, primeval drama of its birth and death as well as of its filial relations. *The Lost Steps* led to the assumption of self-referentiality that *The Kingdom of This World* eluded; "Manhunt" plays on the terrors of self-referentiality—the reification and fragmentation of self that we observed in our reading of that novel. In no other text of Carpentier's (with the possible exception of *Reasons of State*) is reading more compulsively present: the ticket seller reading Beethoven's biography and the ordinances of his job, the fugitive reading the book of prayers, the inscriptions on buildings, newspaper clippings, books on architecture.

The question of the artist in contemporary society is, as in *The Lost Steps*, the manifest theme of "Manhunt," and this Romantic topic of the artist's alienation is couched in terms of a longing for the absolute, for oneness and restoration. This desire involves once more returning to a lost paradise, the world of nature and the mother, and a search for God, the maker of order and giver of meaning in the universe. The search takes various general forms: love, religion, art, and political action. Although distinct echoes of

192 Alejo Carpentier

Joyce (*Ulysses* and *Portrait of the Artist as a Young Man*), Huxley (*Point Counter Point*), Kafka (*The Trial*), and Sartre (*La nausée*) abound, the context of the quest is thoroughly Romantic, and more specifically Romantic through the emblem of the Gothic.[46] If Beethoven's symphony is an overwhelming presence in the novella, architecture is the most revealing symbolic code; there is a proliferation of mansions, churches, fountains, colonnades, monuments, sarcophagi, as well as an abundance of more technical architectural terms, such as cornices, acanthi, dentils, capitals, peristyles, and the like.

In what appears to be a passing allusion, the hunted one asks himself, as he attempts to find refuge in some part of the city: "Why were men today denied that ancient privilege of sanctuary that he had read about in a book on the Gothic?" (p. 168). The book alluded to here is one that had a tremendous impact on Carpentier's generation: Wilhelm Worringer's *Formprobleme der Gotik*, based precisely on the notion of religion as a refuge from terror.[47] Immediately after mentioning this "book on the Gothic" (which is part of his pure but abandoned past as a student of architecture), the fugitive sees a church: "Out of the night shone a church, surrounded by ficus and palm trees, gleaming through all the finials of its white bell-tower rising slender above the lights reflected from the sward. Its stained glass windows took fire; the purples and greens of its rose window came aflame. And suddenly the doors of the nave opened, a pathway of red carpet leading to the altar blazing with candles. The hunted one slowly approached

46. In "Renuevo de la novela," *El Nacional*, October 14, 1953, p. 30, Carpentier speaks about some of these authors; see the quotation from this essay on pp. 66–67, above.

47. In "Ortega y Gasset," *El Nacional*, October 20, 1955, p. 16, Carpentier refers to Worringer as one of the authors whom he read in the *Revista de Occidente*. Worringer's book first appeared in 1912 under the title *Formprobleme der Gotik*; in 1907 a theoretical preamble had appeared under the title *Abstraktion und Einfühlung*. Ortega devoted a series of articles to Worringer in *El Imparcial* (Madrid), during the summer of 1911, and later had the book translated into Spanish. Worringer had some influence on Spengler as well as a wide impact on Latin America. Quotations here are from *Form in Gothic*, trans. Sir Herbert Read, 2d ed. (New York, 1957).

the proffered Haven; he passed under the ogive of one of its side doors and stopped, bedazzled, at the foot of a column whose stone oozed incense" (pp. 168–69).

That this Gothic cathedral does not offer the fugitive the refuge that he seeks is significant for reasons that we shall soon see; but its significance here is that it brings together the many Gothic motifs strewn throughout the text, not the least of which is the tower in which he takes refuge at the black woman's house, which is reached through a spiral staircase. In *The Lost Steps* the narrator-protagonist, after enduring the "Second Trial" (the storm), sees the mountainous rocky masses as a Gothic cathedral, and in *El libro de la Gran Sabana* Carpentier had described the ogival arches of the rustic church built by the Franciscan friars at Santa Elena de Uairén. The reiteration of the Gothic is not merely a motif, but a sign of the nature of the hunted one's quest. Worringer had spoken of what he considered to be the two main aspects of the Gothic: the rapturous, sensual desire for transcendence and union with God, the mystical side, and the rationalistic, scholastic side, which followed a logical, even mechanical ascension to God. Worringer associated the mystical side with the interior of the Gothic cathedral and the scholastic with the exterior. These two aspects of the Gothic are also those of the fugitive's quest. On the one hand he believes to have discovered God with the clarity of reason, following the steps of the cosmological argument:

The astounding new thing was God. God, who had revealed himself in the cigar lighted by the old woman the evening before she took sick. Suddenly, that gesture of taking the ember from the fire and raising it to her face . . . had grown pregnant with overwhelming implications. As it raised the ember, the hand carried a fire that came from remote ages, fire that antedated the matter consumed and transformed by the fire—matter that would be only a possibility of fire without the hand that kindled it. But if this present fire were an end in itself, it required a previous act to achieve it. And this action postulated another, and others prior to it, which could come only from an Initial Will. It was necessary that there be an origin, a point of departure, a Fountainhead of fire which, through the ages beyond reckoning, had illuminated the faces of men. And this First Fire could not have kindled itself. [P. 138]

Later, when he is concealed in the theater (earlier in the text, of course), he applies the same logic of the cosmological argument to his predicament. All that has occurred to him is part of a divine plan of a God who was always in the *afterwards* of events, who knew in advance: "I stand before the Lord made manifest in song [the symphony], as He might have been in the burning bush; as I glimpsed Him, lighted, blinded, in that ember the old woman raised to her face. I know now that no offender was ever more carefully observed, more exactly placed in the Balance of the Divine Regard, than the one who fell into the snare, into the supreme trap —led by the inexorable Will where a language without words has just revealed to him the expiatory meaning of these last days" (p. 118). While reason thus leads him to discover the plan behind the "train of events" that has taken him to his present state, he also experiences mystical raptures during which he longs to feel the presence of God:

He did not want to eat. He offered to God the emptiness of his stomach as the first step toward purification. He felt light, rewarded, understood. And it seemed to him that a glowing understanding put him in intimate contact with matter, with the eternal reality of the things around him. He understood the night, he understood the stars, he understood the sea which came toward him in the reflector of the searchlight, uncomplainingly tormented each time its turning brought it full against his gaze. But this understanding was not in words or images. It was his whole body, his pores, his mind become being that understood. His body had become integrated for a moment with the Truth. He dropped face down on the brick tiles that still gave off the heat of the previous day. He sobbed from so much clarity at the foot of the Tower in shadows. [Pp. 134–35]

All of the hunted one's musing about stone, about the stony labyrinth in which he is trapped, are reflections of Worringer's analysis of the presence of scholasticism in the Gothic. In both there is, as Worringer puts it, the "same logical frenzy, the same methodical madness, the same rationalistic expenditure for an irrational aim" (p. 107). That irrational aim is, of course, knowledge of God and fusion with Him, pursued both in the "petrified scholasticism" of the cathedral and the desire to dematerialize stone. The verticality in the descriptions in the novel—columns, lighthouse, and particularly the belvedere in which the hunted one takes refuge—are signs of this vertical desire for transcendence.[48] So, of course, are the character's waverings between his anxiety to keep intact his physical integrity (the fear of castration that leads him to "sing") and his yearning to be rid of his body, to soar away from that material self that the has to labor to keep hidden from his pursuers.

But the Gothic is an inverted emblem, for its signs constantly betray the fugitive. As in *The Lost Steps*, the protagonist's quest ends in failure. He is thrown out of the church where he seeks sanctuary because the book of prayers that he carries contains the wrong cult (the Afro-Cuban), and he dies on the floor of a theater that has become a cathedral with its "five doors" and the actions of the spectators: "the almost imperceptible movement of hands, of sleeves, of fingers, the getting up, the checking of belongings, which in church goes with the *Ite misa est*" (p. 177). He is thrown out of all the houses in which he attempts to hide. The house-temple turns into a house of terrors (the fortress), a house of death (the old woman's house), a trap (the concert hall), a house of treason (Estrella's), or a wall-less house (the House of the Effort). This house without walls, the dismantled mansion that leaves him unsheltered for the last time—like Ti Noël at the end of *The Kingdom of This World*—is an ironic inversion of the Gothic church and of the desire to dematerialize stone. According to Worringer, the thrust upward, the shifting of weight away from the sides of the Gothic cathedral, was a movement whose ultimate goal was the abolition of the wall: "The pressure of the vault was concentrated on the four corner piers supporting the vaulting, thereby removing the pressure from the walls between the piers. It was the first step on the road which ended in the complete dissolution of

48. Harriet de Onís translates *mirador* as "tower," but in "Manhunt" it is a belvedere, defined by Webster as "an open, roofed gallery in an upper story, built for giving a view of the scenery." This sort of construction apparently originated in port cities, to allow relatives of a mariner to see ships coming in at a distance. Belvederes are usually surrounded by an open balcony called a "widow's walk," from which the wife of a seaman could scan the horizon and anticipate her husband's safe return home.

the wall" (p. 156). The house of the magistrate has been reduced to pillars without a roof and without walls: "the fugitive reached the dark street of the sad cafe, with its columns of green wood that imitated a squalid Tuscan, and with long strides covered the distance to the corner where the House of the Effort, wall-less, was but a group of columns still standing on a marble floor covered with stones, joists, plaster that had fallen from the ceilings. The window grilles had been carried off, and the lions holding a ring in their mouth. An inclined wheelbarrow track crossed the great drawing room, where several shovels formed an **X** above a pile of formless rubble" (pp. 162–63).[49] Instead of the apex, the converging point of the spiral, where all lines meet at the top of the Gothic cathedral in a metaphor of space conquered, of the absolute, the wall-less house is total chaos, the boundlessness and meaninglessness of the unparceled void.

That unmarked space of the dismantled house—that **X**—is premonitory of the protagonist's death, of the ultimate dissolution of consciousness that is the only liberation afforded him. That dissolution had been prepared by the constant horizontal movement of the protagonist: "He advanced from column to column—as he had previously done from tree to tree—timidly approaching, step by step, the communion table" (p. 169). This asymptotic displacement toward communion is punctuated by repetition—a repetition that evokes, as opposed to the Gothic, Classical architecture:

In Classical ornament there is a general inclination toward repetition of the selected motif the opposite way round, as in a mirror, thereby avoiding the appearance of endless progression produced by repetition. By repetition of this reversed kind, a feeling of serenity, of completion in the rhythm, is created; this successive arrangement gives an effect of restful addition which never mars the symmetry . . . [In the Gothic]

49. Sánchez conjectures, on the basis of his exhaustive research (which allows him to locate with great precision on a map of Havana all the buildings mentioned and the route of the fugitive), that this house may very well have been designed by Georges Carpentier, the author's father; "La elaboración," p. 142, n.29. The **X** signifying an absence is also used in *The Lost Steps*, where the protagonist's boss is always called by his initials, X.T.H., *Exteeaych*, and in *Reasons of State*, where the deposed dictator is called "the Ex."

ornament repetition does not bear this restful character of addition, but has, so to speak, a character of multiplication. The intervention of any desire for organic moderation and serenity is here lacking. A continually increasing activity without pauses or accents is set up and repetition has only the one aim of giving the particular motif a potential infinity. [P. 55]

The opposition between the horizontal repetition of the Classical ornament and the potential infinity of the Gothic forecloses both the serenity of the former and the converging thrust to the apex in the latter. In "Manhunt," as in *The Lost Steps*, no such convergence or serenity is to be found; instead there are the infinitely receding sequences. This infinity-bound progression, terminated only by death in "Manhunt" and by plurality-in-the-present in *The Lost Steps*, destroys the symmetry that was found in the work of the forties—that of *The Kingdom of This World*, for example, where the text is divided into symmetrical halves. In *The Lost Steps*, symmetry is undermined not only by the composition en abîme but also by the repetition of Saturdays at the end of the novel. In "Manhunt," repetition leads to death and/or fragmentation, to a convulsive multiplication observed precisely in the narrators.

The most striking and confusing aspect of "Manhunt" is its Faulknerian multiplicity of narrators, a bewildering technical *tour de force* that makes the novel the most inaccessible of Carpentier's texts.[50] No antecedent can be found in Carpentier's work for this experimentation with narrative voice except in *The Lost Steps*. The plurality-in-the-present realized by the narrator-protagonist at the end of *The Lost Steps* is, as it were, blown up in "Manhunt," a text narrated by an omniscient third-person and two first-person narrators, who are themselves pluralized. The displacement of narrative voice between third and first person in *The Lost Steps* and the subsequent unfolding of the protagonist into several selves that

50. In an extremely negative critique of "Manhunt," Marinello said that the novel was of the kind to interest only a small number of specialists; "Sobre el asunto en la novela: a propósito de tres novelas recientes," in Marinello's *Meditación americana* (*cinco ensayos*) (Buenos Aires, 1959), p. 72.

comment upon each other are concretely re-enacted in "Manhunt" in the political activist and the ticket seller, who meet fleetingly but whose lives are intertwined without their knowledge. The same interaction between "I" and "he" is found here between two separate consciousnesses which do not know each other but which the reader is bound to confuse and must try, in the first chapter, to pry apart. Their separation as well as their proximity is suggested by their living in contiguous buildings and above all by their visiting the same prostitute, Estrella. In a sense they are like brothers. In the concert hall, the hunted one recognizes Beethoven's symphony because he has been hearing it for the past few days on the old scratchy records of the ticket seller. Both can follow and anticipate the various motifs of the symphony because of that common memory that they unknowingly share, like the body of the prostitute. There are many other parallels between them. They both come from rural towns (the fugitive from the east, the other from the west), where they have left a past now contemplated as filled with purity and innocent erotic longings, and they both seek recognition in a city that entraps them and thwarts their desires. In frustration they both seek reintegration through the erotic favors of Estrella. (Because she is obviously mulatto, the fugitive associates her with the black wet nurse.) The name of the prostitute (Estrella, star), of course, denotes the fusion of their destinies; she is the inverted high point where their lives and quests meet.[51] Like Perro and Cimarrón in "Los fugitivos" they follow common destinies but are separate consciousnesses ultimately at war with each other. The counterfeit bill that they both handle underscores this lack of communication and hostility. When the

51. Frances Wyers Weber writes: "The meshing of the visits paid by both to Estrella is a descriptive, static device, because the prostitute, as her name implies, is a fixed point of convergence, the motionless, timeless center in the lives of her clients and the pivot between *acosado* and *taquillero*" ("*El acoso:* Alejo Carpentier's War on Time," *PMLA*, 78 [1963], 442). While this is true, the same could be said of the black wet nurse; toward the end of the action, after his failure to engage Estrella because of the false bill, the ticket seller also thinks of the old woman and decides to take her some sweets. Both protagonists are left in the no man's land between the dead old woman and Estrella—two centers that no longer provide comfort.

ticket seller recognizes the body of the hunted one at the end and speaks about him, it is only to add to the list of his crimes by accusing him of passing counterfeit money.

The text of the novella is composed mostly of recollections of these two parallel yet separate consciousnesses and by their actions in a brief fictional present that is supposed to comprise the forty-six minutes that it takes to play Beethoven's Third Symphony (chapters 1 and 3, encompassing five subchapters). But the fragmentation of the narrative voice occurs not only through the splitting of the narrator-protagonist but also within the consciousness of the hunted one and in the presence of the third-person narrator. While the activities of both characters in that fictional present of the last night of the action are narrated in that third-person, free indirect style, akin to the first/third person of *The Lost Steps*, and for the most part in the imperfect, the moments of recollection are narrated in the present. The correlation between that present and memory is vitally significant, and brings us back to architecture. The hunted one contemplates his criminal past and says to himself: "(Although I have tried to bury it, to silence it, it is here [*presente*], always here [*siempre presente*], after months of forgetting that was not forgetting—when I found myself in that afternoon again, I would shake my head to rid myself of the image, like a child who sees dirty thoughts clinging to the body of his parents)" (p. 157). The permanent present of memory is associated here, as throughout the text, with the idea of the fall, of the character's sinful actions from which he tries to escape vainly, and serves as a counterpoint to his present actions (chapters 1 and 3). The present glides into the imperfection of the recent past ("discourse" and "history" mingle, to use Benveniste's categories), to fuse with the past that is fixed and become an eternal present, where the whole story is ordered like the symphony. The "I-he" of the present struggles against the fixed "I" of his fall—the story of his political activities, of the assassinations, of his cowardly vote against a fellow student (who, like him, "sang"), and his own treason. "I will not leave" (p. 177), thinks the hunted one in the last episode while he is hiding in the theater; but there is no possible salvation, for his death is the unavoidable end of that repeatable story, the only event that will furnish it with a coherent teleological and eschatological finale—the point at which all the tenses will become one in the present. As Frances Wyers Weber writes in her brilliant analysis of the novel: "The principal characters, the *acosado* and the *taquillero*, see the course of their own lives not as a psychological unfolding but as a kind of timeless, mythical drama of primal innocence destroyed by the fall into sin."[52] The climax of that drama, the present, death, is associated throughout the story with lifeless bodies: the *cuerpo presente* of the old woman and the athletic body of the executed student, as well as that of Estrella, always seen by her as cut off from her head.[53] The *cuerpo presente* is a liturgical expression denoting an absence, that of the soul, and its inverted correlative is the presence of God in the Eucharist. Death, of course, is the only permanent presence: the true apex where all the different lines will merge in one uninterrupted continuum. It is the only vantage point from which the totality of self may be recovered and from which the whole story can be narrated in a single tense. The *cuerpo presente* is the text, as it fuses with that archtext of the repeatable drama, the stony labyrinth in which the hunted one is trapped, the iced body of the old black woman. It is through association between the body and the text that "Manhunt" unveils its self-referential drama.

Though the plot progression is begun at a different point, "Manhunt" follows the same pattern of fall and redemption found in *The Lost Steps*, and as in the earlier novel, the protagonist does not achieve redemption. Like his predecessor, the fugitive seeks that redemption through art. But he is also compelled to abandon that path, attempting instead a return to the mother. He is sent to

52. Ibid., p. 440.
53. Eduardo G. González has written illuminating commentaries on the presence of the body in the novel from which I have profited here. See "El tiempo del hombre," esp. pp. 75–78. Part of González's work on "Manhunt" appeared in "*El acoso:* lectura, escritura e historia," in *El cuento hispano-americano ante la crítica,* ed. Enrique Pupo-Walker (Madrid, 1973), pp. 126–49.

Havana to study and to live with his former wet nurse; later he leaves her in order to be free to bring women into his apartment. When he is forced to betray his associates, he seeks refuge again with the old woman to escape from their vengeance, leaving when she dies to seek sanctuary at Estrella's. When the prostitute fails him, he decides, after discovering that the House of the Effort has been leveled, to return to the house of the old black woman, hoping to find safety at her wake. As in *The Lost Steps*, the surrogate mothers multiply (Ruth-Mouche, Rosario-María del Carmen; old woman–Estrella), or betray him. The wet nurse dies, bringing danger of exposure and casting him out of the belvedere; Estrella reveals what she knows about him to his pursuers to set in motion the last stage of the chase. As in *The Lost Steps* love is not a way back to lost innocence, a reintegration. Sexuality as return to the womb appears not as a restoration but as a mechanical repetition of an act that is a corruption of the initial union with the mother. Sexuality is not a rebirth but a redeath, a stroking of the body. The infernal scene at the public baths, where the hunted one went with the scholarship holder instead of returning to the black woman's wake, brings about the fugitive's death; he is unarmed when surprised by his enemies and has to flee into the theater, where his death is a kind of inverted birth: "They will lock the five doors with padlocks, and I will lie down on that red carpet of that box—the one where those in the back row are already getting up—curled up like a dog" (p. 178). By dying in the theater, the hunted one completes the journey of the narrator-protagonist of *The Lost Steps*, who had begun his adventure in the theater. In the theater he will replay in his memory the story of his life up to that point, and die after realizing the inexorable order of the events which have led him there. The death in the theater signals the betrayal of art, religion, and love as paths back to innocence. The only reintegration achieved is with the theater itself in a material sense; the killer, at the end, fires, not at the fugitive, but "toward the floor" (p. 179).

The last subchapter of the novel (the second of chapter 3, or the eighteenth) opens, as did the first, with a quotation from the biography of Beethoven that the ticket seller is reading: "*After this prodigious Scherzo, with its whirling and its arms, comes the Finale, a paean of joy and liberty, all festival and dances, its exultant marches, and the rich spirals of its variations. When suddenly, in the midst of it, Death appears, which lies beyond victory. But, once again, Victory turns its back. And the voice of Death is drowned out by the shouts of joy*" (p. 178). The Romantic victory over death proclaimed by the biography is in ironic contrast to the victory of death in the fiction. Rather than a liberation, the concordance of symphony and plot is a negation of freedom.[54] The presence of that exalted biography of Beethoven indicates the distance between the redemption promised by art and the unredemptive, death-bound thrust of life, the impossibility of attaching a permanent meaning to signs except when ordered and fixed through death. Like the book of prayers that the fugitive wants to use to gain access to the church, the biography of Beethoven fails to give the ticket seller access to the realm of art. The biography and the prayerbook, like the (falsely) counterfeit bill, betray the protagonists. The bill, significantly, turns out to be good, but only after the hunted one has died and it has been taken from the ticket seller. All texts betray the protagonists; all signs become enemies because their meaning is always postponed to an afterward that they will never reach. The presence of that fragment from Beethoven's biography also points to the questions of biography that the novel raises, and thereby to the arrangement of the plot.

There are at least two ways of reordering the hunted one's life to glean its potential meaning; by rereading the novel, or by reading chapters 1 and 3 before chapter 2.[55] In "Journey Back to the Source," because of the magic of Melchor, there is the possibility of a first reading that is already a rereading, since Marcial's life is

54. González writes of the "terror" of order that hangs over the protagonists, as opposed to the falsely "beneficent" order of music and the mass; "El tiempo del hombre," p. 86. As we shall see, that terror is manifest in the threat of petrification.

55. Anderson Imbert suggests that "upon a second reading the chaos is illuminated as a splendid geometry" (as quoted by Weber, "El acoso," p. 443, n.8).

narrated from his death backward. The reading suggested by "Man-hunt" (chapters 1, 2, and 3 read in succession) leads the reader to the brink of the protagonist's death and then to a review of the events that bring him to such a predicament. The first two read-ings suggested give the reader access to a point beyond death that the character seeks but can never reach. The reader, in other words, practices a reading of the *whole* text parallel to that of the events in chapter 2 practiced by the protagonist, when he recollects the "train of events" leading to the theater. This chapter, which is composed of the protagonist's recollections, and his recollections of recollections, does not have the chronological sequence that we can give it by retelling the plot but exists on a horizontal time line without depth—the eternal present of memory—with its mirror-house illusion of simultaneity and the concomitance of spatiotemporal moments. Whereas the chronological reading re-veals the inexorable concatenation of events analogous to the cos-mological argument, the actual sequence is connected by a series of motifs that acquire meaning outside the temporal chain. Both these arrangements belie the *textual* nature of chapter 2, which is very much like that of the stories of the forties. But the protagonist is only dimly aware of the relationships outside the temporal chain that we as readers can exhaust; he is caught in the desire to find theodicy in the concatenation of events; we know better and can look for other meanings that escape him. Chapter 2 is that per-petual present of memory that can be re-enacted—a present lived, a present body (the text, memory) which, like that of the dead woman preserved in ice, is oblivious to past and future. By reading the past as we read the novel, that present lived begins to assume the interconnectedness and meaningful arrangement that we give the entire novel as readers, but a definitive reading is foreclosed for the protagonist.

It is not fortuitous, then, that chapter 2 is subdivided, like the stories of the forties, into a significant number of subchapters (thirteen) and that it comprises the last six days of the fugitive's life. It is as if Carpentier had enclosed one of the stories of the forties in a biographical pattern in order to experiment with the two directions his fiction had taken until then. The coincidence of the fugitive's last two weeks with the redemption cycle and of his final days with Holy Week strengthens this relation and further emphasizes the self-referentiality of the novel.[56] It is the final irony of the novel that the protagonist dies on Resurrection Sunday, and that his passion is parallel to Christ's. The Sunday that is not reached at the end of *The Lost Steps* is the one in which the present action of "Manhunt" takes place, the (false) Resurrection Sunday from which his life attains meaning. But it is a fictitious meaning in death. The fugitive's reading of his own biography is shortsighted, for he fails to see the relationship between his passion and that of Christ. We as readers perceive the irony and the defeat; we see that the only significance which the novel accords to the fugitive's life lies in the repetition of an archetypal pattern of passion and resurrection.

It is the error of that naive reader, the ticket seller, to seek a pattern of redemption through art in a literal reading of Beethoven's biography; and it is an illusion for the hunted one to attempt to discover a redemptive theodicy in a reading of his own life. Only the reader, provisionally and fictively situated on the far side of death, can see the "total" biography of the fugitive and establish the final connections; only the reader can see "all the lights" that the protagonist fears will reveal him to his pursuers. Even that "final connection," of course, has to be tentative, as the reading is incorporated into each reader's life, since the reader can read and reread the novel at different moments. The perfect reading always has to be deferred, or made fictional, which amounts to being "transmortal"—but at that point the reader is inevitably absorbed by the text, something that, as we shall see, also happens to the author. Thus the act of reading "Manhunt" attains the same status as the hunted one's reading of his own biography: neither can assign a permanence to signs except through a leap in fictionality, a suspension of temporality and of death.

The reading of biography emerges as a self-stimulatory exercise, the re-enactment of a ritualistic death; like sexuality, it is the re-

56. See Sánchez, "La elaboración," p. 117.

hearsal of a deferred death. As in the erotic search of the two protagonists, reading and copulation become a stroking of the body, which, like Soliman's caresses of the statue of Pauline Bonaparte, cannot breathe spirit into the body to induce a resurrection. As in *The Kingdom of This World* and *The Lost Steps*, the imposition of order and meaning threatens somatic petrification, the fusion of the protagonist with the stony labyrinth that surrounds him (like Henri Cristophe immured in his own fortress), and the fusion of the reader with the text. For as the past becomes perpetual present it turns into an epitaph, a fixed and final text. This textual fixity is visible in the repetition throughout "Manhunt" of the Horatian sentence engraved in bronze on the façade of one of the buildings of the university: *Hoc erat in votis* ("This was what I wished"). With its counterpoint between the present-evoking *hoc* and the imperfective past *erat*, this intratextual epigraph is precisely the emblem of the petrification of desire. This is also the ultimate meaning of the ubiquitousness of buildings, monuments, columns, and the rest, and clearly the motive for Marinello's shrewd comment that "Manhunt" is "a sculpted narrative, carved out of a stone far from its quarry."[57] If the past as source, as mother, is the realm of formlessness, the past as present is the apotheosis of form, of the father—of *archtextuality*. That father is the *Deus architectus* of classical and medieval tradition, the maker of the stony labyrinth and the master of its secret code.[58] His power is a compendious imperialism that constantly threatens to reduce the text to a mere contingency.

The reversion to that archtext combines both the self-reflexiveness of allegory and the retrospective gesture of autobiography. On the most immediate level, allegory results in the transition from the specificity of the story into the generality of History. Allegory

57. "Sobre el asunto en la novela," p. 60.
58. "In the Platonic mythopoeia of the *Timaeus*, God appears as demiurge, that is, as architect and maker of the cosmos. . . . For *artifex* . . . the *Thesaurus* gives examples from Cicero, Seneca, Apuleius, and the fathers. In the same sense *architectus* occurs in Cicero, Apuleius, Irenaeus" (Ernst Robert Curtius, *European Literature and the Latin Middle Ages*, trans. Willard R. Trask [New York, 1953], p. 544).

reflects itself as symbol, but in doing so becomes other, as it is subsumed by a larger, abstract system of signification. Autobiography too, as we saw, always results in turning the self into another.[59] Thus the backward gesture of both allegory and autobiography entails a distancing and a reification. That reification is what accounts for the emblematic quality of allegory, its appeal to the material and visual aspects of the sign; for allegory is the residue of signification, a sign hollowed out, emptied of a meaning that has always already fled (*allos agoreien*, discourse of the other). The hieratic fixity of allegory stems from this constant flight of meaning. As the fugitive runs through the city, each sign reminds him of his story. Signs attain meaning for him in this way, but it is a fleeting meaning. By virtue of their abstractness the signs are there to subsume any story and reduce its protagonist to contingency. We as readers know that there is no specificity to the hunted one's story, that it is also part of a larger context. The most obvious suggestion of this is the similarity between the predicaments of the fugitive, the ticket seller, the traitor who is executed (the athlete). Less obvious (particularly to him) is the similarity between his passion and the Passion, a lack of recognition that is repeated when he fails to see the perverse coincidence of his having just "killed" his mother and the fact that he hears, as he passes the university, lines from Sophocles' *Electra* (he is one more Orestes). The specificity of his story is lost in all these analogies and similarities. This generality is what accounts for the various upper-case phrases scattered through the text: not only HOC ERAT IN VOTIS, but also BY EXPRESS, FREE FILL, HYPOTENUSA, IHS. (Although FREE FILL fits our discussion particularly well, because it suggests an emptiness and lack of substance, the original,

59. Eugene Vance has noted how in the *Confessions* Augustine shifts from the narrative of "the particular self" to "universals," centering his text "on the arch-narration of the Author-of-all in whose image Augustine is made and in terms of whom all language signifies. Simultaneously, then, as Augustine's soul is suffused with the Christ-logos, the narrative of his own origins returns to the narrative of universals, to the source of 'narrativity' itself" ("Augustine's *Confessions* and the Grammar of Selfhood," *Genre*, 6 [1973], 13).

SE REGALAN ESCOMBROS, is not as obvious.) The impersonal, emblematic nature of these inscriptions is a sign of the impersonality and detachment of the signs that surround the protagonist and that threaten him by their capacity to absorb his story. As in *The Kingdom of This World* and *The Lost Steps*, that threat is somatic petrification, a severing of flesh and spirit that will reduce him to an empty body and that is most poignantly present in the scene where the police threaten to castrate him: "And now they were going to mutilate him of himself; they were going to dry him up in life, depriving him of the center of his being where the body had placed its seal, its most intimate pride, boasting of the infallibility of a force that came from itself" (p. 165).

The first instance of the hunted one's bodily fixation occurs when the fugitive's father, who is a tailor, cuts a suit for him before sending him to Havana; it is, appropriately, the suit he wears on the night of his death. But what abounds in the text are allusions to petrification, linked to the notion of fear. When the fugitive is starving on the roof of the old woman's house, he compares his hunger to "that of a new-born infant abandoned beside a cemetery wall, who wails its misery, seeking its mother in the stone" (p. 137). Later, when he is leaving the rubble of the House of the Effort, "After sinking up to his ankles in mud crusted with plaster, he reached the street" (p. 168); and when he thinks of the church as a sanctuary, he longs to "lie face downward on the chill of the pavement, with this burden of stone I drag about me—my cheek against the cold stone, my hands on the cold stone; my fever, and this thirst, and this burning that sears my temples allayed by the chill of the stones!" (p. 168). Toward the end, the scholarship holder speaks of erecting a monument to those who, like the fugitive, "preserved, in times like this, a heroic spirit" (p. 172). And at the end, the fugitive's pursuer does not shoot him but fires into floor of the theater, as if the protagonist had already become a part of the building. The hunted one is not the only one destined to congealment or immurement. The old black woman's body is kept in ice, and when Estrella takes stock of her actions, she realizes that she has become the word that describes her: "It was no longer five simple letters that come to her lips; it was the ignoble Word, charged with abjection and death by stoning; the insult always to be found on the walls of prisons, latrines, asylums and passage-ways" (p. 150). Finally, the man shot by the fugitive is evoked by his acne-pocked neck: a sort of blank, inverted face on which marks have been carved.

The fear of petrification, of being subsumed and fixed by the archtext, is part of the erotics of writing as posited by the text. Desire in "Manhunt" is a fascination with texts and bodies that leads to the terror of petrification; eros, then, is a dialectic of desire and fear, of return and flight. This process evokes the myth of Medusa, seen in the persistent separation of Estrella's head and body and in the attraction she exerts over both protagonists.[60] In a brilliant article, John Freccero has examined the relation between the figure of Medusa and writing, and concludes that "in Dante's text, it is the power of the Letter to enthrall the beholder that makes of it a Medusa, an expression of desire that turns back to entrap its subject in an immobility which is the very opposite of the dynamism of language and desire [Paolo and Francesca con-demned to read over and again the same text and repeat the same gestures]. To see beyond it, however, is to see in the spiritual sense, to transform the Eros of the Medusa into the transcendent Eros of Caritas. This is Dante's achievement as a love poet: a refusal of the poetics of reification, sensual and verbal, for the poetics of 'trans-lation,' as Scribe of the Spirit which is written on 'the fleshy tab-lets of the heart.' "[61] In Dante such reification is averted because

60. The Medusa is also subtly suggested by the dark glasses worn by the fugitive when he goes to Estrella's house, although it is already night. The two statues in the garden of the House of the Effort, which will serve Estrella as points of reference, are Pomona and Diana. The first evokes not only the notion of a temple destroyed, but the metamorphosis of Actaeon, who chanced to *see* her nude. Pomona too suggests a story of metamorphosis; that of Anaxarete's petrification when she sees the dead body of her suitor Iphis, told the goddess by her own suitor Vertumnus.

61. "Medusa: The Letter and the Spirit," *Yearbook of Italian Studies* (Florence, 1972), p. 17.

in the fiction of the *Commedia* the pilgrim-poet narrates from an afterward where he has undergone a conversion that allows him to translate the letter into the spirit of faith. This, however, is constantly denied to the fugitive, who in addition, has left his native Sancti-Spiritus (a real town in Cuba) for the corrupt and stony Havana. The fugitive's only "translation" is his treason, when he "sings" to preserve the integrity of his body, of his manhood, conceived as his "being" (p. 165). The ticket seller is enthralled by an idolatrous reading of Beethoven's biography and only closes the book to go visit the prostitute. His only "translation" is a treason also, when he explains that the bill given him by the fugitive is counterfeit (a treason to the second power for, by turning out to be good, the "text" has also betrayed him, as the hunted one's treason turns back on him by unleashing the fury of his betrayed associates). While in Dante "the Book of Memory has as its author God Himself [and in this sense] Dante's poem is neither a copy nor an imitation of the Bible [but instead] is the allegory of theologians in his own life,"[62] modern secular literature, by its fetishistic claim to originality, falls into a guilt-ridden repetition of the materiality of the Word—it becomes an allegory of its own materiality. *The Kingdom of This World*, *The Lost Steps*, and "Manhunt" conceal their lineage only to reveal the trace of earlier texts surreptitiously assimilated like the nourishment the fugitive steals from the black woman. The drama played out in "Manhunt" is that of the text's attempted escape from its sources, its fear of repeating, like a protagonist, an archetype, an archtext.

Marinello's negative critique issues from his view that "Manhunt" presents, in too abstract a fashion, real conflicts of recent Cuban history; the characters, as he puts it, "have no last name."[63] But "Manhunt" conceals, in fact, the possibility of a more specific reading. Sanchez's exhaustive research has shown that the action of the novel is constructed through a collage of real incidents of Cuban political history, drawn from journalistic sources—sources followed so closely as to border on copying—and that the geogra-

62. Ibid., p. 17.
63. "Sobre el asunto en la novela," p. 72.

phy of Havana has been respected in all details.[64] The abstract, contemporary history of *The Lost Steps* has turned here into a concrete and documentable history—which Carpentier lived from his Parisian exile—and the setting, instead of being the Latin American Capital, the Metropolis, is the Havana that the author had rediscovered upon his return from Europe in 1939 but abandoned again in 1945. Both history and setting have been reconstructed by an act of recuperation analogous to the one practiced with Haitian history in the composition of *The Kingdom of This World*. The rigorous collation of those sources and the specificity of the geography of Havana reveal the predicament of the author: he is caught, like the hunted one, in the repetition of an archtext, upon which is laid, as *en filigrane*, the text of his novel. This process of composition by assembling newspaper clippings is self-reflexively present in the novel: "And [the fugitive] found in the other room whatever the old woman could provide him in the way of meat or stew that one could get one's teeth into, and the morning paper which he avidly scanned to see if he could find any news that had a bearing on his fate. Often the most interesting page was nothing but a fringe from which the patterns of shoulder pads, sleeves, had been cut for the students of the Academy of Dressmaking and Design—which was the name the dressmaker gave the room where she kept her dress forms and red velvet cushions bristling with pins, and taught the making of blouses and simple skirts" (pp. 128–29). The association here between the body and the text of history is clear; the most important part of the news, of history, has been hollowed out to form patterns to cover the body, while the fugitive has to content himself with the fringes, the residues. Like the fugitive, Carpentier has to content himself with the fringes, with the residues of a text that has already been shaped and hollowed out in predetermined patterns.

In a 1954 interview following the publication of *The Lost Steps*, Carpentier spoke of "Manhunt" as taking place "in Havana today."[65] Carpentier's statement is revealing in the same way as those

64. See "La elaboración," chap. 3.
65. Dorante, "Contrapunto entre selva y ciudad," p. 44.

about the composition of *The Lost Steps*, since it is provable that the incidents in "Manhunt's" plot took place in the thirties and forties. Since 1952 Batista had ruled in Cuba; his *coup d'état* signaled the collapse of everything the revolutionaries of 1933 had struggled for, the demise of all the ideals of Carpentier's and of the hunted one's generation. By claiming contemporaneity for the novel, Carpentier is attempting to make of it a political act, but at the same time he is defusing it by indirectly turning history into a series of repetitions: Batista has come to replace Machado, as the hunted one replaced the scholarship holder in the novel. The text is an empty sign that will contain all contingent historical events. Carpentier is falling into the same trap as his protagonist. He is, as it were, reconstructing his past life and attempting to find in it a transcendental pattern of redemption. But if history repeats itself, then its very generality excludes him as author, as maker; if it does not, it turns his text into an aesthetic exercise, a mere contingency. As with *The Lost Steps*, Carpentier's attempt to insert himself into his text condemns him to re-enact it, and in doing so to become a character instead of an author. The author's predicament in all self-referential writing is that, rather than achieving a resurrection of the subject, it turns him into a predicate. Marinello's statement that the characters lack *last* names in "Manhunt" is interesting because in a sense the author lacks a *first* name, a sign that will replace and distance the cipher of his last name—that of his father.

The Lost Steps and "Manhunt" take to its limits and subvert the metaphor of nature as logos, of the fusion of creative consciousness and nature as the source of narrativity. The conversion suggested by the autobiographical nature of *The Lost Steps* is found in the displacement of this metaphor, as signaled in "Manhunt" by the dead mother around whom the text is woven and the prostitute Estrella who constitutes the other focus of the narrative. The conversion is also found in the suggestion of a different source of narrativity in "Manhunt": political history. The hunted one has gained access to that magic Sunday denied the protagonist of *The Lost Steps*; but the last day, although completing the story that the narrator-protagonist of the previous novel had to leave unfinished, signals death and somatic petrification in the absence of desire. In *The Lost Steps*, Saturday was the day of writing; but Saturday, the day of Saturn, afforded only the paroxysms of desire in the falsehood of masks; in "Manhunt" Sunday is the day of writing, but the final day engenders only writing as an *officium tenebrae*. What beckons is Monday, the day of beginnings and of the future; the day of history in the making.

The stories written before 1953 hinged on the metaphor binding history and writing into an uninterrupted continuum, a flow from the same source—nature—lost in the past but subject to recall. The attempt to return to that source shows in *The Lost Steps* that no such unity exists, that writing unveils not the truth, nor the true origins, but a series of repeated gestures and ever renewed beginnings. After 1953, Carpentier's fiction assumes another origin, discarding the metaphor of natural writing and fantastic literature. In "Manhunt" Carpentier offers an alternate origin, political history, delving into the background of today's Cuba. In *Explosion in a Cathedral*, his next novel, Carpentier returns to the eighteenth century in the Caribbean as a means of telescoping into the present and beyond (by means of strategic anachronisms) the historico-political process undergone by the New Continent. In *The Kingdom of This World*, as we saw, Carpentier finished his narrative with a "green wind," an unchecked natural force that wipes out the work of men as if divinely ordered to frame the historical process in a natural cycle. *Explosion in a Cathedral* ends in the streets of Madrid on May 2, 1808 (the beginning of the wars of independence against Napoleon), with the characters' resolve to do something and with the implied prophecy of the Latin American wars of independence and revolutions yet to come. The quest for origins in the natural fusion of history and consciousness in a utopian past is abandoned in favor of a political history whose origins are to be found in the dissemination of the texts of the French Revolution throughout the New World. The myth of a past utopia has been replaced by the correlative myth of the future, when all versions of history will at last be one, and all steps will finally be found.

5. Memories of the Future

La Revolution spécialement, dans sa rapide apparition, ou
elle réalisa si peu, a vu, au lueurs de la foudre, des profondeurs
inconnus, des abîmes d'avenir.

Michelet, *Histoire de la Revolution Française*

(El cabalista que ofició de numen
A la vasta criatura apodó Golem;
Estas verdades las refiere Scholem
En un docto lugar de su volumen.)

Borges, "El Golem"

Yannes offered me passage on the boat in which he was sail-
ing the next day, the *Manatí*. I would sail toward the burden
awaiting me. I raised my burning eyes to the flowery sign of
Memories of the Future.

The Lost Steps, VI, 39

When Carpentier returned to Havana in 1959, after the triumph
of the Cuban Revolution, he carried in his luggage the manuscript
of a finished novel: *Explosion in a Cathedral*. This sweeping historical romance set in the eighteenth century opens a new period
in his writing, a recapitulatory period. After the radical questioning
of the relationship between writer and history in *The Lost Steps*
and "Manhunt," Carpentier will return to re-evaluate and in a
sense rewrite the fictional world he created before 1953. The question of origins in both history and the narrative undergoes a major
transformation, and Carpentier rescues Surrealism and Hegel from
his own past. One could say, in fact, that in this last period Carpentier attempts a revindication of the avant-garde, a reaffirmation
of both its ludic and its revolutionary spirit. The momentous
events of which he soon became a part obscured these changes.

According to Carpentier's testimony, the new realities that he encountered in Cuba led him to postpone submission of his new novel to a publisher, in order to make it more responsive to the revolution.[1] *Explosion in a Cathedral* had been written in Caracas between 1956 and 1958,[2] when the Cuban revolutionaries were fighting against Batista's regime and the prospects for a radical change in Cuban society appeared very dim. The fifties had been a period of consolidation for Carpentier, both in his work at Publicidad Ars and in his position in the field of literature; during this period he traveled to France to receive a literary prize and to Hollywood to negotiate the filming of *The Lost Steps*.[3] In spite of this disassociation from political activity, the theme of the new novel was hauntingly coincidental with events in Cuban history: revolution. Carpentier's statement that he had made changes in the novel gave rise to speculation hostile to the Cuban Revolution, particularly when he declared his allegiance to the new government and was made director of the state publishing house. These speculations were rekindled when, in 1968, he was removed from that position and made cultural attaché of the Cuban delegation in Paris (where he remains).

If he had changed the novel, had he done so in order to make it comply with the policies of the revolutionary government?[4] Those who thought of Carpentier as the author of *The Kingdom of This World*, *The Lost Steps*, and *War of Time* could not help but

1. Luis Harss and Barbara Dohmann, *Into the Mainstream: Conversations with Latin American Writers* (New York, 1967), p. 64.
2. Ibid.
3. For these and other details of Carpentier's years in Caracas, see Rafael Pineda, "Alejo Carpentier en la ciudad de las maquetas," *Imagen*, March 14, 1972, pp. 2–3. In answer to a survey of Venezuelan intellectuals carried out by *Cruz del Sur*, Carpentier spoke of his plans in terms of the translations of his works and of solidifying the growing base of his emerging popularity; "¿Qué piensan hacer los intelectuales venezolanos en 1958?" *Cruz del Sur*, 3, no. 35 (1957), 9. In a review of the English translation of *The Lost Steps*, Charles Poore called for a Nobel Prize for Carpentier; "Books of the Times," *The New York Times*, June 20, 1957, pp. 12–13.
4. "It has been rumored that *Explosion in a Cathedral* exemplifies revolutionary failure and only the poorest interpretation of the novel can lead to such a conclusion" (César Leante, "Un reto a la novela moderna: *El siglo de las luces*," *Revolución* [Havana] April 8, 1965, p. 3).

wonder, when his work most readily evoked for them the avant-garde and a circular conception of history. They could not contemplate a conversion on the part of a man whose political position had always been regarded as ambiguous without assuming a large dose of bad faith. Many set out to discover in *Explosion in a Cathedral*, if not the traces of a hasty rewriting, then at least a counterrevolutionary view of the Cuban regime, or even a code that would reveal Carpentier's portrayal of the French Revolution to be a *roman à clef* about the Cuban Revolution. With his return to Cuba and subsequent (and continued) allegiance to the regime, and with the growth in popularity of the Latin American novel in the sixties, Carpentier and his work became polemical.

Carpentier insisted later, in a way recanting his earlier statement, that the changes he made in *Explosion in a Cathedral* were not substantive, that he had merely rewritten the episode of Víctor and Sofía's break many times in an effort to avert melodrama.[5] Anyone intimately familiar with Carpentier's work and unwilling to accept counterrevolutionary propaganda will probably have to accept this version, for in works as intricately woven and organically connected as his, major changes would be difficult after a certain point. Total rewritings, as in the case of *The Lost Steps*, yes; but alterations that would significantly modify the structure of the plot, very doubtfully. Furthermore, a clear picture of Cuban history in the early years of the revolution reveals that external events could not have pressured Carpentier into changing his novel significantly, and that if *Explosion in a Cathedral* differs from Carpentier's earlier production, it does so for other reasons.

It is a common mistake of coarse historical criticism to think of 1959 as the watershed, when Cuban political and social life suddenly changed into what they are today. Such a naive view of history ignores many important facts. In 1959 the revolutionary government assumed power in Cuba, but it was naturally several years before the country's social, economic, and political structures changed so as to conform to a Socialist model. The reasons behind

5. Carpentier has repeated this in several interviews, and to me in Paris in the summer of 1973.

Carpentier's own return to Havana in 1959 provide a good example of the nature of political and socioeconomic life in Cuba during that first year of revolution. Carpentier returned to Cuba in that year because of his involvement in a business venture organized by the Peruvian writer and publisher Manuel Scorza. In 1958 Scorza had begun a series of book festivals at which he had managed to sell an unprecedented number of books at extremely low prices. The festivals began in Peru and moved to Caracas, where, as Scorza says, "I met two extraordinary persons; the novelist Alejo Carpentier (25,000 copies of The Kingdom of This World had been sold in Lima in one week), and the poet Juan Liscano. Thanks to the collaboration of both, a Venezuelan festival was organized. We sold 300,000 books in one week. From there I went to Bogotá and the success was the same."[6] In time, a festival was organized in Havana (two were eventually staged), with Carpentier, whose experience in public relations and advertising must have made him suitable for the position, as director.[7] By this time a wide-ranging organization was set up, called Organización Continental de los Festivales del Libro, with Manuel Mujica Gallo as president, Manuel Scorza as general director, and a board of directors from each of the participating countries: Miguel Scorza in Peru, Alberto Zalamea in Colombia, Jorge Icaza in Ecuador, Juan Liscano in Venezuela, and Carpentier in Cuba.[8] The group's downfall came as a result of the economic and political changes that began to take place in Cuba from 1960 to 1961.[9] It was not until April 1961, in the wake of the aerial attacks that preceded the Bay of

6. Julio Ortega, "El libro en la calle" (interview with Manuel Scorza), *Mundo Nuevo*, no. 23 (May 1968), p. 84.
7. César Leante offers a brief evocation of Carpentier as director of the Cuban festival in "Un reto a la novela moderna," p. 3.
8. See unnumbered pages at the end of Félix Lizaso, *El pensamiento vivo de Varona* (Havana, n.d.), one of the books published under Carpentier's directorship.
9. Scorza says: "We took all of our assets to Cuba, but then the well-known crisis came; all the Batista people left, taking with them all the money, and the government forbade taking out dollars. Our accounts were blocked. The Peruvian government, very eager to back up any demand against Cuba, offered to intervene diplomatically. But I talked with [Che] Guevara, then Minister of Industry, who told me: 'Cuba does not even have the money to

Pigs Invasion, that Fidel Castro declared the revolution Socialist, and radical changes in the socioeconomic fabric of Cuba did not occur until much later. And it was not until August 1961, after the First Congress of Cuban Writers and Artists, that cultural activity in the island was centralized.

At that point Carpentier was made executive director of the Editorial Nacional. And then, perhaps even more than now, the cultural policies of the revolution were broad enough to include the publication in state-sponsored translations of authors such as Proust, Kafka, Joyce, and Robbe-Grillet.[10] *Explosion in a Cathedral* first appeared in Mexico on November 24, 1962, so even if one were to allow that after the summer of 1961 there was pressure on Carpentier to alter the manuscript of his novel substantially (an unlikely event), there is simply not enough time for such a change, taking into account the location of his publishers, publication schedules, and the like.[11] When in October 1968 he was asked by *Casa de las Americas*, "What fundamental change has been ef-

buy penicillin for children; choose whether you are going to behave as a writer or as a publisher.' I went back to Lima, as a matter of fact, with at least a shirt on my back" ("El libro en la calle," p. 85).

10. See Carpentier's own testimony of his work in "La actualidad cultural en Cuba," *Sur* (Buenos Aires), no. 293 (March-April 1965), pp. 61–67.

11. The exact date of publication is given in *El siglo de las luces*, 2d ed. (Mexico City: Cía. General de Ediciones, 1965), on the verso of the title page. In 1959 Carpentier had published various fragments of the novel in the *Nueva Revista Cubana* (see Bibliography). In my experience, when Carpentier publishes part of a novel or story it is already finished. There are two items of interest concerning the genesis of the novel in Araceli García-Carranza's list of exhibits from the 1974 exhibition of Carpentier manuscripts held in Havana. One is forty-one pages of notes dated 1952, and the other some scribblings on the menu of a restaurant in Guadeloupe, which apparently has no date. I suspect that the latter must be from 1954, since it was then that Carpentier traveled to Paris to receive the award won by the French translation of *The Kingdom of This World*, and he has stated in several interviews that during that trip his plane made an emergency landing in Guadeloupe, where he had the first idea for *Explosion in a Cathedral*. The 1952 notes, however, would disprove that assertion, but as we saw in connection with *The Lost Steps*, Carpentier tends to establish links between the geneses of his novels and adventures in his life that must be understood symbolically, rather than literally. See Araceli García-Carranza, "Bibliografía de una exposición," *Revista de la Biblioteca Nacional José Martí*, 3d series, 17, no. 1 (1975), 62.

fected on you by the Revolution between 1959 and today?" Carpentier gave the following answer:

The Cuban Revolution has not effected changes in me, because I was expecting it since the days of my adolescence, although not knowing how it would come about. But, beyond that expectation, it has realized a great deal more with respect to my activities. It has given an orientation, a meaning, to my labors. Today I know that I can act in the name of something, today I know that the desires, the indignation, the rebelliousness, that simmered within me since the days of my fraternal friendship with Rubén Martínez Villena—not forgetting my friendship, my conversations every afternoon, not many years after, with César Vallejo—did not mature in vain. I have acquired the awareness, as never before, that the task of writing, of expressing ideas by means of the printed or spoken word, can be carried out as a useful function. That, I owe to the Cuban Revolution.[12]

The distinction that Carpentier establishes between the self that has not been radically altered by the revolution because it expected and wished for it and the self that has been given a meaning in its activities is revealing. Clearly, the revolution put an end to the double life that he had been forced to live, particularly in Caracas between 1945 and 1959, and for over a year in Havana. The revolutionary expectations of his writings and his daily activities were no longer at odds with each other. The Cuban Revolution marked for Carpentier an overcoming of alienation, a return home without the ambiguities and duplicities of 1939. But in that other self that remains unchanged by the revolution, the transformation goes back further, as he admits. That process, which in his life had to await the sixties, is to be found in the evolution noted from the fiction of the forties to The Lost Steps and "Manhunt." Neither Explosion in a Cathedral nor any of Carpentier's work after 1959 may be considered novels of the Cuban Revolution, if by that it is meant that they issue from a conversion directly incited by the political events of the past seventeen years. Carpentier has stated that both Reasons of State (El recurso del método, 1974) and Concierto barroco (1974) were "prepared" along with Explosion in a Cathedral, that is to say, in Caracas during the fifties.[13] The coinci-

12. "Literatura y revolución (encuestas)," Casa de las Américas, nos. 51–52 (1968–69), p. 127.
13. "As I was finishing Explosion in a Cathedral I had already on the way

dence of this "revolutionary" phase in Carpentier's writing with the emergence of the Cuban Revolution was propitiated by Carpentier's constant appeal in his fiction to historical beginnings and apocalyptic events. Paradoxically the actual occurrence of the revolution opens a new question that Carpentier has not yet come to terms with: that of writing, not about an expected revolution, but within one that has actually taken place. Carpentier is one of the few post-Romantic writers who has been allowed to live his dreams of revolution and follow his characters into the fray of history.

The paper delivered by Carpentier at the First Congress of Cuban Writers and Artists in the summer of 1961, widely circulated as an essay in *Tientos y diferencias*, is as crucial a text as any in the articulation of Carpentier's new orientation,[14] although because of the context in which it was produced it is full of false leads. It was delivered in a climate of increasing radicalization, barely five months after the Bay of Pigs invasion, at a congress that asked the inevitable questions about the new interplay between politics and the arts. The speech is one of many texts produced in Cuba since, revising the history of Latin America literature to distinguish writers who took an active interest in politics from those who did not, and attempting to find the correlations between literary and political traditions. The usual gallery of heroes and villains appears in Carpentier's essay. He places the origin of national and political consciousness at the beginning of the nineteenth century, and proceeds to trace a sketchy and somewhat conventional history of the political commitment of Latin American intellectuals. But the essay is important because of the way in which Carpentier reviews the accomplishments of his own generation, which is remembered as one "that is keenly concerned with

---

the material for two novels that are those two new ones coming out now" (quoted in Jacobo Zabludovsky, "Habla Alejo Carpentier," *Siempre!* [Mexico City], July 25, 1973, p. 44). For other publications of the sixties and seventies, see Bibliography.

14. The paper first appeared in *Memoria del Primer Congreso Nacional de Escritores y Artistas de Cuba* (Havana, 1961), pp. 49–54. I am quoting here from *Tientos y diferencias* (Montevideo: Arca, 1967), where it appears as "Literatura y conciencia política en América Latina."

the political and social destiny of Latin America." What follows, however, is not a apologia for his own generation, but a critique: "Soon some of the writers begin to understand that politics is not a game. That political commitment carries with it many inconveniences. And it is then that, with a false aura of novelty, with a sense apparently modified, appears 'our americanism' . . . To disengage themselves from the tremendous reality that is beginning to assert itself to the east of Europe, some begin to speak of the future of 'Our America' in the language of magicians and prophets, proclaiming as much more immediate and close at hand what the dreamers of the beginning of the century [Darío et alii] thought to be very remote." This new type of escape took on various forms, according to Carpentier. One, based on the myth of "Latinity" (an allusion to Rodó, no doubt), on the genius of the race, would bring about a "solution different from all those imagined or to be imagined: something American, very American, situated perhaps between Miranda's Neo-Incan state and Campanella's Heliopolis, with a lot of folklore in the background. There would be a lot of El Dorados and Potosís in all that." Another would be Hispanism: "The linguistic community would create a particular destiny on the planet, oblivious to the economic laws that govern the modern world." Finally, there was a third made up of those who "'socialized haphazardly,' ignoring the scientific foundations of Socialism. This gave way to the flowering in Europe, as well as in America, of very well-intentioned books which, ultimately, solved no problems and explained nothing." This "haphazard socializing," Carpentier adds, "carries the risk of leading us to dead ends such as 'cosmic races,' 'latinity,' and other gibberish that was very well regarded thirty years ago." The essay significantly ends with a confessional note: "Those of us who have abandoned local lyricism, a messianic rhetoric that only fooled ourselves, acquiring a more ecumenical and universal conscience of Latin American problems, know that when he said his prophetic words, José Carlos Mariátegui [the Peruvian Marxist] was at an hour of truth."[15]

15. *Tientos y diferencias*, pp. 81, 82, 83, 85–86. This ending does not appear in the original version of the essay printed in *Memoria del Primer*

If one takes into account Carpentier's essays on the decline of Europe, as well as his prologue to *The Kingdom of This World*, it should be obvious that in "Literatura y conciencia política en América Latina," he is denouncing a part of his own past, clearly that part covering his production until 1949. But such about-faces are never simple. When in 1964 he reprinted this speech, along with other essays, in *Tientos y diferencias*, he included among them the prologue to *The Kingdom of This World*. In the book, the prologue was expanded in a very curious and revealing fashion. The prologue constitutes the last section of a longer essay, or travel journal, in which Carpentier recounts a trip undertaken in the sixties, as member of an official Cuban delegation, through China, India, Czechoslovakia, and the Soviet Union. The first words of the prologue are worked into the middle of a paragraph, an accompanying footnote reads: "I pass on here to the prologue to the first edition of my novel *The Kingdom of This World* (1949), which did not appear in subsequent editions, although today I consider it, except for a few details, as valid as it was then. Surrealism has ceased being for us, through an imitative process still very active fifteen years ago, an erroneously interpreted movement. But the 'real marvelous' remains, which is of a very different nature, more visible every day and beginning to proliferate in the work of some young novelists on our continent."[16]

One is hard put to explain such a statement after reading "Literatura y conciencia política en América Latina," particularly when Carpentier's tirade against committed literature in the prologue has been left intact.[17] An attempt to force the conciliation of these contradictory statements would be futile. To appreciate Carpentier's decision to allow them to stand side by side one must remember that, for the first time, because of the notoriety he had gained as a result of the Cuban Revolution and the "boom" of the

---

Congreso, but was added in the first edition of *Tientos y diferencias* (Mexico City: Universidad Nacional Autónoma de México, 1964).

16. "De lo real maravilloso americano," *Tientos y diferencias*, 1967 ed., p. 116.

17. It appears in the 1967 edition on p. 119.

Latin American novel, Carpentier was having an impact on Latin American literary circles. This impact, as noted, was conveyed primarily through The Kingdom of This World and War of Time, and also through a reading of The Lost Steps deriving from those works, the second of which was generally considered to have been written after The Lost Steps. Denying the prologue to The Kingdom of This World at such a moment would have meant abdicating the paternity rights that he was exercising then over younger novelists such as Carlos Fuentes, who had spent some time in Cuba in the early sixties and had written his best-known novel, The Death of Artemio Cruz, under the influence of Carpentier.[18] A reader of Tientos y diferencias must exercise caution and take note of its recapitulatory nature—and as such of its heterogeneity and lack of a unified position. The attempt to blend positions fifteen years apart in the amalgam of the longer version of "De lo real maravilloso americano" is the most blatant example of this unevenness, caused by the desire to recover and recast theoretical statements from the past.[19]

The most revealing contradiction in the essays revolves around

18. Carpentier devotes a laudatory sentence to Fuentes in "Problemática de la actual novela latinoamericana," Tientos y diferencias, 1967 ed., p. 15.

19. In the sixties and seventies "magical realism" came under attack in Cuba by Portuondo and Marinello. The latter, whose opinion of Carpentier's works has always been guarded, insists on the value of Carpentier's most recent production (namely, Explosion in a Cathedral) in an article where he celebrates the inclusion of the works of Carpentier and Nicolás Guillén in the curriculum of French universities; see "Un homenaje excepcional," Bohemia (Havana), August 7, 1964, pp. 94–95. On Carpentier's seventieth birthday, when he was awarded a doctorate honoris causa by the University of Havana, and other honors, Marinello spoke of Carpentier's forthcoming novel about the Cuban Revolution, which ends with the Bay of Pigs invasion, as having a "good ending, but a better beginning. From there on should the most accomplished aspects of his mastery begin." In "Homenaje a Alejo Carpentier: palabras a nombre del Comité Central del Partido Comunista de Cuba." Revista de la Biblioteca Nacional José Martí, 3d series, 17, no. 1 (1975), 17. Portuondo, one of the first critics of "magical realism," opposes to that concept a Marxist-Leninist portrayal or reality, in a review of Manuel Cofiño López's La última mujer y el próximo combate; "Una novela revolucionaria," Casa de las Américas, no. 71 (1972), 105–6.

Carpentier's concept of the baroque, which he now puts forth as the distinguishing characteristic of Latin American literature, and which has come to replace the "real marvelous."[20] The recourse to such a concept also involves a recapitulatory gesture, for its dissemination throughout Latin America goes back to Spengler, Worringer, and other thinkers and art historians published by the *Revista de Occidente* in the twenties.[21] It is also an attempt to recover a Sartrean legacy on the theory of contexts, and to legitimize Surrealism.[22] The contradiction centers on the status of literary language. On the one hand, Carpentier maintains that the baroque nature of Latin American literature stems from the necessity to name for the first time realities that are outside the mainstream of Western culture. On the other, he states that what characterizes Latin American reality is its stylelessness, which results from its being an amalgam of styles from many cultural traditions and epochs: Indian, African, European, Neoclassical, Modern, etc. With the first statement Carpentier is, of course, resurrecting the Blakean and generally Romantic topos of Adam in the Garden after the fall, having to give names to the things that surround him. But the second claim runs counter to the first insofar as the reality in question, if it is the product of manifold traditions, would have already been "named" several times, and by different peoples. If what characterizes Latin American reality is that mélange of styles that Carpentier discovers in the architecture of Havana—mixing the Neoclassical with Gaudí and Californian

20. Discussion of the baroque is found in two essays in *Tientos y diferencias*: "Problemática de la actual novela latinoamericana," and "La ciudad de las columnas."

21. To Spengler the baroque was a kind of "third style," as Carpentier will call the style of Latin America, born out of the tensions between Classical art and the Gothic. For a more detailed history of the concept, see my "Apetitos de Góngora y Lezama," *Revista Iberoamericana*, 41 (1975), 479–91.

22. As seen in the note appended to the new version of "De lo real maravilloso americano," Carpentier has changed his views on Surrealism. This reassessment had begun in the fifties; see "Renuevo de una escuela," *El Nacional*, July 21, 1954, p. 30.

from the twenties and thirties—then the act of naming that reality is a renaming.[23]

The baroque as a new metaphor, a new conceit designating that which is particularly Latin American, is quite different, however, from the concept of "marvelous American reality" woven in the forties. To begin with, Carpentier insists now on defining cities, not the jungle or the world of nature. More importantly, though, in the concept of "marvelous American reality" the mediator between that reality and the literary text was the self; the conceit was that of the writer as a spontaneous, unreflexive mediator between the transmutations of nature and those of writing. The new theory of contexts, on the other hand, establishes a new relationship. If there is an inherent tension between the desire to name for the first time and a reality that has already been named several times, the theory of contexts assumes and subsumes that tension: it provides for a writing that purports to name for the first time even while it is conscious of naming for the second time, of being a renaming. The text is a context, which is already inscribed in the hybrid reality issuing from previous conceptions; the text, in other words, is a ruse, an evasive gesture that points to itself as a beginning that never was, but knows that it is instead a future of that beginning, its ultimate end. Latin American writing will then be that third style that is the future of all styles; their degradation in heterogeneity, when their codes lose their referentiality: "Not serene and classical styles by means of the prolongation of a previous classicism, but by a new disposition of elements, of textures, of embellished ugliness, by fortuitous approximations, enervations and metaphors, by allusions to things that are 'other things,' which are, in sum, the source of all known baroquisms."[24] The negative way in which Carpentier describes this third style, as that which has no style, provides the clue for the grounding element of the new conceit. If the narrative must go beyond itself to contexts and at the same time constitutes, in a sense, those contexts, then the text is the empty space opened by that negation; it is the point at which

23. "La ciudad de las columnas," *Tientos y diferencias,* p. 62.
24. *Tientos y diferencias,* p. 16.

things cease to have a style and the locus where they shift from one level to the other. Whereas the theory of "marvelous American reality" assumed a complicity between nature and the self, here they are, so to speak, pulverized in the explosion of that negation, scattered in the stylelessness of the text.

This has nothing to do with the apparent and overt intention of "Problemática de la actual novela latinoamericana," which on the surface seems to be a pious call for novelists to direct their attention to contemporary realities. The most obvious proof of this contradiction is found in Carpentier's return in his fictions to the eighteenth century, after his sally into contemporaneity in *The Lost Steps* and "Manhunt." The pristine moment of beginning or origination sought by the concept of "marvelous American reality" lay in a prehistory—the colonial or pre-Hispanic utopia toward which the narrator-protagonist of *The Lost Steps* traveled (the singular moment before plurality and difference that always multiplies and eludes him, the purity that always turns murky and heterogeneous). Carpentier returns to the eighteenth century not only in the obvious historical sense, as in *Explosion in a Cathedral* and *Concierto barroco*, but also to explore its problematics, as in *Reasons of State*, which rekindles the debate between Descartes and Vico. It is a return that constitutes a rewriting of the fiction of *The Kingdom of This World* and *War of Time*, a return that will assume the secondary and historical nature of the eighteenth century as the birth of Latin American culture and writing.

At the end of *The Lost Steps*, when the narrator-protagonist decides to abandon his quest for the single point of origin in the jungle and return to the city, he gazes at the sign with the name of the café where he has heard about the fate of Rosario and his other companions of the previous voyage: *Memories of the Future*. This is the last threshold he crosses in memory toward the point from which he has written or rewritten his account of the voyage, the threshold of assumed self-reflexivity and history, of writing in the city, in that third style that is the future of all styles remembered. *Explosion in a Cathedral*, *Reasons of State*, and *Concierto barroco* will all be written, so to speak, in that future perfect where the beginning of history is already history.

2

Everything begins with reproduction

Derrida

Nowhere more than in *Explosion in a Cathedral* does the reassessment of an eighteenth-century problematics which subtends Carpentier's recent production appear more minutely deployed—a problematics that could be defined as the search for the common source of all symbolic activity, the master code of the universal mind. And given that the eighteenth century was the first period to consider itself modern, the novel constitutes, as it were, a counterpoint between self-conscious modernities: the Enlightenment's and our own.[25] The novel problematizes the idea of modernity by its own apparently anachronistic form. So traditional is *Explosion in a Cathedral* in its outward form that a critic has called it "a challenge to the modern novel," in the sense that it seems to spurn the experimental nature of the modern narrative in favor of a dated historical and realistic design.[26] This temporal questioning that a most superficial consideration of the novel elicits is evidence, however, that beneath its outward appearance *Explosion in a Cathedral* conceals a radical experiment with history and the narrative. Though the voluminous historical research that went into the writing of the novel obviously links it with *The Kingdom of This World*, Carpentier's return to the era of revolutions does not imply a continuation of his experiments of the forties, but a revision.[27] The most salient and deceptive feature that issues from this revision is the detailed attention to historical, social, and geographical particularities; the

25. "In a more general way one may say that the eighteenth century considered itself to be a modern period. It is perhaps the first period to do so, for the Renaissance is, as its very name implies, a rebirth; in the eighteenth century we have the consciousness of a radical new beginning," Herbert Dieckmann, "Esthetic Theory and Criticism in the Enlightenment: Some Examples of Modern Trends," in *Introduction to Modernity: A Symposium on Eighteenth-Century Thought*, ed. Robert Mollenauer (Austin, 1965), p. 66.

26. Leante, "Un reto a la novela moderna," p. 3.

27. For a list of some of Carpentier's sources, see *Alejo Carpentier: 45 años de trabajo intelectual* (Havana, 1966), pp. 10–11 (unnumbered).

conventional and gradual development of the characters and the focusing of the action on the destiny of a household. On this level, where the novel appears almost as a nineteenth-century popular historical novel of adventure, *Explosion in a Cathedral* allows for a rather conventional thematic reading.

Though ranging over a vast geographical expanse encompassing portions of the Caribbean, France, and Spain, *Explosion in a Cathedral* is set more specifically at a crucial point in Cuban history: a period of socioeconomic revolution in the aftermath of the English occupation of Havana from 1762 to 1763. Because of the occupation, Cuba was the first Hispanic country to come into direct contact with the incipient industrial revolution.[28] New industrial and commercial ideas and practices revolutionized the socioeconomic fabric of the island and forced the Spanish colonial regime to liberalize its rule after regaining Havana. These changes began to erode the colonial system that had been in force since the sixteenth century and had kept the island outside the mainstream of intellectual, social, and historical currents. The second half of the eighteenth century prepared Cuba for the convulsive economic and social era around the turn of the century, when the Haitian Revolution sent Cuba into the frenzied ups and downs of the sugar market. *Explosion in a Cathedral* covers the two decades from 1789 to 1809. Trade with England and later with the newly independent United States and with more than one Spanish port (a lifting of a previous restriction) brought about not only a commercial transformation but also an influx of ideas in sharp conflict with colonial rule and the outmoded ideology of the metropolis. The scenes of the bustling Havana port in *Explosion in a Cathedral*, with vessels from various nations at the docks, as well as the general store of the protagonists' father, replete with stock from all over the world, are clear indications of the historical setting of the beginning of the novel.

28. See Hugh Thomas, *Cuba: The Pursuit of Freedom* (New York, 1971), esp. pp. 53–57. For details and extensive quotations from documents of the period, see José Luciano Franco, *La batalla por el dominio del Caribe y el Golfo de México: revoluciones y conflictos internacionales en el Caribe, 1789–1854* (Havana, 1965).

The family whose evolution is depicted in *Explosion in a Cathedral* is the archetype of the new Cuban *haute bourgeoisie* of the period. The father, a prominent retailer born in rural Spain who has established a fortune in the colony by adhering faithfully to the old ways, is a typical *indiano*.[29] His fortune will allow his children to move into the upper class, while he remains bound to traditional and rustic ways. But by creating an upper-class mentality in his children and providing the economic foundation to sustain it, the old retailer has doomed his succession to failure, for his children will scorn his values. His death signifies, in the novel's synchronization of family history and social history, the death of the old ways. In the period in question this destruction of succession is revolutionary. The new commercial aristocracy of the late eighteenth century in Cuba—and even more so in the nineteenth century as its wealth increased, being dependent on the fickle wealth of sugar—was given to frivolity with a *carpe diem* frenzy unknown to the class of laboring small farmers that preceded it, which had a long-range view of growth. Dependent on the fluctuations of a foreign market, with the rigors and tedium of labor just one generation behind them, the new class built mansions in Artemisa and Almendares, or in Havana itself, and squandered their money on the long-awaited amenities of gentility.[30]

Carpentier has set *Explosion in a Cathedral* in a historical moment parallel to the one lived by the Haitian colonists in *The Kingdom of This World*. But if in that novel the colonists' demise began with a slave revolt carried out in complicity with nature, in *Explosion in a Cathedral* the process is a slower though equally revolutionary one, brought about by precise historical socioeconomic factors.[31] The invasion of the colonial household by Víctor Hugues, the man without origins who embodies the new mercan-

29. *Indiano* is the term for a Spaniard who comes to America to amass a fortune and returns to die in Spain. The *indiano* became a literary figure in nineteenth-century Spanish fiction.

30. Marcial, in "Journey Back to the Source," is a good example of this.

31. Carpentier's most direct source for this background is Humboldt's *Ensayo político sobre la isla de Cuba* (Havana, 1960 [1826]). Some of the descriptions of Havana in the first chapter of the novel come from this book.

tile ideas, reminds us here of Macandal's alliance with nature. Before the youths can set out in search of the worlds they yearn for, Víctor Hugues must put in order the business affairs of the household. Rearranging the house, explaining the true function of scientific instruments, balancing the books of the store, all of these measures taken by Víctor Hugues are a small-scale revolution following the chaos caused by the death of the father. That period of chaos when everything goes topsy-turvy and objects dissociated from their uses become toys is the amorphous historical moment following revolution—the Carnival, the inversion—before a new order is established. In *The Kingdom of This World* and the stories written in the forties, this period involves a transition between cyclical movements and repetitions. Here the transition is to a new world. The changes brought about by Víctor Hugues are irrevocable. Whereas the old father died in the paroxisms of debauchery, Víctor, as the surrogate father, will lead Carlos, Sofía, and Esteban into the maelstrom of history. Víctor is a merchant, a Mason, a freethinker, a pragmatist—a new man of action oriented toward the future, whereas the old father embodied the traditions that died with him.

In the end Esteban and Sofía will surpass Víctor. He dies defending the interests of the new bourgeoisie; they will join the first revolution to challenge those values and will die in the streets of Madrid fighting Napoleon's troops. The chronology of the novel leads from the bourgeois to the popular revolution, from France in 1789 to Spain in 1808.[32] Víctor, as a father figure, initiated a succession—a revolutionary one. In *The Kingdom of This World*, the ruins were the evidence of a circular historical process; in *Explosion in a Cathedral*, a succession of mansions are closed as the characters move forth in history. When the last mansion is shut, Esteban and Sofía have died in the streets.

32. It is much easier to determine the dates in *Explosion in a Cathedral* than in *The Kingdom of This World* because of the former's precise reference to historical events. The characters in the former arrive in Santiago Bay in 1791, two years after the beginning of the action of the novel. They would coincide there, of course, with M. Lenormand de Mézy and Ti Noël.

Esteban's trajectory is the most significant in this process; it parallels that of the narrator-protagonist of The Lost Steps, except that his is a completed trajectory. Esteban's first sally into history and revolution is as spectator, cut off not only from historical action but from himself. In France he views the revolution as theater or a street parade, just as the protagonist of The Lost Steps saw the revolution in the Latin American Capital as a mindless struggle between Guelphs and Ghibellines. While Víctor makes the revolution, Esteban moves on the fringes as witness and judge, assuming the position of the intellectual and the artist. Indeed, his job in the revolution is that of a translator. His return to Havana on the eve of the century's end marks the beginning of a contemplative phase, when he attempts to recover his past through an exercise of memory, much as the autobiographical writer—like Ti Noël at the end of The Kingdom of This World, or like the protagonist in The Lost Steps. This process of recapturing time past turns into a game, a rediscovery of his toys and of his adolescent longings for Sofía, the lover/mother. Sofía spurns his advances, and the new century opens with her determination to seek out Víctor Hugues, after Jorge, her husband (who is a descendant of the British families who came to Havana during the occupation), dies. Her path will cross Esteban's again in Madrid, but under different circumstances. By then, Sofía has abandoned Víctor, who has become a shadow of his former self. Whereas he once represented the forces of progress, by persecuting the slaves he has turned into an agent of the reaction. Víctor is defeated by nature in Cayenne, and abandoned by Sofía, who at this point begins to embody a new force ushered in by the new century—not the power of reason of the bourgeoisie but that of passion and nature as represented by the massess of the oppressed. The forces that Sofía now embodies are those that defeat Víctor. With the disappearance of this second father, Sofía and Esteban finally unite. Their fusion at the end is the fusion of knowledge and love, of science and nature. He incarnates the new committed intellectual; she, the maternal, natural force turned into an active political agent of history. Unlike Rosario, who marries Marcos and remains in the jungle to run out the course of her existence, Sofía and Esteban join each other and the masses to form a new marriage bond that will bring forth a rebirth of history, for it must be remembered that Spain's war of independence set off the Latin American wars of independence and the birth of the new republics. Esteban accomplished by uniting with Sofía what the protagonist of *The Lost Steps* was unable to accomplish: the redemptive marriage of nature and knowledge. The ending of *The Lost Steps* was an admission of impotence; that of *Explosion in a Cathedral*, of fecund beginnings.

Esteban's new awareness comes after his return to the paternal household. There he realizes, after an initial period of recall and playfulness, that his work as translator had borne fruit. In Havana, in the midst of political unrest, he sees Spanish versions of *The Social Contract* and other revolutionary texts that he recognizes as his own work. The revolution has gone on, absorbing his work and making it anonymous. His willingness to set Sofía free and aid her in escaping to join Víctor is his first conscious act of revolutionary significance. Unlike Carpentier's previous characters, Esteban and Sofía are allowed a second sally after the return home; self-consciousness after the return no longer signals the end but constitutes a new beginning. From the Proustian moment of recollection of time past and regressive flight into the maternal abode, the characters set forth into action and into the future. From now on Esteban's actions and thoughts run on converging paths with Sofía's until they merge at the end. For her the reawakening will come after finding that Víctor, the surrogate father, the one who ushered her into a new life, no longer stands for freedom, but only represents the past.

Carlos, the heir, although the most marginal among the protagonists, plays an important role at the end of the novel. Until then he has had to carry on his father's enterprise; he has kept the business going and presided over Sofía's marriage to Jorge. Significantly, he opens as well as closes the novel. At the beginning he is crossing Havana Bay to attend his father's funeral; at the end he pieces together the story of Esteban's and Sofía's last sojourn in Madrid. He always presides over the aftermath of a significant event, and at the end of the novel he is the one who returns, the one who will carry on with what Sofía and Esteban had begun. Wealthy, but with the liberal ideas garnered through his contact with the revolution, he is the one who will bring about the wars of independence. This suggestion is inescapable in the novel. Not only was it the uprising against Napoleon that set off the wars of liberation in the Spanish colonies, but it was a wealthy Carlos— Carlos Manuel de Céspedes—who in 1868 declared his slaves free and marched against the Spaniards in Cuba.

Explosion in a Cathedral is set, then, within a period of socio-historical transformation that signals the end of colonial rule and the beginning of the wars of independence in Latin America. The emphasis in the novel is on social change, as seen through the children of a family whose evolution appears as the microcosmic representation of the changes that the world around them is undergoing.[33] Even in this broad, historical reading of the novel, however, there are indications of a different Carpentier.

Carpentier offers in this novel a radical revision of the historical process he portrayed in *The Kingdom of This World*. The difference lies in the breaking of the daemonic circle in which history, moved by natural forces, was entrapped in the earlier novel. The clearest indication of this is found not only in the minute details of the social and ideological evolution of the characters, but also in the absence of circularity and in the characters' ability to return to the fray of history after they have completed a first cycle of their lives. As we saw, Esteban, after his return to the paternal home and to Sofía, is able to begin again, now in a self-conscious manner, a new period of his life. And Sofía, who seemed at the beginning to be caught in the natural cycles of her feminine existence, manages to break with Víctor and become an active, conscious, and free agent of history. Self-consciousness is now a return from which a new departure may take place. There are repetitions and returns in

---

33. For a lucid interpretation of the role of the house in this and other novels of Carpentier, see Eduardo G. González, "El tiempo del hombre: huella y labor de origen en cuatro obras de Alejo Carpentier" (Ph.D. diss., Indiana University, 1974).

Explosion in a Cathedral, but not historical cycles that mirror each other and create a vertiginous *composition en abîme*. The characters return to what appears to be a previous moment in their lives, as history appears to repeat itself in certain events. But the return is not to the same point; it is rather to one that is merely similar and creates the illusion of sameness but is really far removed from the previous one: instead of identical cycles, history in *Explosion in a Cathedral* follows a spiraling movement. And history is no longer determined by cosmic cycles complicitous with nature, it is man-made.

It is the attention to social, historical, and political details, in addition to the apparent absence of technical *tours de force*, that has led Carpentier's critics to view *Explosion in a Cathedral* as a traditional and anachronistic novel. This, together with its publication at the beginning of the Cuban Revolution, has contributed to a reading of the novel that underscores its historical and realistic values. But this is an illusion. *Explosion in a Cathedral* conceals under a tranquil surface a highly complex experiment with history and the narrative, an experiment whose relation to others by Carpentier should soon become evident. Some critics have noticed that the novel contains what appear to be blatant anachronisms.[34] For example, the first sentence of *The Communist Manifesto* is inserted in a discussion between Víctor and Ogé: "And we shall continue to go without news because the governments are frightened, terribly frightened, of the phantom that is stalking through Europe" (p. 71).[35] There are many others, including an allusion to modern painting: "Esteban had a taste for the imaginative and the fantastic, and would day-dream for hours in front of pictures by modern artists representing monsters, spectral horses, or impossible scenes—a tree-man with fingers sprouting from him, a cupboard-man with empty drawers coming out of his stomach" (p. 18). Although there is in that reference allusion to "pre-Surrealistic"

34. The first to note this was Edmundo Desnoes, in "El siglo de las luces," *Casa de las Américas*, no. 26 (1964), p. 107.
35. Quotations are from *Explosion in a Cathedral*, trans. John Sturrock (Boston: Little, Brown and Co., 1963).

paintings of the late eighteenth century, there is also oblique mention, as Ramón García Castro has shown, of twentieth-century pictures such as Dalí's "The Anthropomorphic Cabinet" (1936).[36] And this is not the only anachronistic reference to Surrealism in the novel. Concerning the many occult practices and doctrines of the eighteenth century, we read that "Extremes of subtlety had been attained in the interpretation of dreams, and by means of automatic writing, they had held converse with the basic 'ego' ["yo profundo"], conscious of previous existences, which lies concealed within every one of us" (p. 103). The text also contains veiled, anachronistic allusions to Fernando Ortiz, as when Víctor refers to the Caribbean as "a timeless marginal world, suspended between tobacco and sugar" (p. 69), and the overall vision of the political questions discussed by Víctor and Ogé is strangely anachronistic, with its mention of class struggles. Furthermore, Esteban's dilemma between aesthetic contemplation and action is post-Sartrean, as is Sofía's decision to "do something" at the end of the novel.

There can be no question that Carpentier is establishing an analogy between the modernism of the eighteenth century and that of his own time, and the futuristic quality of the novel is put within the future-oriented thought of the eighteenth century, with its desire to abolish the past and its proliferation of cities of the future and the like. As Paul Hazard writes: "The ancient fabric which had provided such indifferent shelter for the great human family, would have to come down. The first task was of demolition. That well and truly completed, the next thing was reconstruction. Foundations must be laid for the City of the Future."[37]

But what is peculiar about the future evoked in Explosion in a Cathedral is its quality of being simultaneously a past. The difference between the futurism of the eighteenth century and that of Carpentier is made clear if we consider for a moment a suggestive allusion in Explosion in a Cathedral. Among the new books that

36. "La pintura en Alejo Carpentier," to appear in Tlaloc.
37. The European Mind (1680–1715), trans. J. Lewis May (London, 1953), p. xviii.

Carlos, Esteban, and Sofía read is "a modern novel, set in the year 2440" (p. 25)—no doubt Sébastien Mercier's *L'an deux mille quatre cent quarante: Rêve s'il en fût jamais* (London, 1772). Mercier's utopian novel portrays the future as the time when all the ideals of the Enlightenment have become realities. His protagonist, who suddenly wakes up in the year 2440, establishes an ironic counterpoint between the eighteenth century, with all of its unachieved ideals, and the twenty-fifth century, when they have finally been put into practice: " 'Your century hardly enjoyed the glory of doing such a thing.' 'Oh, my century experienced the greatest difficulties when faced with the smallest undertaking.' . . . 'The most beautiful things were built on speculation; and language and the pen seemed to be the universal tools. Everything at its proper time. Ours was that of numberless projects; yours that of achievement. I congratulate you. I am glad to have lived so long.' "[38] The future appears in Mercier's utopian text as the kingdom of bourgeois virtue and reason from which metaphysics and rhetoric have been banished. In *Explosion in a Cathedral*, on the other hand, there is no counterpoint between ideal project and historical execution but a constant re-enactment of the gap between project and execution, as well as an affirmation of their indissoluble link. By making the future also past, history becomes the dynamic textual counterpoint between means and ends. In other words, the future that the history narrated in the text implies is, of necessity, nothing but the text—which forecloses any projections beyond its own specificity but allows for linear free play within itself. Contradictions are not bypassed and resolved in the novel, but merely begun again and again within the text's own dialectical free play. Whereas Mercier's idealistic utopia posits a future in which language would be reduced to pure functionality, in Carpentier's novel language is deployed in a present that is a composite of conflicting desires: a self-annihilating thrust to indistinctiveness and a constant reaffirmation of difference and order. Temporality, in the guise of an ever present future, dissolves any

38. I am translating from the Cornell University Rare Book Collection copy of Mercier's novel (p. 32).

possibility of fixed meanings. The most concrete manifestations of this in *Explosion in a Cathedral*, and in most of Carpentier's fiction since the forties, is the mixture in his prose of archaic and modern words and turns of phrase. The allusion to Mercier's *L'an deux mille quatre cent quarante* as a "modern novel" is precisely an indication of both the inherent naïveté of the future and its potential subversiveness: a self-referential sign, in short, of the mechanics of history and the narrative in Carpentier's novel.

The question of history and the narrative was at the very core of Carpentier's experiments in the forties and of the concept of "marvelous American reality." There, as we saw, it was the recovery of history from the texts that contained it that motivated Carpentier's enterprise—turning the fictional text into a pastiche of the texts from which history was recovered, and recovering with those texts the concert of history, already present as an organic continuum with nature. But breaking away from such a metaphor, in which the narrating self was effaced, subsumed in texts that were merely repeated, made the position of the self and its situation in history problematic. Once the illusion of repeating history in the text is done away with, the position of the writer is left in suspense. How is it possible to narrate history? Who narrates and from where in time? The common strategy in the historical novel is to bypass the problem and narrate *as if* the text were contemporaneous with the action of the novel. But Carpentier has not allowed himself such an easy way out of the dilemma. He obviously narrates history from a perspective that is *already* the future of that history. Historical narrative is, of necessity, always in the future: at the moment when history and its outcome are one. (The process by which Carlos reconstructs the last day of Esteban and Sofía in Madrid is indicative of this.) The anachronisms perform the function of pointing at the density of the historical field encompassed by the text, which integrates the past and the future on a single horizontal level. History, the grounding object of narration, and the text, its outcome, are one.

The thematic counterpart of this experiment is inscribed in another reading that *Explosion in a Cathedral* conceals. Carpentier has said that the Spanish title of the novel—*El siglo de las luces, The Century of Lights*—is ironic, that it contrasts, in its evocation of the light of reason, with the irrational and even barbaric history of the eighteenth century.[39] The historical process followed by the revolution as narrated in the novel would lend credence to this. It is obvious that in the tortuous course of the narrative the ideals of the revolution, once put into practice, turn out to work against the noble intentions on which they are founded: thus, the repeal of the law abolishing slavery, and the slave ship roaming the Caribbean under the name *The Social Contract*. Víctor Hugues's transition from libertarian to ruthless tyrant bent on the subjection of blacks in Cayenne is obviously the best example of this gulf between ideals and praxis. A less somber but equally significant instance, given in an emblematic scene typical of Carpentier, is when Billaud-Varenne, now a prisoner in Cayenne, is portrayed with his mulatto mistress: "Billaud-Varenne was writing by the light of a candle in the next room, having taken off his shirt because of the heat. From time to time he would kill some insect which had settled on his shoulders or the back of his neck with a powerful smack. Beside him the young Brigitte lay naked on a bed, fanning her breasts and thighs with an old copy of *La Décade Philosophique*" (p. 235).

But it is mostly in the presence of the occult, in sects such as the Masons and the Rosicrucians, that the irrational appears in *Explosion in a Cathedral*, investing the gap between reason and action with a quasi-religious and symbol-producing quality. It is by means of this reference to the occult that the text itself partakes of that symbolic quality, the allegorical configuration that invites a reading that goes beyond the peripety of the action and the development of the characters. The most consistent code to which this reading alludes is the Jewish Kabbala, which had a notable resurgence during the eighteenth century and the presence of

39. Miguel F. Roa, "Alejo Carpentier: el recurso a Descartes" (Interview), *Cuba Internacional*, no. 59 (July 1974), p. 50.

which in this text is a clear indication of Carpentier's reconciliation with his Surrealist past.[40] The first of the two epigraphs preceding the text of the novel—"words do not fall into the void"—
is taken from the Zohar, or Book of Splendors, one of the fundamental texts of kabbalism, written in Spain in the thirteenth century by Moisés de León.[41] The lights in the title of the novel not
only refer ironically to those of reason as defined by the Enlightenment, but also to those of the emanational doctrines of the Kabbala.
The Kabbala becomes the metaphoric link between history and
writing, a new "mock" theology of narrative. As we read in the
Zohar: "Throughout the expansion of the sky which encircles the
world, there are figures, signs by which we may know the secrets
and the most profound mysteries. These signs are formed by the
constellations which are to the sage a subject for contemplation
and delight. . . . He who travels in the early morning shall look
carefully to the east. He will see there something like letters march-
ing in the sky, some rising, others descending. These brilliant
characters are the letters with which God has formed heaven and
earth."[42] That divine text emanating from the hidden creator is

40. "In the eighteenth century magic and philosophy, politics and religion,
were so intimately mingled that it is difficult and perhaps impossible to define
the true character of the secret societies that now flooded Europe" (Kurt
Seligman, *Magic, Supernaturalism and Religion* [New York, 1971], p. 310).

41. For details on the Zohar, see Gershom G. Scholem, "The Zohar, I:
The Book and Its Author," in his *Major Trends in Jewish Mysticism* (New
York, 1961), pp. 156–204.

42. As quoted by Seligman, *Magic*, pp. 246–47. *Explosion in a Cathedral*
abounds in references to the celestial dome, which in a Carpenterian typology
has come to replace the exploded *domus*, or house. In "Manhunt," when the
fugitive finds the rubble of the House of the Effort, he enters "under the
open sky of the drawing room" (*Noonday*, 2 [1959], p. 167). In the first
chapter, after the death of the father, Esteban, Sofía, and Carlos climb to the
roof of their house, where "they fell asleep, after talking, with their faces
turned upwards to the sky, about habitable—and surely inhabited—planets,
where life would perhaps be better than it was on this earth, everlastingly subjected to the processes of death" (p. 23). And at the end of chapter 1, when
Víctor and Esteban sail to France: "The *Borée* sailed slowly with the night
breeze, beneath a sky so brilliant with stars that the mountains to the East
showed like intrusive shadows, cutting into the pure geometry of the constellations. . . . Towards the East the mind's eye could descry a Pillar of

not merely a reflection of Him or of the cosmos, but constitutes His only visible extension. "The Ancient One, the most Hidden of the hidden, is a high beacon, and we know Him only by His lights, which illuminate our eyes so abundantly. His Holy Name is no other than these lights."[43]

By appealing to the Kabbala, Carpentier is recasting the pattern of fall and redemption, of exile and return—of all his writing—within a system that centers precisely on these themes. And the Kabbala as metaphor was popular for this very reason in Romantic literature and all chiliastic writing. But beyond these thematic considerations, the importance of the Kabbala in *Explosion in a Cathedral*, as in Borges's work, is its concern with the nature of symbolic action, its centering on a hermeneutics whereby writing is accorded a crucial role in the composition of the world—as is well known, for kabbalists the world issues from the letters of the Hebrew alphabet. Thus its presence in the novel is not, like history, an external referential code but one which attempts to explicate the text of the novel itself. The metaphor of light is of primary importance in this connection, for although light emanates from a given source, its dissemination through space is so fast that both source and illumination appear as one. The analogy between this metaphor of light and that of the explosion in the painting "Explosion in a Cathedral" is clear; for an explosion is so sudden that cause and effect coincide and constitute a single experience, a sort of instantaneous movement: "But [Esteban's] favourite painting was a huge canvas by an unknown Neapolitan master which confounded all the laws of plastic art by representing the apocalyptic immobilisation of a catastrophe. It was called 'Explosion in a Cathedral,' this vision of a great colonnade shattering into fragments in mid-air—before it dashed its tons of stone on to the terrified people beneath" (p. 18). But it is not only on this metaphoric level that the novel and the Kabbala are linked.

Fire, standing upright and magnificent, guiding the ship towards the Promised Land" (p. 90).

43. Charles Poncé, *Kabbalah: An Introduction for the World Today* (San Francisco, 1973), p. 101.

The correspondence of kabbalistic doctrine and text in *Explosion in a Cathedral* becomes even more evident when we notice that the characters in the novel, and their relationships, share qualities with the *sephiroth* (or *sefiroth*), the vessels, through which divine light emanates to the world. As Charles Poncé explains: "These sefirothic lights manifest themselves in three triads, each triad representing a particular value as was originally contained in the *En-Sof* [without end or beginning, God] *in potentia*. The first triad is composed of the *Sefiroth Kether, Hokhmah* and *Binah*. This is the most important of the three triadic divisions of the *Sefiroth*, for it symbolizes the dynamic function of a thought process anterior to the world, and therefore an archetypal model." *Kether*, the first *sephirah*, is also known as "the Crown," a fact that becomes significant when it is considered that Esteban's name derives from the Greek *stephanus*, which also means "crown." Esteban's characteristics correspond to those of the *sephirah Kether*, which "is just the first impulse of *En-Sof* toward manifestation. It is the first expression of God's primal will, a will to will, an impulse and nothing more as yet. . . . Within this *Sefirah* reside all opposites in peaceful union. They exist in a state of potential separation. It is not until the two following *Sefiroth* come into being that the idea of balance appears. *Kether* represents equilibrium as a force or power residing at the central axis of a fulcrum. It is that point where two contending and opposing forces are counterbalanced. This is the significance of *Kether's* attribute of 'The Primordial or Smooth Point.'" Esteban is essentially passive and needs the presence of Víctor or Sofía to be moved into action; it is with the Marsellan that he makes his first sally into the world, following him as a lover would ("With almost feminine susceptibility Esteban grieved over Víctor Hugues' increasing loneliness," p. 165), with a mixture of admiration and fear. And it is with Sofía that he makes his second sally, playing a more masculine role. Esteban seems to possess both the feminine quality of Sofía and the masculine of Víctor. A neutral, latent force, he contains them both and needs each in turn to transform his energy into action, his contemplative nature into an active force. Esteban's sickness, his suffering for lack of air, is also consistent with a kabbalistic reading: "The energies of the second and third *Sefiroth*, *Hokhmah* and *Binah*, in that they are representative of all that is extreme in polarities, are contained by *Kether* in a point. It is the intensity of these powers residing in one space which cause *Kether* to 'suffer,' as it were."[44]

Víctor, the entrepreneur and revolutionary, represents the second *sephirah*, *Hokhmah*, "the *Sefirah* of God's wisdom [who] contains within him, in potential, the whole creation set within the catalyst of a will to create. In *Kether* we had the plan as intimated to him by *En-Sof*; in *Hokhmah* we have not only the plan but the impetus, the 'current,' the bursting desire to put forth the plan of creation." Víctor's appearance sets the other characters in motion as he assumes the position of a second father to them. *Hokhmah* is, according to Poncé, "the archetype of fatherhood, for he is referred to as the 'father of fathers.'" Sofía, on the other hand, assumes throughout the novel a maternal position with regard to Esteban: "she took special pains to be a mother to Esteban, a mother who was so possessive in her new functions that she did not hesitate to undress him and bathe him with a sponge" (p. 23). In this respect she most closely resembles the *sephirah Binah*, who is "the supernal Mother, *Imma*, within whose womb all that was contained in Wisdom finally becomes differentiated."[45]

The kabbalistic code in *Explosion in a Cathedral* contains the basic elements of Carpentier's new concept of writing, his new metaphor to link writing and history. If Carpentier's fiction in the forties sought its foundation in a theological, transcendental source from which it received order, his new writing will have a much more dialectical conception of the source. Earlier fiction sought an original source, a single fountainhead of origination from which writing flowed in a continuum. In *The Lost Steps* the irrevocable

44. Ibid., pp. 110–11, 114–15, 116.
45. Ibid., pp. 119, 121, 122. The relationship between *Binah* and the name Sofía (wisdom) is made precisely by this power to differentiate, for *Binah* "can be taken to signify not only 'intelligence,' but also 'that which divided between things'" (Scholem, "The *Zohar*, II: The Theosophic Doctrine," in *Major Trends*, p. 219).

absence of that source is made manifest, while "Manhunt" issues from the terror of its presence. In *Explosion in a Cathedral*, for the first time, there is a clear separation between worldly and divine realms. The presence of the Kabbala points precisely at the secondary status of writing and of the world. History after the original Fall is the province of man, not of the Divine: "As above so below: the Fall of Adam in the Garden was understood as inevitable in that the archetypal drama of the Fall had already taken place in Adam Kadmon [an original Adam previous to the one in the Garden]. . . . The aim of Kabbalism is the restoration of the divine man in the medium of mortal men."[46] Paradoxically, this does not mean that the cosmos is independent of its creator, since the cosmos emanates from Him; but the point of that emanation is a void, like the center of an explosion—the first, lost source is the *En-Sof*, which is without end or beginning. The point of arrival of the emanation, being the self, is also a void, a nothing: "The Hebrew word for nothing, *ain*, has the same consonants as the word for I, *ani*—and as we have seen, God's 'I' is conceived as the final stage in the emanation of the *Sephiroth*, that stage in which God's personality, in a simultaneous gathering together of all its previous stages, reveals itself to its own creation. In other words, the passage from *ain* to *ani* is symbolical of the transformation by which the Nothing passes through the progressive manifestations of its essence in the Sephiroth, into the I—a dialectical process whose thesis and antithesis begin and end in God."[47] In kabbalistic terms, then, being is nothingness, and the source of being, also nothingness. Both the cosmos as the emanation from negativity (from that which is not) and being, its reflection, are postponed, delayed echoes of something that was not. Writing, in other words, is always the future of a past that does not exist, that is re-created.

This conception of writing and history explains the secondary status of Caribbean history as it appears in the novel. Of the French Revolution, as it were, there is little in *Explosion in a Cathedral*, only some of its repercussions in the Caribbean. The

46. Poncé, *Kabbalah*, p. 140.
47. Scholem, "The *Zohar*, II," p. 218.

cause of the effect is lost; effects stand as their own causes, merely alluding to a prime mover that is remote in space and time. Evidence of this is found everywhere in the plot of the novel. While he is a ruler in Guadeloupe, Víctor Hugues attempts futilely to keep up with the transformations of the revolution, but his actions always lag behind because of the time it takes for news to reach the Caribbean. He remains, for instance, an epigone of Robespierre when the latter had already been deposed. We do not know, until much later in the novel, that Sofía gave herself to Víctor when the Arrow was anchored off Santiago Bay, and therefore cannot take this into account in our reading of her actions until the revelation is made. The source is present, but as an erasure, an absent or delayed presence. The text begins, in other words, with the second Adam, the one in the Garden, not the ontological Adam Kadmon.

The multiplicity of protagonists, which had already begun in "Manhunt" with the counterpoint between the hunted one and the ticket clerk, is obviously related to this conception of writing and constitutes, in a sense, an assumption of the results yielded by The Lost Steps (in which the sought unity of the narrator-protagonist refracts manifold selves and images). The conceit of writing as the result of the communion between nature and the self is abandoned in favor of the writer as medium, transmitter or conductor, of the emanations from a plenum of nothingness. Esteban's delayed recognition of his translations, which are circulating anonymously through Latin America, is a clear indication of this. A more concrete instance, bearing upon Carpentier himself, is the concealed identification between Esteban and the author. Carpentier has left a coy clue in the text to the effect that Esteban's name (whose coincidence with Joyce's Stephen has been noted by Desnoes),[48] beyond the other connotations that we have indicated, was not randomly chosen: "That morning there was a Grand Dinner in the dining room; they made believe it was in Vienna, because for some time now Sofía had loved reading articles

48. "El siglo de las luces," p. 299.

extolling the marble, glass and rocaille of that incomparable musical city dedicated to Saint Stephen—the patron saint of Esteban, who had been born in this house one December 26th" (p. 39). (In the Spanish text Carpentier puts three dots after the date, a mark he uses often to underline the oblique meaning of something, particularly in his journalistic work.) Carpentier, of course, was also born on December 26th, in Havana, on the feast of Saint Stephen, the protomartyr. Carpentier's identification is suggestive on many counts. As we saw, within the context of the kabbalistic reading, Esteban stands for a latent force, composed of both the masculine and the feminine forces represented by Víctor and Sofía. Within this mythology of writing, Esteban is a catalyst, a conductor of the will of the masculine power and the differentiating power of the feminine one—thus his role as translator. But as the embodiment of the first *sephirah*, Esteban is also the closest to *En-Sof*, and the nearest to the source of emanation. He is the closest to nothingness, then, identified by the absence of a name in his translations, the sickly emaciated "smooth point" that bears within him all the contradictions and can only become something at the end when he joins Sofía and loses himself in the crowd (his ailment, which manifests itself as lack of air, is also significant, for in Kabbalistic doctrine air mediated between water and earth, the other two elements composing the universe). On both ends he is annulled; he suffers (the association with the protomartyr is important here) because he is that void which must bear the warring contraries that produce signification.

Although the relationship of this conception with the Romantic archetype of the sickly, sensitive, alienated writer is obvious, the point is that in *Explosion in a Cathedral* Esteban is moved to positive action at the end. By uniting himself to the feminine power in an incestuous bond (he and Sofía are first cousins) he gains strength to differentiate and to take action. This is not merely a political statement, nor is his dissolution in the crowd a return to the seed. The writer, being here the point of arrival of the emanation, returns to it without repeating it, without regressing. The fact that he and Sofía are linked by consanguinity stresses both their fusion and their separation, the repetitiousness and the originality of their act. Their fusion is a new fall, a new original sin, as it were, that will propel the course of history forward, not to an original union that is lost in the past. Esteban's journey is not circular but spiral. The fusion with nothingness at the end is one more point in the chain of returns that never go back to a primal source, to *the* source, but to phantasmatic, secondary images of it. Esteban and Sofía cannot become the original couple; he is not Adam Kadmon, but the second (third, fourth, and so on) Adam, just as he, born the day after Christmas, can re-enact the suffering of the protomartyr but not of Christ. The writer is bound to the nothingness from which his consciousness springs; writing, his product, is that spiral trajectory of traces, a signifying machine that annuls him.

Although it is Carlos who opens and closes the fiction proper, the text of the novel is preceded by an epigraph (besides that from the *Zohar*) of Esteban's mediations on the arrival of the guillotine in the New World, as he sails with Víctor to the Caribbean. That first-person meditation is unsigned; the reader is given no indication of who speaks. Only after we read the novel can we identify Estaban as the speaker and realize that the words must have been uttered by Esteban at a point more or less in the middle of the action. Esteban stands anonymously at a point before the beginning of the text and comments upon a central episode that we have not yet read—an episode in which he is returning home at a crucial point in his life, when he is passing from adolescence to adulthood. The whole of the novel is contained within Esteban. But because his voice is not identified at the beginning, he is the embodiment of the erased source, the postponed presence that can only attain meaning in the future, a future that we read but whose meaning is suspended. Writing and the self can only merge at a point that is constantly postponed and at the same time remembered; in the meantime, we are allowed to revel in the evocative beauty of the passage.

This complex deployment of time becomes significant when we examine two memorable scenes in the novel: Esteban's meditation on a beach while contemplating a conch shell, and the festivities at

Jorge's country estate during the Christmas and New Year holidays. The meditation on the shell occurs at the beginning of chapter 3 and at the end of subchapter 24; that is to say, in the center of the text, since the novel has forty-seven subchapters, followed by one (subdivided in two) unnumbered subchapter in chapter 7 that would make it forty-eight. Esteban is on a beach in the Caribbean (the English translator has erroneously rendered "conch shell" as "snail"):

Or else, with the point of his chin resting on the cool leaves of an uvero, he became absorbed in the contemplation of a snail—a single snail—which stood like a monument, level with his eyes, blotting out the horizon. This snail was the mediator between evanescent, fugitive, lawless, measureless fluidity, and the land, with its crystallisations, its structures, its morphology, where everything could be grasped and weighed. Out of a sea at the mercy of lunar cycles—fickle, furious or generous, curling and dilating, forever ignorant of modules, theorems and equations—there appeared these surprising shells, symbolising in number and proportion exactly what the Mother lacked, concrete examples of linear development, of the laws of convolution, of a wonderfully precise conical architecture, of masses in equilibrium, of tangible arabesques which hinted at all the baroquisms to come. Contemplating a snail—a single snail—Esteban reflected on how, for millennium upon millennium, the spiral had been present to the everyday gaze of maritime races, who were still incapable of understanding it, or of even grasping the reality of its presence. He meditated on the prickly husk of the sea-urchin, the helix of the mollusc, the fluting of the Jacobean scallop-shell, astonished by this science of form which had been exhibited for so long to a humanity that still lacked eyes to appreciate it. What is there round about me which is already complete, recorded, real, yet which I cannot understand? What sign, what message, what warning is there, in the curling leaves of the endive, the alphabet of moss, the geometry of the rose-apple? Contemplate a snail. Te deum. [P. 180]

Seen in the broader context of Carpentier's earlier work the most striking feature in this passage is the opposition between the sea and the shell. As we saw in The Lost Steps, the watery world to which the protagonist regresses is the region of formlessness and ambiguity, of shifting meanings and perpetually emerging forms. In Explosion in a Cathedral the same associations are made: the novel opens with Carlos on a boat crossing Havana Bay under a glimmering sun that blurs the contours of things and creates mirages of light on the water's surface. The spiral of the conch shell, however, mediates between the formlessness of water and hardened shapes of earth; it embodies the fluidity of form, as opposed to the formlessness of water and the chiseled, symmetrical shapes of stone. The conch shell is neither multiplicity nor unity, but the relationship, the play between unity and multiplicity. The temporal connotations of the spiral are clear: it establishes a relationship between the circle and a moving center and signals not atemporality but recurrence, or, as the text reads, "the laws of convolution." The spiral evokes a controlled image of infinity, as opposed to the abysmal infinity of the receding sequences. Like the contained formlessness represented by the painting "Explosion in a Cathedral"—in which the opposition between shapelessness and architecture is evident—the spiral is generated by a movement around a movable center. But precisely because that center moves along a perpendicular axis, the circle around it moves on an incline that will return all of its points to the same vertical position but on a different horizontal plane, and the center itself will disappear to constitute itself again. The process is one of perpetual construction and deconstruction, in which each movement is always the potentiality of the next. Again, as opposed to the specular reflection, which offered identical or reversed images of itself *ad infinitum*, the spiral projects future images of each of its points, as well as a nebulous shade of its past trajectory always in dissolution. The central position of the spiral in the novel could not be more suggestive, but its implications become clearer when examined in conjunction with the scene of the festivities at Jorge's country estate.

The significance of the scene stems from its temporal disposition. After his adventures with Víctor Hugues, Esteban returns to Havana and finds Sofía married to Jorge. It is 1799 and the Christmas holidays are near; Sofía, Jorge, Carlos, and Esteban are invited to spend the season at a country estate near Havana belonging to Jorge's family. Esteban and Sofía leave first, while Carlos and Jorge promise to go "eight days later" ("a week" in the English translation), after concluding some business matters. The action begins, therefore, on December 16, for Esteban and Sofía go to the gates of the estate on the 24th to await the arrival of Carlos and Jorge: "On the evening of the 24th of December, whilst some of the party were eagerly completing the arrangements for Christmas Day, invading the kitchen at intervals to make sure that the turkeys were browning in the ovens, and that the sauces were beginning to give off their eloquent aroma, Esteban and Sofía went to the entrance of the finca, with its monumental iron gates, to wait for Carlos and Jorge who would soon be arriving" (p. 269). While they are waiting, and after taking refuge in a gazebo from a sudden rainstorm, Esteban declares to Sofía his long-repressed passion for her. There is no indication of temporal transition during this climactic scene. At the end of it Esteban and Sofía are witness to a ritual celebration of Christmas Eve: "The rain had stopped; the undergrowth was full of lights and fancy dresses. Shepherds appeared, and millers with floury faces, negroes who were not negroes, old women aged twelve, men with beards, and men with cardboard crowns all shaking maraccas, cow-bells, tambourines and timbrels" (p. 271). The celebration is followed in the text by lines of a traditional *villancico*, and then by this startling transformation: "Behind the clumps of bougainvillaea, the house was a blaze of candelabra, lamps and Venetian lustres. Now they would have to wait for midnight, surrounded by trays of punch. Twelve strokes would ring out from the tower, and everyone would have to gulp down the traditional twelve grapes. Then would ensue the interminable dinner, prolonged by a dessert of hazel-nuts and almonds broken open with nut-crackers" (p. 271). The celebrations described here are no longer those of Christmas Eve, but of New Year's Eve, when the symbolic twelve grapes are eaten at midnight. There has been a transitionless forward temporal displacement of one week: from December 24 to December 31. The presence of the heavy iron gates of the finca, of fires and lights, and of the Carnivallike display of masks clearly suggests that something portentously symbolic is lurking underneath what appears to be a fairly traditional novelistic scene. The fact that it is not merely the end of a year but the end of a century that is being celebrated is no doubt significant here, and even more so since the transition from 1799 to 1800 marks the chronological center of the action (1789–1809). (The importance of this transition from the point of view of the plot may be gauged by the new turn that Sofía's life immediately takes, with the sudden death of Jorge and her subsequent decision to seek out Víctor to join him again; her husband's death, twelve years after her father's, opens a new cycle of Sofía's life.) It cannot be discounted either that the temporal displacement, which, like the anachronisms already noted, is a forward shift toward the future, occurs in subchapter 37, a number that brings together not only two privileged numbers in the Kabbala (3 and 7) but two numbers that add up to an even ten: the number of *sephiroth* and of lights. The connotations of the dates involved, Christmas Eve and New Year's Eve, no doubt also enter into the symbolic network of subchapter 37. If in "Manhunt" Carpentier had set the action during Holy Week, here we have (as in *The Kingdom of This World*) the other high point of the liturgical year, Advent, encompassing the birth of Christ and the beginning of the New Year.

The two weeks in question, extending from December 16 to December 31, swirl vertiginously in a single movement analogous to that of the spiral. The constant numerical proportion guarantees the return of all the points in the circle to a place perpendicularly even with their previous position: the sixteenth becomes the twenty-fourth and then a thirty-first that will become the first (thus the conditional in the quotation above, "they would have to"). For just as *The Lost Steps* ends on the last day of the year, a Saturday that announces a Sunday and a New Year that never comes, subchapter 37 ends announcing a New Year, at the end of the first chronological half of *Explosion in a Cathedral*. The presence of the masked figures at the chronological midpoint in the action is reminiscent of the pivotal Carnival scenes in Carpentier's fiction of the forties; but the difference is as great as that established by the fact that the announced New Year does indeed come in *Explosion in a Cathedral*. In *The Kingdom of This World* and the stories collected in War of Time, the textual and chronological centers of the narrative coincided, dividing the plot into two mirrorlike halves. Here, on the other hand, the textual and the chronological centers do not coincide, for, as we saw, the meditation on the conch shell occurs in subchapter 24, which is the middle subchapter, while the end-of-the-year scene is in subchapter 37. It is no coincidence, it also seems, that there are thirteen subchapters between 24 and 37, making the latter then the beginning of a new cycle (12 + 1), nor that there are twelve subchapters between 37 and the end of the novel (counting the two unnumbered subchapters in chapter 7). This displacement of centers is analogous to the spiral's. The centers do not constitute a fixed chronological or textual fulcrum, but instead provide, as does the spiral, a movable, phantasmatic axis, constantly doing and undoing itself, around which the action of the novel revolves: a "law of convolution," not of mirror images, presides over the structure of the novel. That New Year's Day for which Esteban and Sofía would have to wait to consummate their union is the one that appears in the last chapter, when Carlos arrives in Madrid, after Sofía and Esteban have vanished, joined now as they could not join each other in 1799. Carlos arrives in Madrid on January 1, 1809, the tenth year after the scene at Jorge's estate, and the twentieth of the action.

Christmas Day 1799 is skipped in the novel, as are in analogous fashion all founding or beginning actions and dates in history. If the birth of Christ, the pivotal point in the liturgical year and the archetypal revolution in Western thought, is skipped, so are political revolutions, which provide the historical axis of the novel's historical context. Víctor arrives from Boston, where he had been profiting from the aftermath of the American Revolution; most of the novel relates the repercussions of the French Revolution, and even when the action takes places in Paris, we are given only the marginal incidents of a postrevolutionary period from the perspective of marginal characters; the historicopolitical actions ends after the uprising against Joseph Bonaparte on May 2, 1808. Not only de we find a recurrence of revolution, as a future already past, but the novel offers only its outer edge. The paternal figures in the novel suffer the same fate, being constantly replaced or made prematurely obsolete. The *pater familias* is dead when the novel begins, and upon discovering his licentious activities later, Sofía stamps on his portrait and caves it in; Remigio is proven by Víctor to be an embezzler; Jorge dies young; Víctor himself becomes weak and corrupt, and Sofía not only leaves him but gives herself to one of his underlings. If there is a correspondence between history and the family, there is also a parallel in this pattern of centerlessness. The historical and familial center is a void like the vacuum at the point of detonation in "Explosion in a Cathedral," or that of the whirl of constellations in the celestial dome—in kabbalistic terms, the hole in the celestial dome through which the blinding flash of the Hidden One projects Its emanations unto the cosmos.

It is, appropriately, in Esteban's meditation in the second epigraph of the novel that the connotative range of this deferred centerlessness of the text is given through the most prominent emblem in the novel, the guillotine:

I saw them erect the guillotine again to-night. It stood in the bows, like a doorway opening on the immense sky—through which the scents of the land were already coming to us across an ocean so calm, so much a master of its rhythm, that the ship seemed asleep, gently cradled on its course, suspended between a yesterday and a to-day which moved with us. Time stood still, caught between the Pole Star, the Great Bear and the Southern Cross—though I do not know, for it is not my job to know, whether such in fact were the constellations, so numerous that their vertices, their sidereal fires, mingled and combined, shuffling the allegories they symbolised. And even the brightness of the full moon paled beside the whiteness—how portentously renewed at that moment!—of the Milky Way.

But the empty doorway stood on the bows, reduced to a mere lintel and its supports, with the set-square, the inverted half-pediment, the black triangle, and its bevel of cold steel, suspended between the uprights. Its naked, solitary skeleton had been newly raised above the sleeping crew, like a presence, a warning, which concerned us all equally. . . . Here the Door stood alone, facing into the night above the tutelary figurehead, its diagonal blade gleaming, its wooden uprights framing a whole panorama of stars. [Pp. 7–8]

The association between guillotine and door throughout the novel is clear because of the persistent allusions to the doors of the family's house in Havana and Madrid, as well as to the gates of Jorge's estate. And in the Kabbala the relation between doors and lights that we find in Esteban's meditation was already established in a text contemporaneous with the Zohar, Joseph Gikatilla's *Gates of Light* (*Sha'are Orah*), disseminated in Paulus Ricius' Latin translation, *Porta Lucis* (Augsburg, 1516).[49] The guillotine is constantly presented in the novel as a door without walls and an empty frame ("la puerta sin batientes" in the text)—an arbitrary threshold in the endless void.

In the context of Carpentier's persistent evocation of buildings and ruins, the guillotine appears, then, as a frame left standing after the demolition of a house, or before its construction, as the empty, demarcated space around which the house is built. In "Manhunt," the walls of a building constituted the apotheosis of form, the petrification of the text and of desire. The building— house, church, theater—was the enclosure of being. Here, on the other hand, what is continuously suggested is the demolition of the monument, and the door-guillotine remains (like the conch shell) as the mediator, the boundary between the unstructured void and the region of form—entrance and exit constituted by a single frame that is immovable yet is displaced through space (as the boat). As Cirlot explains, the door "contains all the implications of the symbolic hole, since it is the door which gives access to the hole; its significance is therefore the antithesis of the wall. There is the same relationship between the temple-door and the altar as between the circumference and the center: even though in each case the two component elements are the farthest apart, they ar nonetheless, in a way, the closest since the one determines and reflects the other. This is well illustrated in the ornamentation of cathedrals, where the façade is nearly always treated as if it were an altar-piece."[50] The double meaning of the door-guillotine as

49. See Scholem, "The *Zohar*, II," p. 212. The significance of Gikatilla's work is that it "analyzes the motives which determine the correlation between the Sephiroth and their Scriptural symbol," according to Scholem.

50. J. E. Cirlot, A *Dictionary of Symbols*, trans. Jack Sage (New York, 1962), p. 81.

gateway and exit is paralleled by its contradictory meanings in history, being both the symbol of freedom and of death. Whereas the wall denotes fixity and completion, the door stands as both beginnings and ends, in the same way that the circle is its center expanded around a virtual though absent point. Like the spiral in the conch shell, the door-guillotine is the dynamic mediator between formlessness and fixity; as such, door-guillotine, spiral, and the painting "Explosion in a Cathedral" stand as emblems of the text itself, of its constitution at an unstable point where past and future are one for an instant. In Esteban's meditation the guillotine frames, like a page, the signs, the stars and constellations, projected against the celestial dome.

The central metaphoric chain in *Explosion in a Cathedral* revolves, then, around these emblems of the constitution of the text itself and of its inner dialectics. Rather than a self-reflexiveness of a thwarted return to the source and to a grounding notion of beginnings, as we found in *The Lost Steps*, *Explosion in a Cathedral* posits a kind of writing that appears as a series of returns to origins that turn with the same movement: revolutionary writing in its etymological sense, in that it revolves around an absent axis that is constituted by the very movement of its periphery. If, in Hegel's famous dictum, world history is world judgment, in *Explosion in a Cathedral* history and judgment are one—writing is history. It is in this context that the epigraph from the *Zohar* acquires its ultimate meaning: as in kabbalistic thought, writing is the world. The text is the first and last measure of itself.

The constitution of the text, its crystallization in movement, is given by the "constellations, so numerous that their vertices, their sidereal fires, mingled and combined, shuffling the allegories they symbolised." The elaborate symbolic structure of *Explosion in a Cathedral* attempts to come to grips with the relationship between the movement of history and the fixity of emblems, not only in an abstract sense, but in the very concrete mode in which Carpentier's historical fiction tends, by its allegoric and archetypal quality, to move into an ideal realm of signification. Julio Ortega has written perceptively on this subject:

The novel itself opens with other emblems: the death of the father and the chaos of the physical world coincide in exemplary fashion. . . . The disappearance of that father comes in a world invaded by rains, covered with lime, with mud; those repeated images suggest resonances of chaos; the novel begins from that shapeless world and the lives of the three young protagonists are reordered from that beginning. Thus from the first pages we notice already the almost fatalistic significance that the relationship between the characters and a correlative setting that defines and judges them possesses. A significance that is constantly expanding the actuality of fiction in the anachronism of the emblem. The novel also shows the fatalistic progress of an emblematic history that imposes itself. Lastly, this code of the typical announces the very construction of the novel as a parodic redoubling, as theater that unveils itself through the emblems of its elaborate staging.[51]

If we reflect upon the presence of the theater in *Explosion in a Cathedral*, and in scenes such as the "execution" of the costumes in chapter 1, in addition to what has already been observed about the possibility of an allegorical reading through the doctrines of the Kabbala, we cannot escape the feeling that Ortega's formulation is correct. And it is, except that the coexistence of a fatalistic element in that emblematic history and the parodic aspect that Ortega mentions appears suspect. While retaining the idea that there is a visible synchronization of action and emblem, and thus a redoubling, I would suggest that the anachronistic relationship between the redoubled elements excludes the possibility of fatalism (in a sense of predictability of recurrence). What the allegorical self-referentiality of the novel opens up is precisely the gap manifested by the anachronism, the perpetual shuffling of allegory—its emptying out of meaning. Through that gap the parodic and the humorous, as opposed to the tragic evoked by fatalism, explode in the text.

At this point *Explosion in a Cathedral* reveals its radical reassessment of Carpentier's previous writing and marks a turning point whose more visible manifestations are only seen later in

51. "El siglo de las luces," *Asedios a Carpentier: once ensayos críticos sobre el novelista cubano*, ed. Klaus Müller-Bergh (Santiago, Chile, 1972), p. 193.

Reasons of State and Concierto barroco. The clue here is what Ortega calls "emblem," which one could define as the physical, visible manifestation of a codified symbol—an allegory. It is the materiality of the emblem, in this as well as in previous novels by Carpentier, that has the most significance. Carpentier's insistence on the guillotine, on costumes, on buildings, on paintings and statues, obviously related to his use of capital letters, is an attempt to invest a character or event with a solid, materially fixed meaning. But what allegory constantly reveals is an emptying process, by means of which each one of those emblems can only attain meaning by alluding to something else. Just as "Explosion in a Cathedral" points to the dismantling of the domus dei, of the fixed, petrified text (which forebodes an abolition of desire), so the shuffling of allegories in the novel uncovers the ultimate fluidity of the emblem—its constant state of dissolution. The fluidity stems from its being a code rotating around an empty center, like the constellations, which can signify only by its elusive and allusive movement. If the guillotine framing the stars can evoke the essential fluidity of the page, it can also evoke the theater: the frame of the proscenium arch. The parodic element emerges both from the degradation of signification by making it material and from the gesture toward the void that separates each figure from the next. It is the same temporal displacement that we have noted throughout the novel: the emblem is not a meaningful object, but is already the gesture toward another figure in the future that it already contains. The "spirit" of each of those material figures has already escaped (like the animal from the shell), has already moved on, and only the hollow husk is left as an epitaph for its source.

It is this quality that accounts for the anachronistic external form of Explosion in a Cathedral. The novel is not only reminiscent of nineteenth-century novels but is also cast in the mold of popular adventure novels of that century. Carpentier has inscribed within the format of the popular romance a meditation on history and thought, emptying out and vulgarizing, as it were, the core of Western culture—as indeed the popular nineteenth-century romance did. If Explosion in a Cathedral deals with very ponderous

intellectual matter pertaining to the Enlightenment, it does so by
degrading them, by reducing them to the allegorical play of an
outwardly simple romance. The frequent allusions to Goya, whose
titles head many chapters of the novel, are the clearest indication
of this corrosive, parodic impulse—of the novel's reveling in the
materiality of a world abandoned by the gods but bent on resurrection through the very pleasure of unredeemed matter. Sofía's
heady call to action at the end of the novel implies this as much
as a call to political action. Revolution is not a remote future, but
the future become present in the textual activity of the novel.

3

Hegel remarks somewhere that all facts and personages of
great importance in world history occur, as it were, twice. He
forgot to add: the first time as tragedy, the second as farce.

Marx, *The Eighteenth Brumaire of Louis Bonaparte*

What emerges from Carpentier's experiments in *Explosion in a
Cathedral* is parody: parody that results from the confrontation of
the future with a source, a pre-text, whose ideal, phantasmatic form
is violated to allow for a textual free play. In historical terms, the
parody results from the overturning of the core of Western civilization by the popular culture arising at the juncture of the eighteenth
and nineteenth centuries. In terms of writing, parody becomes
the locus created by the fissure, now assumed, between thought
and its signs—a humorous allegory that underlines the hollow
materiality of signs and the temporal gap between meaning and
its representation. If up to *The Lost Steps* and "Manhunt" Carpentier's writing was grounded on a veiled self-reflexiveness that
posited a return to the source, now self-reflexiveness is embraced
and both the return and the source multiply and proliferate; history has become parodic repetition, its own end, and the sources
of the text are revealed in their deformed, desecrated condition,
instead of being concealed and covered to safeguard their originality and that of the text. The most superficial indication of a
change is the absence of solemnity; humor was almost completely
missing in Carpentier's earlier production (with the exception of

"El milagro de Anaquillé"). Stemming from this new element and from the recapitulatory nature of Carpentier's works from *Explosion in a Cathedral* on, which recover themes and topics of his earlier works, there is also an element of self-parody that is obviously related to self-reflexiveness. These are the elements that predominate in *Reasons of State* (1974), *Concierto barroco* (1974), "The Chosen" (1970), "Right of Sanctuary" (1972), and the published chapters of Carpentier's next novel, *La consagración de la primavera*: he has assumed, as it were, that third style he defined in his essay on the new Latin American novel as a nonstyle.

Faithful to the implications of that new style, the newest narratives constitute a return to the city—not to the city as the stony labyrinth of architecture (of *arch-texture*) but to the city become a mock-up, a stage for comic opera. As we read in *Reasons of State*:

> The poor lived in Foundation Palaces, dating from the days of Orellana and Pizarro—but now given over to filth and rats—while their masters inhabited houses belonging to no tradition, native, baroque or Jesuitic, but theatrically got up in Mediaeval, Renaissance or Hollywood-Andalusian colour-schemes, and without the smallest connection with the country's history, or else in large buildings aping the Second Empire style of the Boulevard Haussman. The new Central Post Office had a superb Big Ben. The new head Police Station was a Temple from Luxor in eau-de-nil. The country house of the Chancellor of the Exchequer was a pretty miniature Schönbrunn. The President of the Chamber kept his mistress in a little Abbaye de Cluny, swathed in imported ivy. . . . And by the same token the Head of State remembered his long-cherished but now realizable desire to install an Opera House inside the Opera-City, the Capital of Fiction, and offer his compatriots a spectacle like those to be seen in Buenos Aires and Rio de Janeiro—towns that had always kept their eyes on the arts and refinements of the Old World. [Pp. 175–76][52]

It is in this setting, or a *fin de siècle* Paris, or eighteenth-century Venice at Carnival time, that Carpentier locates the action of his new narratives. The imposing buildings of the University of Havana in "Manhunt," the Sans-Souci or La Ferrière of *The Kingdom of This World*, the palatial country home of Marcial in

52. *Reasons of State*, trans. Frances Partridge (New York, 1976).

"Journey Back to the Source" lose their proportions, becoming either too small or preposterously large, and the consistency of their material is turned into cardboard and papier-mâché. It is a décor whose proportions and materials remind one of the scenario for "El milagro de Anaquillé."

This degradation of the architecture reflects a similar process in the texts themselves. Now, more than ever, and with increasing impunity, they are a mixture of styles and sources; historical and fictional characters mingle on the same level. Bits and pieces of other literary texts are brought together in a textual amalgam, as in this passage from *Reasons of State*, where a mutilated title from Proust is juxtaposed with a fragment of one from Ciro Alegría: "se había desviado hacia sucesos *anchos y ajenos. Sosiego y reposo hallaba, por fin, el Primer Magistrado, a la sombra de los cañones en flor*" (p. 146, my italics; the allusions are lost in the English translation). Parody and humor rule in Carpentier's new writing.

The ponderous titles of Carpentier's two most recent novels, *El recurso del método* and *Concierto barroco*, seem to indicate quite the opposite. But their solemnity, which at first glance makes them evoke weighty erudite treatises, belies their parodic nature, for just as *El siglo de las luces* meant precisely the opposite, so do these titles mock rather than designate their overt referents. In 1974, Carpentier said of *Reasons of State*: "It is Descartes's *Discourse on Method* turned upside down, for I believe that Latin America is the least Cartesian continent imaginable. And so *Le discours de la methode* turns into *Le recours de la methode, El discurso del método/El recurso del método*, for all the chapters—there are twenty-two—are linked in deadpan fashion, by Descartes's reflections taken from the *Discourse*, the *Philosophical Meditations*, and the *Treatise on Passions*, which, in spite of the rigidity of their thought, are the justification for totally delirious acts."[53] It is precisely the inversion already present in the title that rules over these new narratives. Let us observe its effects in *El recurso del método*, which is the major text of the post-1956 period.

53. Roa, "El recurso a Descartes," p. 50.

By the opposition *discourse/recourse*, Carpentier is not only undermining Descartes but pointing to the source of his inversion: Vico. The presence of Vico in this new phase of Carpenterian writing is enormously significant. In a sense Vico has come to replace Spengler as a philosophical underpinning for Carpentier's fictions and performs a function homologous to the Kabbala. If Spengler posited a circular history whose cycles were repeated throughout the universe, Vico offers an idea of return that does not deny historicity, but affirms it. As opposed to Spengler, whose concept of history and culture is grounded in a complicity between spirit and nature, Vico offers a history that begins when man begins to make history, in a second beginning by which the Christian idea of genesis is not dismissed but its relevance diminished. That second beginning is the Flood, when man begins anew, but by himself, to remake history. It is not by chance that one of Carpentier's stories of this period, "The Chosen," uses as its theme the convergence of many arks, constructed by the many Noahs of different religious traditions, who must remake the world after the universal Flood. "The Chosen" is a Vichian fable of origins, the story of the second beginning of history—of the first recourse, as it were. Vico, to be sure, furnishes more, in particular the idea of a history whose import must be read not only in a few privileged monuments but in the laborious *fabulations* of the people: a decentering of culture, so to speak, that undermines the imperialistic centrality of thought posited by Descartes.

But the opposition between discourse and recourse implies much more. The crucial passage in Descartes's *Discourse* is the one where, after rejecting all received ideas as potentially false, he proclaims the essential unity of truth and of the self: "And since all the same thoughts and conceptions which we have while awake may also come to us in sleep, without any of them being at that time true, I resolved to assume that everything that ever entered into my mind was no more true than the illusions of my dreams. But immediately afterwards I noticed that whilst I thus wished to think all things false, it was absolutely essential that the 'I' who thought this should be somewhat, and remarking that this truth

'*I think, therefore I am*,' was so certain and so assured that all the most extravagant suppositions brought forward by the sceptics were incapable of shaking it, I came to the conclusion that I could receive it without scruple as the first principle of the Philosophy for which I was seeking."[54] It is this unity and truthful status of the discoursing self that was found lacking in *The Lost Steps* and which *Reasons of State* parodies. For *discourse* is here equated with *method*, with system, implying the tautological nature of Descartes's very title—the discourse of discourse or the method of method—by the duplicatory connotation of the prefix re. This, I believe, helps to explain the somewhat obscure meaning of Carpentier's Spanish title, which could be translated as "The Recourse of Method," meaning the turning back of method onto itself, but more appropriately, "Method's Recourse," meaning the method's availing itself of itself—method's recourse to protect itself. Either way, what the title implies is the illusory nature of discourse, in its oratorical, pedagogical, or grammatical sense. Discourse is a constant turning onto itself, an areferential play of signifiers that revert to themselves to acquire meaning. It also implies the dissolution of the discursive self as the source of truth and order. Discourse and self are only apprehended "in the recourse"; that is to say, they emerge only at that point when they turn onto themselves to manifest, not their rigorous unity, but their constant dispersal and discontinuity.

The parody of Descartes in most other instances is rather obvious and direct, not only in the epigraphs of each chapter but also in the many direct allusions to him or to his work by means of which the protagonist justifies his actions. But ultimately the parody is not as important as the implications of the opposition between discourse and recourse. Descartes merely becomes the emblem of rational thought and of the rationality of history. The Head of State is the embodiment of this opposition.

Carpentier's dictator is a *déspota ilustrado*, as opposed to

54. "Discourse on the Method," in *Rules for the Direction of the Mind* . . . , trans. Elizabeth S. Haldane and G. R. T. Ross, Great Books of the Western World, vol. 31 (Chicago, 1952), p. 51.

Asturias's, who appears as the personification of latent telluric forces in the tradition of Sarmiento's portrayal of Rosas or Carpentier's own Henri Christophe. Whereas these are the result of mysterious natural or supernatural transmutations, the Head of State personifies the future of the eighteenth-century Enlightenment—the product of the bourgeois revolution. The Head of State is the second coming of Víctor Hugues, armed again with the philosophical traditions of France, an old Víctor Hugues, adrift in the babblings of countless readings and the erotomania of old age. Carpentier has combined in him the traits of Estrada Cabrera, Gerardo Machado, Rafael Leónidas Trujillo, and other dictators in the worst Latin American tradition who, drunk with power and their own liberal rhetoric, became entrapped in the ludicrous image of their own making. The Head of State is surrounded not only by coarse, obsequious goons, but by academicians, writers, artists; he can quote Renan from memory and order the best wines. He is a tragicomic figure, attempting to emulate ghosts from the past or the European present, but always falling short or going too far. In his portrayal Carpentier has abandoned the traditional format that he had used in *Explosion in a Cathedral* to revive the theatrical tradition of the *figurón*. The Head of State is constantly equated with a mummy, a mannequin, a puppet. The text manifests this dehumanizing multiplicity and hollowness, for the point of view oscillates between that of the Head of State and a third-person "free indirect" style that establishes an ironic counterpoint between the protagonist's babbling contradictions, imperious commands, and oratorical rhetoric. But it is through the association between the Head of State and the mummy that Carpentier's conception of history in *Reasons of State* emerges.

While campaigning against the rebel general Ataulfo Galván, the Head of State and his men take refuge from the rain in a cave. There they find, in a scene reminiscent of "Los fugitivos," the funerary relics of an ancient culture: thirteen mummies in earthenware jugs. The relics, which frighten his men, turn out to be just what the Head of State needed to deflect attention away from his latest atrocities. He orders that a description of the site be fabricated and the mummy in the center of the group repaired and sent to the Musée de l'Homme. Throughout the rest of the novel, the relic is turned into a mimicking monster evoking the past, a past falsified and used to guarantee the Head of State's position in power. It is dubbed by him and his men, as a publicity stunt, "America's Grandfather," and sent on a tour of Europe which clearly parallels those of the dictator. The mummy becomes an emblem of the past, of origins, but also a memory of the future: "It was like some gigantic fleshless foetus, that had gone through all the stages of growth, maturity, decrepitude and death—and returned to its foetal state in the course of time [por recurrencia de transcurso]—sitting there, beyond and yet closer to its own death . . . " (p. 57). The Head of State is himself the grand-father of a fetus, his daughter's aborted child—"that thing"—con-ceived while she was on one of her gallivanting sprees. On his hammock, at the moment of death, he also, like the mummy, takes on a fetal appearance. Whereas in Carpentier's fiction until Ex-plosion in a Cathedral the avatars of family history embraced only the relationship of fathers and sons, now the novelistic universe has been expanded to include the grandfather, who becomes the symbol of a distant and decrepit source, as well as of the future, invoking and inverting the medieval (and baroque) topic of the puer senex.[55] Like the spiral in Explosion in a Cathedral or the missing Christmas Day, the distance of the grandfather, one step removed, stresses the tenuous presence of the source (the father is not mentioned); he is death and birth, the two loci of nothing-ness, the two poles between which Marcial's life was suspended in "Journey Back to the Source." The mummy and the Head of State are Carnival masks, the two central figures in the recourse of method. The chronological sequence of the novel, as in Explo-sion in a Cathedral, projects this transience by its futuristic orien-tation, its temporal décalage.

Carpentier has said that "The novel [Reasons of State] begins very precisely in the year 1913, but its action expands concretely

55. Ernst Robert Curtius, European Literature and the Latin Middle Ages, trans. Willard Trask (New York, 1953), p. 101.

by a synchronization of events and epochs until the year 1927, with allusions to various historical events. But later there is a period that takes my central character toward the thirties, forties, with a small epilogue of two pages [one in the printed version] that is titled '1972.' "[56] This chronology can be easily corroborated by tracing some of the historical events that are mentioned in the novel, such as the Battle of the Marne, the entry of the United States into World War I. The year 1927 at the end is easily corroborated because The Student, who is patterned after Rubén Martínez Villena and Julio Antonio Mella, is going to the Anti-Imperialist Conference in Brussels, which took place in that year.[57] But the synchronization of dates and events does not follow the rigorous and symmetrical historicism of *The Kingdom of This World*; it is more like the forward-leaping spiral structure of *Explosion in a Cathedral*. The most obvious feature of the temporal and textual structure of the novel is the multiples of seven. The novel contains seven chapters and twenty-one subchapters, plus the epilogue. The recurring events occur in subchapters that are multiples of seven: the announcement of Hoffmann's attempted *coup d'état*, which occurs in chapter 1, is repeated by that of Ataulfo Galván in subchapter 7; the popular revolt following the bankruptcy of the government occurs in subchapter 14 (to which we will have to return); and the death of the Head of State occurs in subchapter 21, which is, moreover, a Sunday. The rhythm of this textual structure is not paralleled by the chronology. Up to subchapter 13 the various dates and events represented do follow a chronohistorical sequence, which takes us from the fall of 1913 to about 1918, a period of six years that constitutes one-half of the time span discernible in the novel (1913–1927). In subchapter 13 we have the by now familiar Carnival scene, except that here it does not correspond to the liturgical period of the Carnival. It is instead the disturbance caused during a performance of *Aida*, which sends Enrico Caruso in costume into the streets,

56. Roa, "El recurso a Descartes," p. 48.
57. See Hugh Thomas, *Cuba*, p. 588. The third model for the student, particularly in the Paris scenes, may be Carpentier himself.

where he is arrested "for wearing fancy dress when it was not Carnival time" (p. 182). Subchapter 13 does end, however, with the Carnival, but it turns into revolution when the opposition takes advantage of the masquerade to attack the police. A displaced Carnival that begins as opera becomes political revolution.

A curious historical displacement has also begun to take place at the juncture between subchapters 13 and 14. Beginning with subchapter 14, the allusions are to events that took place during Gerardo Machado's dictatorship in Cuba; that is to say, there has been a chronological leap of seven years, from 1918 to 1925. Subchapter 14, which is the first division in chapter 5, would be the virtual center of the text (if the chapters were to round out to an even number) and contains an analogous displacement, but on a liturgical level: the turning of Christmas into the Epiphany, leaping, as it were, over the thirteen days of Advent. The thematic motive for this event is the turning of the Catholic Christmas in the Hispanic tradition into the Protestant Christmas of the Anglo-Saxon tradition, brought into the country by U.S. influence. The gifts of toys given on January 6 are now given by Santa Claus on December 25, thirteen days too early. The leap forward continues, for the Epiphany soon turns into Holy Week, and the first half of the liturgical year ends with the strikes that begin to erode the power of the Head of State and the first appearance of his nemesis, The Student. The dates of the liturgical year skip along to that resurrection when The Student appears to unseat the aging grandfather. The chronological and textual centers of the novel do not coincide, as in *Explosion in a Cathedral*, but constitute in their displacement a vortex of the historical whirlwind that skips years in a spiral movement to the future. The operatic Carnival was in the fall, that which turns into revolution in spring. All of the rituals conceived by the Head of State coincide, like the beginning of the novel, with the fall, and allude to the Day of the Dead. The leap is then from the Day of the Dead to the Resurrection.

The emblem of that displaced, movable center of the text is, as we have seen, the mummy-fetus image of the dictator; but he is only one of several degraded emblems of the center. The correla-

tive emblem of the Grandfather of America is that enormous allegorical statue of the Motherland that the dictator plants inside
the capitol, which is (as in Cuba, for instance) kilometer 0 of all
highways in the land.[58] It is not by chance that work on the
capitol, when the statue is finally housed in the enormous (but not
large enough) dome, comes to an end in subchapter 11—that is to
say, the mathematical center of the text, if divided symmetrically.
It is also at this point, because work on the capitol has been
slowed and will not be finished as planned on the date of Independence, that the central plaza of the city is decorated with
painted palm trees and other props. The view of the city is here,
again, that of a stage set, one of such monumental proportions
that it can only evoke the opera. As in the emblem of the mummy-
fetus, this set acquires here the characteristic of ruins, or unfinished buildings: "And then it happened that in periods of in-
activity the central zone of the capital was transformed into a sort
of Roman forum, an esplanade from Baalbek, a terrace from
Persepolis, while the moon shone down on this strange chaotic
landscape of marbles, half-finished metopes, truncated pillars,
blocks of stone between cement and sand—the ruins, the dead
remains, of what had never been" (pp. 142–43). The dismantled
and stony Mother, who arrives from Europe in various pieces (the
greatest attraction being her one uncovered breast) is housed
within a dome that, like the exploding cathedral of the previous
novel, is a premature ruin. Both her body and her setting are
enormous, hollow props on a stage where the Head of State will
deliver his translation of the *Prayer on the Acropolis*. Discourse
and its setting have become operatic.

The insistence on opera in *Reasons of State* suggests that the
operatic stage is an emblem of the text itself. This appeal to opera
derives clearly from the eighteenth-century problematics that Carpentier deals with in this last phase of his fiction. Opera was
popular in the eighteenth century against the better wishes of the
philosophers of reason and aestheticians, just as Calderonian *autos*
continued to be popular in Spain to the horror of the *afrancesados,*

58. All of these events are taken from Cuban history.

who finally managed to forbid them. The indiscriminate mixture of various arts, the dissolution of genres and styles, is what characterizes opera.[59] But this operatic quality evidenced in *Reasons of State* is not fully developed until *Concierto barroco*, where its apotheosis takes place. If in the first chapter of *Reasons of State* we have the dictator's conversation in counterpoint with the "Für Elise" discordantly played by Ofelia, *Concierto barroco* will be the elevation of disharmony as the very constitution of the text.

The title of *Concierto barroco* is a *contradictio in adjecto*, for the idea of harmony implied by "concert" is undermined by that of disorder and heterogeneity suggested by "baroque." The central scene in the novel, when Handel, Scarlatti, Vivaldi, the girls of the Ospedale della Pietà, and the Mexican traveler and his black Cuban servant join together in a cacophonous "fantastic symphony," is the baroque concert—the indiscriminate fusion of European, American, classical, and popular elements, as well as of instruments of the most varied origins, to produce a new music, a new conglomerate in which there need be no synthesis. The heterogeneous, the amalgam, is also an abandonment of the notion of origins, to which none of the sundry elements need remain faithful; instead it is in itself an origin, a new beginning—it is already the future contained in the beginning. The high point of this bacchanal occurs when Filomeno's Afro-Cuban chant, which goes "Ca-la-ba-són,/Són-són," is sung by others as "Kábala-sum-sum-sum" (p. 45).[60] Occult traditions also mingle in this whirl-windlike center that in its joyous disregard for origins appears as a Nietzschean call to revel in the absence of any grounding genealogies. The somber presence of death in the Carnival scenes in *The Kingdom of This World* have turned into the joy of constant dissolution in the baroque concert.

This concept of the baroque concert is the main theme of the novel. Instead of describing a voyage to America, with its implications of bringing European civilization to the New Continent, *Concierto barroco* describes a return, a *ricorso*. The wealthy Mex-

59. See Hazard, *The European Mind*, p. 380.
60. *Concierto barroco* (Madrid, 1974).

ican and his black Cuban servant go to Europe and there con-
taminate European culture with their own, setting off a series of
events that will lead to a new "Western" culture, of multiple
origins, cut off from any single source that will give it shape. The
text of the novel partakes of this intermingling: when the wealthy
Mexican finds Filomeno in Regla, the black slave tells him his
own version of Silvestre de Balboa's *Espejo de paciencia*, the first
work of Cuban literature, in which a black slave defeats the
French pirate Girón. The description of the action, heavily influenced in the original by Ariosto's *Orlando Furioso*, suffers
further distortions in the version, with commentary, offered by
Filomeno to his master. The most telling scene is when the
wealthy Mexican questions one of Balboa's descriptions, where
the musical *fête* for the victors is portrayed as having been played
by "a hundred rebecks," among other imported and several native
instruments: "for in that universal concert were mingled musicians
from Castile and the Canary Islands, creoles and mestizos, Indians
and blacks. 'Blacks and darks confused in such a frolic?' the traveler
asked himself. 'Impossible harmony! What an unthinkable absurdity, quite badly could the old and noble Romance melodies,
the subtle changes and contrasts of good masters, marry the barbarous din that blacks make when they get hold of rattles and
drums! . . . Quite an infernal charivari would result, and that
Balboa seems to me to have been a great prevaricator!' " (p. 25).
On the night of the Venetian Carnival, however, he will participate
in the very same sort of "impossible harmony."

This same process of mixture is seen at the level of the text,
for if Filomeno relates to his master *El espejo de paciencia*, later
on his master will tell him of the adventures of Don Quijote,
and later, by recounting to Vivaldi the story of Montezuma, will
encourage the Italian to write an opera on the subject. The text is
a composite of stories told again, not in their original version; the
original is forgotten, deformed, by means of the new amalgam.
The difference between this procedure and Carpentier's earlier
fiction could not be more telling; in the earlier fiction Carpentier
attempted to galvanize the mixture of cultural—textual—elements

in one new, homogeneous, cultural entity. In *Concierto barroco* there is an abandonment to the heterogeneity of warring contraries. The emblem of this new nonsynthesis is Vivaldi's *Montezuma*, in which the history of the conquest of Mexico is turned into opera. But Montezuma's story, turned into sentimental melodrama, is not the only one retold. Stories of Hamlet, the Moor of Venice, and other figures are also recounted. The gist of the retelling, of course, is that in their new versions all the stories partake of the absurdity of opera. When Filomeno argues with Handel and Vivaldi about the possibilities of *Espejo de paciencia* for an opera, he reminds them that the homogeneity and reasonableness of European art is a sham, that it is just as devoid of common sense and concert as American culture.

As in *Explosion in a Cathedral* and *Reasons of State*, the temporal disposition of *Concierto barroco* is future-oriented. The action begins in 1709 and continues in that year until the travelers reach Venice. The meeting of the Mexican and his Cuban servant with Vivaldi and Handel takes place on December 26, 1709, the night when the German's *Agrippina* premiered in that city.[61] The action has reached its center, for this meeting takes place in the fourth of the book's eight chapters. From then on, the correspondence with history is lost, and it is suggested that what follows takes place during the forty days of Carnival in Venice—from Christmas to the beginning of Lent. This encompasses the scene of the "impossible harmony" at the Ospedale della Pietà, and the *Don Giovanni*–like scene at the cemetery, where Vivaldi, Handel, Scarlatti, and the two Latin Americans discuss opera and art in general. Violent historical displacements occur in this scene, in which Handel refers to Igor Stravinsky (1882–1971), who is buried in the Venice cemetery where they are picnicking. The next verifiable date appears in chapter 7, when the Mexican awakens, after the debaucheries of the night of December 26, 1709, in the fall of 1733—that is to say, twenty-four years after

61. *Grove's Dictionary of Music and Musicians* (New York, 1959), IV, 39. The central scene, in other words, occurs on the night of what would be Carpentier's birthday.

his Saturnalia on the preceding "days" (a Saturnalia that occurred in chapter 6, on Saturday). The next recognizable date is nine years later, when mention is made of Handel's *Messiah*. This occurs in chapter 8, at the end of the story, when Filomeno decides to go to Paris to attend a Louis Armstrong concert, which, if the same procedure is followed here as in *Reasons of State*, must have taken place in 1924 (42/24). This last chapter is headed by a biblical epigraph ("And the trumpet shall sound") that links Handel's *Messiah* with Armstrong's jazz, and evokes the apocalypse. Jazz is, at the end, the new beginning, that beginning already contained in the jam session of the Ospedale della Pietà: it is the "impossible harmony," the baroque concert. Apocalypse and beginning are marked by that number 8 of the chapter and the hour at which Filomeno abandons his master, becomes liberated after announcing a coming revolution:

"Take care of what's yours," said Filomeno, "and I'll take care of my trumpet."

"You'll be in good company: the trumpet is active and daring, the instrument of ill humor and great events."

"That's why it sounds so often in Major Judgments, at the time of settling scores with fuckers and sons of bitches," said the black.

"For those to disappear you'll have to wait for the End of Time," said the American.

"It's strange, but I always hear about the End of Time. Why not better talk about the Beginning of Time?"

"That'll be the Day of Resurrection," replied the American.

"I can't wait that long," said the black. The long arm of the station clock jumped the second separating it from 8 P.M. The train began to glide imperceptibly toward the night.

"Good bye!"

"Until when? Til tomorrow?"

"Or until yesterday..." said the black, though the word "yesterday" was lost in the long whistle of the locomotive... [P. 80]

The importance of the 8, which in *The Kingdom of This World* designated a new beginning, is that it alludes to the very construction of the novel: "The octogonary, related to two squares or the octagon, is the intermediate form between the square (or the terrestrial order) and the circle (the eternal order) and is, in consequence, a symbol of regeneration. By virtue of its shape, the numeral is associated with the two interlacing serpents of the caduceus, signifying the balancing out of opposing forces or the equivalence of the spiritual power to the natural. It also symbolizes —again because of its shape—the eternally spiraling movement of the heavens (shown also by the double sigmoid line—the sign of the infinite)."[62] As in *Explosion in a Cathedral* and *Reasons of State*, the text is the moment where past and future are one, in permanent revolution; it is the locus of infinite contaminations. Carnival and Apocalypse were the two poles of the pendular movement in *The Kingdom of this World*. In *Concierto barroco* Carnival and Apocalypse are one.

The amalgamation to which *Concierto barroco* points in music is, as we have seen, woven through the text itself by the constant retelling of previous plots, and by the allusion to others (for example, the dinner at the cemetery is a clear reference to the Don Juan myth). It is also present, however, in the two main characters and in their relationship. The wealthy Mexican is an *indiano*, a common figure in Spanish and Latin American literature. But Carpentier has linked him with the picaresque tradition, and more specifically with Quevedo's *Buscón* (there is a direct allusion to the *dómine* in Quevedo's novel, p. 64). The significance of that novel is that at the end the *pícaro* Pablos promises a second part—never written—in which he will travel to America and continue his adventures in the New World. Carpentier's *indiano* is a Don Pablos who has grown old and rich in Mexico and is returning home. He has now become a master, and Filomeno, his servant, the new *pícaro*. But his relationship with Filomeno has undergone a transformation that places the novel within the tradition of the eighteenth-century picaresque, rather than that of the sixteenth and seventeenth centuries. The servant has become the equal of his master and in the end becomes liberated from him. This had already occurred in Quevedo's *Buscón*, for toward the end of that novel Don Pablos has left his upper-class friend to seek a life of his own, but the servant's ascent is

62. Cirlot, *Dictionary of Symbols*, p. 223.

more prevalent in the eighteenth-century variations of the picaresque. Filomeno's freedom from his master is more reminiscent of Lesage's *Gil Blas*, or of Figaro's in Beaumarchais's *La folle journée* than of the Spanish *pícaros*. But this is not the only inversion; by making the original *pícaro* old and rich and picturing him on his way back home, Carpentier is overturning the picaresque tradition after which he has molded his text. And he is also inverting the figure of the *indiano*, for at the end the wealthy Mexican has recognized that he is no longer a Spaniard, that his origins are too remote, and he chooses to return to Mexico. Both master and servant stand at a point of new beginning at the end— a new beginning that is the last of a series of departures leading back to the many journeys of the picaresque protagonist. But this new beginning is a self-conscious one for both, a dissolution of bondage. Home now is self-consciousness and the invitation to the voyage.

As opposed to his earlier work, Carpentier's work of the sixties and seventies contains the possibility of return: Esteban begins a new cycle after returning to Havana, the Head of State returns several times, the politician of "Right of Sanctuary" accomplishes a return to his own country as ambassador from another, and the *indiano* returns to Spain. The narrator-protagonist of *The Lost Steps*, Ti Noël, and the hunted one, never achieve a true return. Ti Noël is blown away from the ruins of his master's house, to which he still felt the need to return, at the end of *The Kingdom of This World*; the hunted one dies on that magic Sunday that he seeks; the narrator-protagonist of *The Lost Steps* finishes his story when he is about to cross the threshold into the memories of the future. The characters of Carpentier's new fiction manage to return and begin anew. The new beginning results only in the consciousness that they must always begin anew, that the steps to the past are lost and those to the future are already here, ready to begin an ever repeated voyage in time whose anticipation is the text itself and their memory of the future voyage. For if the past is lost, the present is never here, except as future, Carnival and

Apocalypse are one, the text is a revolution. Writing will always be that *ailleurs*, that future remembered, where signs will cease to shuffle their meanings and will empty themselves out.

In his latest phase Carpentier traces a return, a recapitulatory journey through his fiction, to erase and reconstitute its point of origin. The new version that emerges is one where the crack at the core of ¡*Ecue-Yamba-O!* is covered through recourse to that part of the novel—the urban, mixed underworld of cultural clashes and indiscriminate assimilation—where hybridness reigns and where the text emerges as the self-conscious outcome of manifold traditions. In a way, Carpentier has opted for that "superficial" view of culture that Marinello suggested as a solution to the problem of presenting Latin American reality, except that it is a superficiality joyously assumed as the condition of writing. The Spengler-Hegel counterpoint of the 1941 essays on the decline of Europe is resolved, as it were, in favor of Hegel. The textual synthesis of Carpentier's late fiction, however, is not Hegelian but post-Hegelian. It is the chaos after the end of history which is simultaneously a self-conscious beginning of history.[63] The search for reintegration is dissolved in a textual amalgam that is at once emanation and source, separation and union, concert and disharmony—concert in disharmony. Carpentier's new style issues from that productive negativity of nonstyle, from that void in which the memory of the source is lost, in which the archtext is exploded.

Fiction is now the Carnival assumed as the permanent revolution, a history whose end and beginning are constantly com-

63. In "Hegel y America," an essay whose importance we mentioned in Chapter 2, Ortega wrote the following: "Here we touch upon a concrete instance of the enormous limitation of Hegel's thought: his blindness to the future. The future unsettled him because it is that which is totally irrational, and consequently that which the philosopher desires most when confronting his frenetic appetite for truth against the imperialistic thrust of his system. Hegel is hermetic to the future. He becomes agitated when it begins to dawn on him, losing his serenity and dogmatically closing all windows to prevent objections from flying in together with new luminous possibilities" (*Obras completas* [Madrid, 1963], II, 573).

memorated and celebrated. Fiction celebrates the consecration of spring.

When José Arcadio Buendía returns to Macondo after his adventures with the gypsies, he reports having seen Víctor Hugues's ship: "In the Caribbean he had seen the ghost of the pirate ship of Víctor Hugues, with its sails torn by the winds of death, the masts chewed by sea worms, and still looking for the course to Guadeloupe."[64] This is not the only link, however, between García Márquez's *One Hundred Years of Solitude* and Carpentier's *Explosion in a Cathedral.* The temporal limit of García Márquez's novel, one hundred years, seems to derive from Carpentier's title: *El siglo de las luces. Explosion in a Cathedral* is not the only novel of Carpentier's that has left a trace in *One Hundred Years of Solitude* either: the hurricane that wipes out Macondo at the end appears to have its textual source in the "green wind" that razes the ruins of M. Lenormand de Mézy's estate at the end of *The Kingdom of This World.* Lunero, the mulatto who raises Artemio—and who is also his uncle—in Carlos Fuentes's *The Death of Artemio Cruz,* came to Yucatan with one of the wealthy families that fled Cuba during the wars of independence. Both Lunero and his masters are direct descendants of the slaves and sugar barons that people Carpentier's fiction. Lunero's very name, evoking the cycles of the moon, is very Carpenterian, and Artemio's recollection of his life in twelve historical moments is an obvious attempt to synchronize personal memory with cosmic and historical cycles in a search for a synthesis of history and fiction.

One Hundred Years of Solitude and The Death of Artemio Cruz are perhaps the two most notorious exponents of what came to be known in the sixties as the "total novel." Carpentier's legacy is this relentless attempt to synthesize history and the self in a form of Latin American writing. While in this sense Carpentier's work has merely repeated a gesture found in all Romantic and post-Romantic literature, he has given that enterprise a particular Latin

64. Gabriel García Márquez, *One Hundred Years of Solitude,* trans. Gregory Rabassa (New York, 1971), p. 95.

American character—not, however, by demonstrating the autonomy of Latin American culture, as he once hoped, or by tracing the precise boundaries of a Latin American context. He has demonstrated, instead, the dialectics of dependence and independence that subtend any effort at cultural definition, and made manifest the pervasive heterogeneity of writing. The total novel is a Hegelian experiment whose failure is the very condition of its existence. By having repeatedly taken it to the limit where its unattainability becomes apparent, Carpentier has made possible the total novel and its ironic counterpart, the antinovel. Both possibilities are already present in *The Lost Steps*, in that "I" that attempts to be one and is at the same time many.

Carpentier once defined his role as "translator," and such it has been, even if not in the way he had hoped. His work, by its encyclopedic and totalizing nature, is akin to the *summae* and cathedrals that appear in thirteenth-century Europe. It is an iconographic storehouse, a monument—the foundation of Latin America's house of fiction.

Bibliography

Carpentier, like all Latin American authors, presents bibliographical problems that are difficult to solve with conventional methods. The most vexing of these problems centers on the meaning of the word "edition." In Spanish a reprint is often called an edition. For example, the second edition of *El siglo de las luces* (Mexico City: Cía. General de Ediciones, 1965) is merely a reprint of the first (1962), yet it is called "segunda edición." Moreover, when Seix Barral in Barcelona issued the same book in 1964, they called it "primera edición," and continued to reprint it as "segunda edición" (1966), "tercera edición" (1966), and so forth.

Guerra del tiempo offers problems all its own. When it first appeared in Mexico City (Cía. General de Ediciones, 1958), it contained three short stories and "Manhunt." The book was reprinted as such by the same publisher in 1966 and called "segunda edición." But when Editorial Sandino in Montevideo issued the book (n.d., 1974?), it did not give an edition number and, furthermore, omitted the novella and included instead two short stories that had not appeared in the 1958 edition: "Los fugitivos" and "Los advertidos." The first of these had first appeared in *El Nacional* in 1946, and Carpentier had chosen not to put it in *Guerra del tiempo.* "Los advertidos" had been included in the 1970 edition of the book brought out by Seix Barral, which also left out "Manhunt." The 1967 French translation of *Guerra del tiempo* contained "Los advertidos" and *El derecho de asilo,* which appeared by itself in Spanish in that year. This translation did not include "Manhunt," and neither does the English. The Seix Barral edition of *El reino de este mundo* (Barcelona, 1969) omits the famous prologue to this novel. The verso of the title page gives 1967 as its copyright date and explains that the "edición original" is the one from Havana (1964). The book was first published in 1949.

This bewildering number of editions and reprints is the result of geographic, economic, and political factors. Whereas a book published in England is easily obtained in the United States and vice versa, it is unlikely that one published, say, in Lima, will be distributed in Madrid, Buenos Aires, or Mexico. When I visited Carpentier in Paris in 1973, I showed him, to his delight, a copy of the 1972 Fondo de Cultura Económica edition of La música en Cuba. He had never seen the book, which by that time was sold out. Even the most established publishing houses in the Hispanic world (such as Fondo de Cultura, Siglo Veintiuno, Sudamericana, the Instituto del Libro in Cuba) cannot overcome the fragmentation of that world. In order to be read, authors resort to multiple editions and reprints in various countries. A detailed history of the printings of a novel such as El reino de este mundo would fill several pages. Suffice it to say that a chapter of that novel was deemed sufficiently unknown in 1959, ten years after the publication of the book, to have been printed in a magazine such as Life en Español (March 9).

One of the consequences of such haphazard publication and distribution is the appearance of unauthorized editions. During the sixties, when the popularity of the Latin American novel reached unprecedented heights, everyone waited for a new Carpentier novel to appear. To take advantage of the situation, Xanandú in Buenos Aires came out with an edition (1968) of ¡Ecue-Yamba-O!, Carpentier's long-forgotten first novel. Four years later, Sandino in Montevideo published Los convidados de plata, which consisted of three chapters of a new novel that Carpentier had published in various journals. Carpentier has told me that the Xanandú edition of ¡Ecue-Yamba-O! is unauthorized, and the opportunism of Los convidados de plata is obvious. But while these are the only cases in which I can be sure that the books in question are unauthorized editions, there may be others. Although all Latin American authors are prey to this sort of practice, the fact that revolutionary Cuba has generally not complied with the

Universal Copyright Convention has made Carpentier more vulnerable to it.

The irony of unauthorized editions is that they have to be used, even in a book such as this. Although I have had access to a copy of the first edition of ¡Ecue-Yamba-O! (at the Rare Book Collection of Cornell's Olin Library), it is the Xanandú edition that is most available, though already out of print. The same applies to *Los convidados de plata*. I have only been able to find one of the installments published, and I suspect that, if the others have been read at all, it has been in the Sandino book. The original of "Los advertidos" I have read in the Sandino edition of *Guerra del tiempo*, and I have used throughout the Arca edition of *Tientos y diferencias*. It would be misleading to call any of these books a reprint or to assign them an edition number. To give the reader a clear picture of the development of Carpentier's works I list his books in the order in which they first appeared and then give the edition and translation used in each case. I do the same with the stories, poems, and scenarios.

The listing of Carpentier's other publications in journals and newspapers is by no means complete, nor does it give all the works read in the preparation of this book. The same applies to my bibliography of Carpentier criticism. Though in both cases I believe that I have read nearly everything available, I have chosen to be selective rather than exhaustive.

Abbreviations

C	Carteles (Havana)
CA	Cuadernos Americanos (Mexico City)
CH	Cuadernos Hispanoamericanos (Madrid)
CLA	Casa de las Américas (Havana)
D	Diacritics (Cornell University)
EN	El Nacional (Caracas)
MLN	Modern Language Notes (Baltimore)
PLEN	Papel Literario de El Nacional (Caracas)
RI	Revista Iberoamericana (Pittsburgh)
RO	Revista de Occidente (Madrid)
S	Social (Havana)
UNEAC	Unión Nacional de Escritores y Artistas de Cuba
YFS	Yale French Studies

Select Bibliography of Carpentier's Works
Books

¡Ecue-Yamba-O! *Historia Afro-Cubana.* Madrid: Editorial España, 1933. On the cover the title reads: ¡Ecue Yamba-O!. *Novela afrocubana.* Edition used: Buenos Aires: Xanandú, 1968. On the cover the title reads: Ecue-Yamba O. *Novela Afrocubana* and on the title page: Ecue-Yamba-O. *Novela Afro-Cubana.*

Viaje a la semilla. Havana: Ucar, García y Cía., 1944. Edition used: see *Guerra del tiempo* below. Translation: "Journey Back to the Source," in *War of Time,* see below.

La música en Cuba. Mexico City: Fondo de Cultura Económica. Colección Tierra Firme, No. 19, 1946.

El reino de este mundo. Relato. Mexico City: Edición y Distribución Iberoamericana de Publicaciones, 1949. Edition used: 2d ed. of Cía General de Ediciones (3d of book), Mexico City, 1969. Translation: *The Kingdom of This World.* Trans. Harriet de Onís. New York: Knopf, 1957.

Los pasos perdidos. Novela. Mexico City: Edición y Distribución Iberoamericana de Publicaciones, 1953. Edition used: 2d ed. of the Cía General de Ediciones (3d of book), Mexico City, 1966. Translation: *The Lost Steps,* 2d. ed. Trans. Harriet de Onís. New York: Knopf, 1971.

El acoso. Novela. Buenos Aires: Editorial Losada, 1956. Edition used: see *Guerra del tiempo* below. Translation: "Manhunt." Trans. Harriet de Onís. Noonday, 2 (1959), 109–80.

Guerra del tiempo. Tres relatos y una novela. Mexico City: Cía. General de Ediciones, 1958. Edition used: 2d ed. of Cía. General de Ediciones, 1966, which is a reprint of the first. Volume contains: "El camino de Santiago," "Viaje a la semilla," "Semejante a la noche," and "El acoso." Translation: *War of Time.* Trans. Frances Partridge. New York: Knopf, 1970. Volume contains: "The Highroad of Saint James," "Right of Sanctuary," "Journey Back to the Source," "Like the Night," and "The Chosen."

El siglo de las luces. Novela. Mexico City: Cía. General de Ediciones, 1962. Edition used: 2d ed. of Cía. General de Ediciones, 1965. Translation: *Explosion in a Cathedral.* Trans. John Sturrock. Boston: Little, Brown, 1962.

Tientos y diferencias. Ensayos. Mexico City: Universidad Nacional Autónoma, 1964. Edition used: Montevideo: Arca, 1967.

La ciudad de las columnas. Fotos Paolo Gasparini. Barcelona: Editorial Lumen, 1970. The text of this book appeared as an essay in *Tientos y diferencias.*

El derecho de asilo. Barcelona: Editorial Lumen, 1972. Translation: "Right of Sanctuary," in *War of Time,* see above.

Los convidados de plata. Montevideo: Sandino, 1972. Contains three chapters of an unpublished novel that appeared in various journals during the sixties.

Concierto barroco. Mexico City: Siglo Veintiuno Editores, 1974.

El recurso del método (novela). Mexico City: Siglo Veintiuno Editores, 1974. Translation: *Reasons of State.* Trans. Frances Partridge. New York: Knopf, 1976.

Letra y Solfa. Selección, prólogo y notas de Alexis Márquez Rodríguez. Caracas: Síntesis Dosmil, 1975. Contains a selection of articles from Carpentier's column in *El Nacional,* "En memoria de Leon Paul Fargue," "Los problemas del compositor latinoamericano," and "Visión de América" (four published fragments of the *Libro de la Gran Sabana*).

Poems

Poèmes des Antilles: Neuf chants sur des textes de Alejo Carpentier, musique de Marius-François Gaillard. (N.p.n.d. Thirty-eight pages of sheet music, obviously printed in Paris, probably in 1929, though copyrighted in 1931. It contains: "Ekoriofo," "Village," "Mystère," "Midi," "Les Merveilles de la science," "L'Art d'aimer," "Fête," "Llanto," and "United Press, Octobre.")

Dos poemas afro-cubanos (Deux poèmes afro-cubains). Música de Alejandro García Caturla. Textos de Alejo Carpentier. Paris: Editions Maurice Senart, 1930. (Eight pages of sheet music, containing "Mari-Sabel" and "Juego Santo.")

"Liturgia." *Revista de Avance* (Havana), no. 50 (1930), p. 260. Reprinted in Emilio Ballagas's *Antología de poesía negra hispano americana.* Madrid: Aguilar, 1935, pp. 65–67.

"Canción." *Antología de poesía negra hispano americana,* pp. 77–78.

Scenarios and Ballets

"Un ballet afrocubano" ["El milagro de Anaquillé"], *Revista Cubana* (Havana), nos. 22–24 (1937), pp. 145–54.

"Manita en el suelo" (Opera bufa en un acto y cinco escenas. Música de Alejandro García Caturla. Libreto de Alejo Carpentier). Small fragment of libretto published in *Boletín* (Dirección Central de Editoriales, Instituto Cubano del Libro), December 15, 1974, p. 6.

Short Stories

"El sacrificio." *Chic* (Havana), May 1923. All information available in Adolfo Cruz-Luis, "Latinoamérica en Carpentier: génesis de lo real maravilloso," *CLA*, no. 87 (1974), p. 48. This "fantastic tale" was the first story ever published by Carpentier, according to Cruz-Luis.

"El milagro" (leyenda). *El Universal* (Havana), 1925. Reprinted without further bibliographical details in *Boletín*, December 15, 1974, p. 6. The retelling of a saint's life.

"Histoire de lunes." *Cahiers du Sud* (Paris), no. 157 (December 1933), pp. 747–59.

"Oficio de tinieblas." *Orígenes* (Havana), 1, no. 4 (1944), 32–38.

"Los fugitivos." *EN*, August 4, 1946, p. 9. Edition used: "Los fugitivos," in *Narrativa cubana de la revolución*, ed. José M. Caballero Bonald, pp. 25–37. Madrid: Alianza, 1968.

"Semejante a la noche." *Orígenes*, 9, no. 31 (1952), 3–11. ("Like the Night.")

"Guerra del tiempo." *PLEN*, July 22, 1954, p. 1. (Fragment of "The Highroad of Saint James.")

"Los advertidos." Probably published in a journal in the late sixties. Included in the 1970 Seix Barral edition (Barcelona) of *Guerra del tiempo*. Edition used here: *Guerra del tiempo*. Montevideo: Sandino, n.d. [1974?], pp. 145–67. ("The Chosen.")

Chapters of Novels

"Lo real maravilloso de América" (prólogo del libro inédito *El reino de este mundo* de Alejo Carpentier). *EN*, April 8, 1948, p. 8.

"Los pasos perdidos—fragmentos." *Cruz del Sur* (Caracas), 1, no. 5 (1952), 38–45.

"Los pasos perdidos." *EN*, March 26, 1953, p. 7. (Chapters 19 and 20.)

"El acoso (fragmentos de novela)." *Orígenes*, 11, no. 36 (1954), 6–16. (Fragments of "Manhunt.")

"El año 59." *CLA*, no. 26 (1964), pp. 45–50. On page 169 of this issue the editors state: " 'El año 59' is the first chapter of a novel with the same title that has already been finished by Alejo Carpentier, and is part of a trilogy that the novelist is writing about the Cuban Revolution." This fragment was reprinted in *Los convidados de plata* as chapter II, pp. 25–40.

"El siglo de las luces." *Nueva Revista Cubana* (Havana), 1, no. 2 (1959), 73–82. (Subchapters 1 and 2.)

"El siglo de las luces." *Nueva Revista Cubana*, 1, no. 3 (1959), 82–98. (Subchapters 3 and 4.)

"La conjura de Parsifal." *Revista de la Biblioteca Nacional José Martí*, 3d series, 17, no. 1 (1975), 25–30. In a note, the editors of this journal explain: "Toward 1943, Alejo Carpentier began to write a novel entitled *El clan disperso*, in which he planned to evoke the period of artistic creativity and political activism of the 'Grupo Minorista' [mid-twenties]. The (unfinished) original manuscript has about two hundred and forty pages, of which we offer today those comprising the first chapter. As will be seen, some of the elements that appear here were incorporated, almost vebatim, into various parts of *El siglo de las luces* and *El recurso del método*."

"La consagración de la primavera." *Crisis* (Buenos Aires), no. 30 October 1975), pp. 46–48. In an interview with Ernesto González Bermejo, Carpentier says that *La consagración de la primavera* [*The Consecration of Spring*] "will be a very long novel, of which I have written more than half already. The novel begins during the Spanish Civil War, in the midst of the International Brigades, where there were many Cubans, Mexicans and other combatants from other regions of our Continent. . . . The action continues, through the great events of the century, until it reaches the Cuban Revolution. *La consagración de la primavera* closes with a description of the battle at the Bay of Pigs, the first victory of a nation in our Continent over Yankee imperialism, and as such, one of the most important battles in the history of America" (ibid., p. 46).

"De *La consagración de la primavera*." *CLA*, no. 96 (1976), pp. 72–76. (The same fragment as in *Crisis*.)

Articles, Essays, and Notes

"La banalidad en el arte." *C*, December 1924, pp. 21, 25.

"Jean Cocteau y la estética del ambiente." *S*, July 1925, pp. 41, 49, 59, 81.

"El arte múltiple de Picasso." *S*, September 1925, p. 29.

"La estética de Debussy." *S*, May 1926, pp. 49, 52.

"Erik Satie, profeta y renovador." *S*, September 1927, pp. 28, 88.

"Stravinski, 'Las bodas' y Papa Montero." *S*, December 1927, pp. 53, 88.

"Montparnasse, república internacional de artistas." *C*, June 24, 1928, pp. 20–21.

"La música cubana en París." *C*, September 23, 1928, pp. 12, 57–58.

"En la extrema avanzada: algunas actitudes del 'Surrealismo.'" *S*, December 1928, pp. 38, 74, 76.

"El arte de los locos." *C*, July 28, 1929, pp. 12, 50–51.

"André Masson, su selva y sus peces." *S*, October 1929, pp. 35, 64.

"Lettre des Antilles," *Bifur* (Paris), no. 3 (1929), pp. 91–105.

"Las nuevas ofensivas del cubanismo." *C*, December 15, 1929, pp. 47–48.

"Temoignage." In *Un cadavre*, p. 4 (unnumbered). Paris: Imprimerie Spéciale du Cadavre, 1930.
"El escándalo de Maldoror." *C*, April 20, 1930, pp. 16, 73–74.
"El gran malestar de Europa en 1930." *C*, May 25, 1930, pp. 16, 69–70.
"Los valores universales de la música cubana." *Revista de La Habana*, 2, no. 2 (May 1930), 145–54.
"Adolescencia." *C*, May 17, 1931, pp. 18, 63.
"América ante la joven literatura europea." *C*, June 28, 1931, pp. 30, 51, 54.
"Leyes de Africa." *C*, December 27, 1931, pp. 46–47, 50.
"Los artistas nuevos y los 'estabilizados.'" *S*, February 1932, pp. 15–16, 80.
"El viaje al final de la noche." *C*, May 12, 1933, pp. 14, 62, 66.
"El radio y sus nuevas posibilidades." *C*, December 17, 1933, pp. 14, 96, 98.
"El momento musical latinoamericano (fragmento de un ensayo inédito)." *Revista Cubana* (Havana), nos. 13–14 (1936), pp. 5–22.
"Numancia." *C*, August 22, 1937, pp. 22, 25.
"España bajo las bombas." *C*, September 12, 1937, pp. 32, 52.
"La muerte de Miguel Hernández." *C*, August 6, 1939, p. 36.
"La Habana vista por un turista cubano." *C*, October 8, 1939, pp. 16–17; October 22, 1939, pp. 18–19; November 5, 1939, pp. 34–35; December 3, 1939, pp. 48–49; December 17, 1939, pp. 30–31.
"Hitler y el parsifalismo." *C*, October 29, 1939, pp. 30–31.
"El ocaso de Europa." *C*, November 16, 1941, pp. 74–75; November 23, 1941, pp. 36–37; November 30, 1941, pp. 44–45; December 7, 1941, pp. 44–45; December 14, 1941, pp. 36–37; December 21, 1941, pp. 36–38.
"L'evolution culturelle de l'Amérique Latine." *Haïti-Journal* (Port-au-Prince), December 23, 1943, pp. 1–2; December 28, 1943, pp. 1, 4.
"La música cubana en estos últimos 20 años," *Conservatorio* (Conservatorio Municipal de La Habana), 1, no. 2 (1944), six unnumbered pages.
"Giovanni Papini la emprende con América." *EN*, June 1, 1947, p. 11.
"La música en La Habana del siglo XVIII." *EN*, July 13, 1947, p. 9.
"Visión de América," general heading: "La Gran Sabana: Mundo del Génesis," *EN*, October 19, 1947, p. 10; "El Salto del Angel en el Reino de las Aguas," October 25, 1947, p. 13; "La Biblia y la ojiva en el ámbito del Roraima," November 9, 1947, p. 8; "El último buscador del Dorado," December 7, 1947, p. 11. Reprinted in *Carteles*, in the same order: January 25, 1948, pp. 34–36; February

22, 1948, pp. 28–30; March 28, 1948, pp. 14–16; May 9, 1948, pp. 14–17. A fifth article also appeared in *Carteles:* "Ciudad Bolívar, metrópoli del Orinoco," June 13, 1948, pp. 14–16. The first four articles have been reprinted in Alejo Carpentier, *Letra y Solfa* (Caracas, 1975), pp. 317–48. (First installment in *Carteles* identifies these as fragments of the *Libro de la Gran Sabana*.)

From "Letra y Solfa," Carpentier's column in *El Nacional* (1951–1959). If an article has been included in the 1975 Caracas volume, the page number is given in parentheses. "Fiebres de primavera," July 18, 1951, p. 12 (*LS*, 24); "¿Qué es un cuento?" September 23, 1951, p. 16; "Destino del escritor latino-americano," September 24, 1951, p. 12; "Este gran don Fernando," October 3, 1951, p. 12; "Un acontecimiento literario," October 26, 1951, p. 4; "Recuerdo de Salinas," December 12, 1951, p. 4; "La vorágine en Europa," December 21, 1951, p. 4; "El mundo del tiempo detenido," January 16, 1952, p. 4; "Poesía del Orinoco," January 26, 1952, p. 4; "Luz del Páramo irá a Venecia en junio," April 18, 1952, p. 12; "Julio Verne y el Orinoco," April 23, 1952, p. 16; "El gran libro de la selva," May 14, 1952, p. 16; "Los hombres llamados salvajes," May 24, 1952, p. 16; "De lo sombrío en literatura," May 29, 1952, p. 16; "Fin del exotismo americano," September 7, 1952, p. 16 (*LS*, 266); "La Biblia y el estilo," April 1, 1953, p. 26; "El por qué de cierta añoranza," September 26, 1953, p. 34; "Renuevo de la novela," October 14, 1953, p. 30; "El hombre y su pasado," October 21, 1953, p. 34; "Lectores de ayer y de hoy," October 24, 1953, p. 36; "Médico y poeta," October 27, 1953, p. 24; "Vitalidad de los clásicos," October 29, 1953, p. 36; "La técnica en América Latina," December 19, 1953, p. 56; "Lo necesario en literatura," December 20, 1953, p. 58; "La era de las peñas," January 15, 1954, p. 30; "El ocaso de la radio," January 16, 1954, p. 32; "De la conciencia en el novelista," January 17, 1954, p. 38; "Julio Verne, profeta a medias," January 20, 1954, p. 26; "Ernesto Hemingway," January 26, 1954, p. 24 (*LS*, 69); "Horizontes de ayer y de hoy," January 29, 1954, p. 32; "Perfiles del hombre americano," April 30, 1954, p. 44 (*LS*, 122); "Un divertido texto," May 27, 1954, p. 32; "Renuevo de una escuela," July 21, 1954, p. 30; "El mito paradisíaco," October 14, 1955, p. 16 (*LS*, 279); "Ortega y Gasset," October 20, 1955, p. 16; "Una página de Humboldt," July 31, 1956, p. 12; "La novela autobiográfica," October 18, 1956, p. 16; "El Kodachrome y la etnografía," October 30, 1956, p. 12.

With Antonio Estévez, Inocente Palacios, Pedro A. Ríos Reyna, and

Vicente Emilio Rojo. "Problemas de la música en América Latina." *Cruz del Sur* (Caracas), 1, no. 4 (1952), 50–59. (Round-table discussion.)

"Intervención de Alejo Carpentier." In *Memoria del Primer Congreso Nacional de Escritores y Artistas de Cuba*, pp. 49–54. Havana: Ediciones Unión, 1961. Reprinted in *Tientos y diferencias* as: "Literatura y conciencia política en América Latina."

"Diego Rivera." In *Orbita de la Revista de Avance*, ed. Martín Casanovas, pp. 147–52. Havana: UNEAC, Colección Orbita, 1965. (Appeared originally in 1927 in the *Revista de Avance*.)

"Autobiografía de urgencia." *Insula* (Madrid), no. 218 (1965), pp. 3, 13.

"La actualidad cultural en Cuba." *Sur* (Buenos Aires), n. 293 (March-April 1965), pp. 61–67.

"Literatura y revolución (encuestas)." *CLA*, nos. 51–52 (1968–69), pp. 125–27.

"Papel social del novelista." *CLA*, no. 53 (1969), pp. 8–18.

"Marcel Proust y la América Latina." *CLA*, no. 69 (1971), pp. 228–29.

"La música popular cubana." *Signos* (Santa Clara, Cuba), 2, no. 3 (1971), 7–12.

"A puertas abiertas." *CLA*, no. 82 (1974), pp. 68–69.

"Carta abierta a Manuel Aznar sobre el meridiano intelectual de nuestra América." *CLA*, no. 84 (1974), pp. 147–50. (Appeared originally in *Diario de la Marina* [Havana] on September 12, 1927.)

"Martí y Francia (primer intento de aproximación a un ensayo posible)." *CLA*, no. 87 (1974), pp. 62–72.

"Palabras pronunciadas por Alejo Carpentier en la presentación del libro *El recurso del método* en la librería 'Lalo Carrasco,' el día 20 de diciembre de 1974." *Boletín* (Dirección Central de Editoriales, Instituto Cubano del Libro), December 15, 1974, p. 5.

"Han terminado para el escritor cubano los tiempos de soledad, para él han comenzado los tiempos de solidaridad" (Palabras de agradecimiento al Comité Central del PCC). *Revista de la Biblioteca Nacional José Martí* (Havana), 3d series, 17, no. 1 (1975), 19–24.

Works Cited

Books

Abrams, M. H. *Natural Supernaturalism: Tradition and Revolution in Romantic Literature*. New York: Norton, 1971.

Aguilar, Luis E. *Cuba 1933: Prologue to Revolution*. Ithaca: Cornell University Press, 1972.

Alegría, Fernando. *Historia de la novela hispanoamericana*. 3d ed. Mexico City: Ediciones de Andrea, 1966.

Alejo Carpentier: 45 años de trabajo intelectual. Havana: Biblioteca Nacional José Martí, 1966. (A bibliography.)

American Realists and Magic Realists. Ed. Dorothy C. Miller and Alfred H. Barr, 1943. Reprint. New York: Museum of Modern Art, Arno Press, 1969.

Aponte, Barbara Bockus. *Alfonso Reyes and Spain: His Dialogue with Unamuno, Valle-Inclán, Ortega y Gasset, and Gómez de la Serna*. Austin: University of Texas Press, 1972.

Arrate, José Martín Félix de. *Llave del Nuevo Mundo; Antemural de las Indias Occidentales; La Habana descripta; Noticias de su fundación, aumentos y estados*. 4th ed. Havana: Comisión Nacional Cubana de la UNESCO, 1964.

Arrom, José Juan. *Certidumbre de América: estudios de letras, folklore y cultura*. 2d rev. ed. Madrid: Editorial Gredos, 1971.

Asedios a Carpentier: once ensayos críticos sobre el novelista cubano. Ed. Klaus Müller-Bergh. Santiago, Chile: Editorial Universitaria, 1972.

Augier, Angel. *Nicolás Guillén: notas para un estudio biográfico-crítico*. Santa Clara, Cuba: Dirección de Publicaciones, Universidad Central de Las Villas, 1962.

Augustine, Saint. *Las confesiones: obras de San Agustín*. Ed. Angel Custodio de la Vega, O.S.A. 5th ed. Madrid: Biblioteca de Autores Cristianos, 1958.

Ballagas, Emilio. *Antología de poesía negra hispano americana*. Madrid: Aguilar, 1935.

Barr, Alfred H. *Painting and Sculpture in the Museum of Modern Art*. 1968. Reprint. New York: Museum of Modern Art, 1942.

Barthes, Roland. *Michelet par lui-même*. Paris: Editions du Seuil, 1965.

——. *Writing Degree Zero and Elements of Semiology*. Boston: Beacon Press, 1970.

Bastide, Roger. *Les Amériques noires*. Paris: Payot, 1967.

Bellegarde, Dantès. *La Nation Haïtienne*. Paris: J. de Gigord, 1938.

Benveniste, Emile. *Problèmes de linguistique génèrale*. Paris: Gallimard, 1966.

Borges, Jorge Luis. *Ficciones*. Buenos Aires: Emecé, 1956.

——. *Discusión*. Buenos Aires: Emecé, 1966.

——, Silvina Ocampo, and Adolfo Bioy Casares, eds. *Antología de la literatura fantástica*. Buenos Aires: Sudamericana, 1971.

Breton, André. *Les pas perdus*. Paris: Gallimard, 1924.

——. *Manifestes du surréalisme*. Paris: Gallimard, 1971.

Bueno, Salvador. *Temas y personajes de la literatura cubana.* Havana: Ediciones Unión, 1964.

Caballero Bonald, José M., ed. *Narrativa cubana de la revolución.* Madrid: Alianza Editorial, 1968.

Castonnet des Fosses, H. *La Perte d'une colonie: la revolution de Saint-Domingue.* Paris: A. Faivre, 1893.

Cirlot, J. E. *A Dictionary of Symbols.* Trans. Jack Sage. New York: Philosophical Library, 1962.

Cole, Hubert. *Christophe, King of Haiti.* New York: Viking, 1967.

Columbus, Christopher. *Los cuatro viajes del Almirante y su testamento.* Ed. Ignacio B. Anzoátegui. 3d ed. Buenos Aires: Espasa Calpe, 1958.

Coulthard, G. R. *Race and Colour in Caribbean Literature.* London: Oxford University Press, 1962.

Curtius, Ernst Robert. *European Literature and the Latin Middle Ages.* Trans. Willard R. Trask. New York: Harper & Row, 1953.

Derrida, Jacques. *De la grammatologie.* Paris: Minuit, 1967.

Desnoes, Edmundo. *Para verte mejor América Latina.* Photographs by Paolo Gasparini; designed by Umberto Peña. Mexico City: Siglo Veintiuno Editores, 1972.

Donoso, José. *Historia personal del "boom."* Barcelona: Anagrama, 1972.

Ellman, Richard. *James Joyce.* New York: Oxford University Press, 1959.

Fanon, Franz. *The Wretched of the Earth.* Trans. Constance Farrington. New York: Grove Press, 1968.

Fernández Moreno, César, ed. *América Latina eu su literatura.* Mexico City: Siglo Veintiuno Editores y UNESCO, 1972.

Franco, José Luciano. *La batalla por el dominio del Caribe y el Golfo de México: revoluciones y conflictos internacionales en el Caribe, 1789–1854.* Havana: Instituto de Historia, 1965.

——. *La presencia negra en el Nuevo Mundo.* Havana: Cuadernos Casa de las Américas, 1968.

——, comp. *Documentos para la historia de Haití en el Archivo Nacional.* Publicaciones del Archivo Nacional de Cuba, no. 37. Havana, 1954.

Gershmann, Herbert S. *The Surrealist Revolution in France.* Ann Arbor: University of Michigan Press, 1969.

Girod, François. *La Vie quotidienne de la société créole: Saint-Domingue au XVIII siècle.* Paris: Hachette, 1972.

Guerra y Sánchez, Ramiro. *Sugar and Society in the Caribbean.* New Haven: Yale University Press, 1964.

Guillén, Jorge. *Cántico*. 1st complete ed. Buenos Aires: Sudamericana, 1950.

Guirao, Ramón. *Orbita de la poesía afrocubana*. Havana: Ucar García y Cía., 1938.

Gumilla, Joseph. *El Orinoco ilustrado y defendido, historia natural, civil y geográfica de este gran río* . . . Madrid: Fernández; Impressor del Supremo Consejo de la Inquisición, y de la Reverenda Camara Apostólica en la casa Baxa, 1745.

Harss, Luis, and Barbara Dohmann. *Into the Mainstream: Conversations with Latin American Writers*. New York: Harper & Row, 1967.

Hazard, Paul, *The European Mind (1680–1715)*. Trans. J. Lewis May. London: Hollis and Carter, 1953.

Hegel, Georg Wilhelm Friedrich. *The Philosophy of History*. Trans. J. Sibree. Introd. C. J. Friedrich. New York: Dover, 1956.

Heidegger, Martin. *Existence and Being*. Ed. Werner Brock. Chicago: Gateway Editions, 1949.

Henriquez Ureña, Max. *Panorama histórico de la literatura cubana (1492–1952)*. 2 vols. New York: Las Américas Publishing Co., 1963.

Henríquez Ureña, Pedro. *Literary Currents in Hispanic America*. 1945. Reprint. New York: Russell and Russell, 1963.

Herder, Johann Gottfried. See *On the Origin of Language*.

Historia y mito en la obra de Alejo Carpentier. Ed. Nora Mazziotti. Buenos Aires: Fernando García Cambeiro, 1972.

Homenaje a Alejo Carpentier. Ed. Helmy F. Giacoman. New York: Las Américas Publishing Co., 1970.

Humboldt, Alexander von. *Viaje a las regiones equinocciales del Nuevo Continente, hecho en 1799, 1800, 1801, 1802, 1803 y 1804 por A. de Humboldt y A. Bonpland*. Vol. IV. Translated from the German. Caracas: Biblioteca Venezolana de Cultura, 1942.

——. *Ensayo político sobre la isla de Cuba*. Ed. Jorge Quintana and Fernando Ortiz. Translated from the German. Havana: Publicaciones del Archivo Nacional de Cuba, 1960.

Kermode, Frank. *The Sense of an Ending: Studies in the Theory of Fiction*. London: Oxford University Press, 1967.

Lévi-Strauss, Claude. *The Savage Mind*. Chicago: University of Chicago Press, 1966.

——. *Tristes tropiques*. Trans. John and Doreen Weighman. New York: Atheneum, 1974.

Levin, Harry. *The Myth of the Golden Age in the Renaissance*. New York: Oxford University Press, 1969.

Leyburn, James G. *The Haitian People*. New Haven: Yale University Press, 1966.

Lizaso, Félix. *El pensamiento vivo de Varona*. Havana: Primer Festival del Libro Cubano, n.d.

Logan, Rayford W. *Haiti and the Dominican Republic*. London: Oxford University Press, 1968.

Lukács, Georg. *Realism in Our Time: Literature and the Class Struggle*. Trans. John and Necke Mander. New York: Harper & Row, 1964.

——. *Estética*. Trans. Manuel Sacristán. 2 vols. Barcelona–Mexico City: Ediciones Grijalbo, 1966.

——. *The Theory of the Novel*. Trans. Anna Bostock. Cambridge, Mass.: MIT Press, 1971.

Madiou, Thomas. *Histoire d'Haiti*. 2 vols. Port-au-Prince: Imprimerie de Jh. Courtois, 1947.

Malinowski, Bronislaw. *Magic, Science and Religion and Other Essays*. Garden City, N.Y.: Doubleday Anchor Books, 1954.

Man, Paul de. *Blindness and Insight: Essays in the Rhetoric of Contemporary Criticism*. New York: Oxford University Press, 1971.

Marinello, Juan. *Sobre la inquietud cubana*. Havana: Editorial Hermes, 1930.

——. *Americanismo y cubanismo literarios*. Havana: Editorial Hermes, n.d. [signed 1932].

——. *Contemporáneos: noticia y memoria*. Havana: Editora del Consejo Nacional de Universidades, Universidad Central de Las Villas, 1964.

Márquez Rodríguez, Alexis. *La obra narrativa de Alejo Carpentier*. Caracas: Ediciones de la Biblioteca de la Universidad Central de Venezuela, 1970.

Marx, Karl, and Frederick Engels. *Selected Works*. New York: International Publishers, 1968.

Mauss, Marcel. *Sociologie et anthropologie*. 4th ed. Introd. Claude Lévi-Strauss. Paris: Presses Universitaires de France, 1968.

Mercier, Sébastien. *L'an deux mille quatre cent quarante: Rêve s'il en fut jamais*. London: N. pub., 1772. (Copy at Cornell University Olin Memorial Library, Rare Book Collection.)

Michelet, Jules. *Histoire de la Révolution Française*. 2 vols. Paris: Pleiade, 1952.

Moran, Charles. *Black Triumvirate: A Study of Louverture, Dessalines, Christophe—The Men Who Made Haiti*. New York: Exposition Press, 1957.

Moreau de Saint-Méry. *Description topographique, physique, civile,* politique et historique de la partie française de l'Isle de Saint-Domingue. Ed. Blanche Maurel and Etienne Taillemite. 3 vols. 1797. Reprint. Paris: Société de l'Histoire des Colonies Françaises et Librarie Larose, 1958.

Morison, Samuel Eliot. *The European Discovery of America: The Southern Voyage*, A.D. 1492–1616. New York: Oxford University Press, 1974.

Morón Arroyo, Ciriaco. *El sistema de Ortega y Gasset*. Madrid: Ediciones Alacalá, 1968.

Müller-Bergh, Klaus. *Alejo Carpentier: estudio biográfico-crítico*. Long Island City, N.Y.: Las Américas Publishing Co., 1972.

Nadeau, Maurice. *Histoire du Surréalisme*. Paris: Editions du Seuil, 1964.

Neruda, Pablo. *Selected Poems*. Ed. Nathaniel Tarn. New York: Delta Books, 1970.

——. *Confieso que he vivido: memorias*. Barcelona: Barral, 1974.

O'Gorman, Edmundo. *The Invention of America: An Inquiry into the Historical Nature of the New World and the Meaning of Its History*. Bloomington: Indiana University Press, 1961.

On the Origin of Language. (Contains Jean-Jacques Rousseau's "Essay on the Origin of Languages" and Johann Gottfried Herder's "Essay on the Origin of Language.") Trans. with afterwords by John H. Moran and Alexander Gode. New York: Ungar, 1966.

Orbita de Emilio Ballagas. Ed. Angel Augier and Rosario Antuña Havana: UNEAC, Colección Orbita, 1965.

Orbita de la Revista de Avance. Ed. Martín Casanovas. Havana: UNEAC, Colección Orbita, 1965.

Orbita de Juan Marinello. Ed. Angel Augier. Havana: UNEAC, Colección Orbita, 1968.

Ortega y Gasset, José. *Obras completas*. Vol. II. Madrid: Revista de Occidente, 1963.

——. *Las Atlántidas*. Madrid: Revista de Occidente, 1924.

——. *The Dehumanization of Art, and Other Essays on Art, Culture, and Literature*. Princeton: Princeton University Press, 1968.

Ortiz, Fernando. *Hampa afro-cubana: los negros brujos (apuntes para un estudio de etonología criminal)*. Madrid: Librería de Fernando Fé, 1906.

——. *Entre cubanos . . . (psicología tropical)*. Paris: Sociedad de Ediciones Literarias y Artísticas y Librería Paul Ollendorff, n.d. [1914].

——. *Glosario de afronegrismos*. Havana: Imprenta Siglo XX, 1924.

——. *El engaño de las razas*. Havana: Editorial Páginas, 1946.

———. *El huracán: su mitología y sus símbolos*. Mexico City: Fondo de Cultura Económica, 1947.

———. *La africanía de la música folklórica de Cuba*. Havana: Ediciones Cárdenas y Cía., 1950.

———. *La antigua fiesta afrocubana del "Día de Reyes."* Havana: Ministerio de Relaciones Exteriores, Depto. de Asuntos Culturales, 1960.

———. *Cuban Counterpoint: Tobacco and Sugar*. Trans. Harriet de Onís. New York: Vintage, 1970.

Pané, Fray Ramón. *Relación acerca de las antigüedades de los indios: el primer tratado escrito en América*. Ed. José Juan Arrom. Mexico City: Siglo Veintiuno, 1974.

Paz, Octavio. *The Bow and the Lyre*. Trans. Ruth L. C. Simms. Austin: University of Texas Press, 1973.

Poncé, Charles. *Kabbalah: An Introduction for the World Today*. San Francisco: Straight Arrow Books, 1973.

Popol Vuh: las antiguas historias del Quiché. Ed. Adrián Recinos. 4th ed. Mexico City: Fondo de Cultura Económica, 1974.

Portuondo, José Antonio. *El contenido social de la literatura cubana*. Centro de Estudios Sociales, Colegio de México, Jornadas no. 21. Mexico City, 1944.

———. *El heroísmo intelectual*. Mexico: Tezontle, 1955.

———. *Bosquejo histórico de las letras cubanas*. Havana: Editora del Ministerio de Educación, 1962.

———. *Crítica de la época y otros ensayos*. Havana: Editora del Consejo Nacional de Universidades, Universidad Central de Las Villas, 1965.

Reyes, Alfonso. *Obras completas*. Vol. XI, *Ultima Tule*. Mexico City: Fondo de Cultura Económica, 1960.

Risquez-Iribarren, Col. Dem. Franz A. *Donde nace el Orinoco*. Caracas: Ediciones Greco, 1962.

Rodríguez Monegal, Emir. *El otro Andrés Bello*. Caracas: Monte Avila Editores, 1969.

Roh, Franz. *Nach-Expressionismus (Magischer Realismus): Probleme der neuesten Europäischen Malerei*. Leipzig: Klinkhardt & Biermann, 1925.

———. *German Art in the 20 Century*. Trans. Catherine Hutter. Greenwich, Conn.: New York Graphic Society, 1968.

Rousseau, Jean-Jacques. *Du contrat social*. Introd. Pierre Burgelin. Paris: Garnier-Flammarion, 1966.

———. See *On the Origin of Language*.

Salazar Bondy, Augusto. *¿Existe una filosofía de nuestra América?*, 2d ed. Mexico City: Siglo Veintiuno Editores, 1973.

Sánchez, Manuel Segundo. *Obras*. Vol. I, *Bibliografía venezolana*. Caracas: Colección Cuatricentenario de Caracas, 1964.

Sartre, Jean-Paul. *La nausée*. Paris: Gallimard, 1938.

———. *Being and Nothingness: An Essay on Phenomenological Ontology*. Trans. Hazel Barnes. New York: Washington Square Press, 1966.

Schoelcher, V. *Vie de Toussaint-Louverture*. Paris: Ollendorff, 1889.

Scholem, Gershom G. *Major Trends in Jewish Mysticism*. New York: Schocken Books, 1961.

———. *On the Kabbalah and Its Symbolism*. Trans. Ralph Manheim. New York: Schocken Books, 1965.

Schomburgk, Richard. *Travels in British Guiana, 1840–1844*. Trans. Walter E. Roth. 2 vols. Georgetown, British Guiana: Published by Authority of the "Daily Chronicle," 1922.

Seligmann, Kurt. *Magic, Supernaturalism and Religion*. 1948. Reprint. New York: Pantheon, 1971.

Shattuck, Roger. *The Banquet Years: The Origins of the Avant Garde in France, 1885 to World War I*. Rev. ed. New York: Vintage, 1968.

Spengler, Oswald. *The Decline of the West*. Vol. I, *Form and Actuality*. Trans. Charles Francis Atkinson. New York: Knopf, 1926. Vol. II, subtitled *Perspectives of World-History*, 1928.

———. *La decadencia de Occidente: Bosquejo de una morfología universal*. Trans. Manuel G. Morente. 11th ed. 2 vols. Madrid: Espasa-Calpe, 1966.

Stevens, Wallace. *The Collected Poems*. New York: Knopf, 1954.

Stewart, T. G. *The Haitian Revolution, 1791 to 1804*. New York: Russell and Russell, 1971.

Tannehill, Ivan Ray. *Hurricanes*. 2d ed. Princeton: Princeton University Press, 1943.

Thomas, Hugh. *Cuba: The Pursuit of Freedom*. New York: Harper & Row, 1971.

Todorov, Tzevetan, ed. *Théorie de la littérature: Textes des formalistes russes*. Paris: Editions du Seuil, 1965.

———. *Introduction à la littérature fantastique*. Paris: Editions du Seuil, 1970.

Uslar Pietri, Arturo. *Letras y hombres de Venezuela*. Colección Tierra Firme, no. 42. Mexico City: Fondo de Cultura Económica, 1948.

Vaissière, Pierre de. *Saint-Domingue: La société et la vie créoles sous l'ancien régime, 1629–1789*. Paris: Perrin, 1909.

Vasconcelos, José. *La raza cósmica: misión de la raza iberoamericana*, 3d. ed. Mexico City: Espasa Calpe, 1966.

Vico, Giambattista. *The New Science of Giambattista Vico.* Trans. from the 3d ed. by Thomas Goddard Bergin and Max Harold Fisch. Ithaca. Cornell University Press, 1972.

Vitier, Medardo. *Las ideas en Cuba.* 2 vols. Havana: Trópico, 1933.

Wahl, François, ed. *Qu'est-ce que le structuralisme?* Paris: Editions du Seuil, 1968.

Weiss, Judith A. "*Casa de las Américas:* An Intellectual Review in the Cuban Revolution." 1975. Unpublished manuscript.

Worringer, Wilhelm. *Form in Gothic.* Trans. Sir Herbert Read. 2d ed. New York: Schocken Books, 1957.

Zea, Leopoldo. *En torno a una filosofía americana.* Centro de Estudios Sociales, Colegio de México, Jornadas no. 52. Mexico City, 1945.

——. *Esquema para una historia de las ideas en Hispanoamérica.* Mexico City: Imprenta Universitaria, 1956.

Dissertations

González, Eduardo G. "El tiempo del hombre: huella y labor de origen en cuatro obras de Alejo Carpentier." Ph.D. diss., Indiana University, 1974.

Sánchez Camejo, Modesto Gaspar. "La elaboración artística de *El acoso.*" M.A. thesis, Trinity College (Hartford, Conn.), 1972.

Articles and Pamphlets

Anonymous. "La muerte del maestro Amadeo Roldán." *Estudios Afro-cubanos* (Havana), 3, nos. 1, 2, 3 and 4 (1939), 109–18.

——. "Entrevista con Héctor Villalobos." *Cruz del Sur* (Caracas), 1, no. 11 (1953), 35–38. (Carpentier is among the critics asked to comment on the Brazilian composer's answers.)

——. "¿Qué piensan hacer los intelectuales venezolanos en 1958?" *Cruz del Sur,* 3, no. 35 (1957), 9. (Carpentier replies.)

——. "Los setenta de Carpentier." *Cuba Internacional,* no. 66 (February 1975), p. 72.

Aguerrevere, S. E., Víctor M. López, C. Delgado O., and C. A. Freeman. "Exploración de la Gran Sabana (Informe que presenta al ciudadano doctor Manuel R. Egaña, Ministro de Fomento, la Comisión Exploradora de la Gran Sabana)." *Revista de Fomento* (Caracas), no. 63 (1946), pp. 183–84. (Reprint of a 1939 report.)

Alegría, Fernando. "Alejo Carpentier: realismo mágico." *Humanitas* (Universidad de Nuevo León, Mexico), no. 1 (1960), pp. 345–92.

Angarita Arévalo, Rafael. "Juan Liscano, su defensa de 'Los fugitivos' y la posición de la crítica actual." *El Universal* (Caracas), September 3, 1946, p. 4.

Barreda-Tomás, Pedro M. "Alejo Carpentier: dos visiones del negro, dos conceptos de la novela." *Hispania*, 55 (1972), 34–44.

Bataille, Georges. "Le Surréalisme et sa différence avec l'existentialisme." *Critique* (Paris), no. 3–4 (1946), pp. 99–110.

Beaujour, Michel. "Flight Out of Time: Poetic Language and the Revolution." *YFS*, no. 39 (1967), "Literature and Revolution," ed. Jacques Ehrmann, pp. 29–49.

Borges, Jorge Luis. "El arte narrativo y la magia." In his *Discusión*, pp. 81–92. Buenos Aires: Emecé, 1966. (Written in 1932.)

Bosquet, Alain. "Alejo Carpentier." *PLEN*, March 16, 1956, pp. 6, 8.

Bueno, Salvador. "Alejo Carpentier, novelista antillano y universal." In his *La letra como testigo*, pp. 153–79. Santa Clara, Cuba: Universidad Central de Las Villas, 1957.

———. "La guerra de Carpentier con el tiempo." *EN*, August 28, 1958, p. 3.

———. "Notas para un estudio sobre la concepción de la historia en Alejo Carpentier." *Universidad de La Habana*, no. 193 (1972), pp. 123–38.

Carlos, Alberto J. "El anti-héroe en *El acoso*." *CA*, 29, no. 1 (1970), 193–204.

"Conversación con Nicolás Guillén." *CLA*, no. 73 (1972), pp. 123–36.

Cruz-Luis, Adolfo. "Latinoamérica en Carpentier: génesis de lo real maravilloso." *CLA*, no. 87 (1974), pp. 48–59.

Depestre, René. "Problemas de la identidad del hombre negro en las literaturas antillanas." In *Diez años de la revista Casa de las Américas*, pp. 51–59. Havana: CLA, 1970.

Derrida, Jacques. "Freud and the Scene of Writing." *YFS*, no. 48 (1972), "French Freud," ed. Jeffrey Mehlman, pp. 73–117.

———. "Structure, Sign, and Play in the Discourse of the Human Sciences." In *The Structuralist Controversy: The Languages of Criticism and the Sciences of Man*, ed. Richard Macksey and Eugenio Donato, pp. 247–64. Baltimore: Johns Hopkins University Press, 1972.

Desnos, Robert, and others. *Un cadavre*. Paris: Imprimerie Spéciale du Cadavre, 1930.

Dieckmann, Herbert. "Esthetic Theory and Criticism in the Enlightment: Some Examples of Modern Trends." In *Introduction to Modernity: A Symposium on Eighteenth-Century Thought*, ed. Robert Mollenauer, pp. 65–105. Austin: University of Texas Press, 1965.

Donato, Eugenio. "Structuralism: The Aftermath." *Sub-Stance* (Madison, Wis.), no. 7 (Fall 1973), pp. 9–26.

D[orante], C[arlos]. "Contrapunto entre selva y ciudad establece la nueva novela de Alejo Carpentier." *EN*, December 18, 1953, p. 44.

———. "Los soldados del tiempo." *PLEN*, July 17, 1958, p. 7.

Dorfman, Ariel. "El sentido de la historia en la obra de Alejo Carpentier." In his *Imaginación y violencia en América*, pp. 93–137. Santiago, Chile: Editorial Universitaria, 1970.

Dumas, Claude. "*El siglo de las luces* de Alejo Carpentier, novela filosófica." *CA* 25, no. 4 (1966), 187–210.

Durán, Armando. "Conversaciones con Gabriel García Márquez." *Revista Nacional de Cultura* (Caracas), 39 (1968), 23–34.

Espina, Antonio. Review of Franz Roh, *Realismo mágico*. *RO*, no. 49 (July 1927), pp. 110–13.

Flores, Angel. "Magical Realism in Spanish American Fiction." *Hispania*, 38 (1955), 187–92.

Freccero, John. "Introduction." In his *Dante: A Collection of Critical Essays*. Englewood Cliffs, N.J.: Prentice-Hall, 1965.

———. "Reader's Report." Cornell University, John M. Olin Library Bookmark Series, no. 36 (April 1968).

———. "Medusa: The Letter and the Spirit." In *Yearbook of Italian Studies*, pp. 1–18. Florence: A publication of the Italian Cultural Institute, Montreal, Canada, 1972.

Fuentes, Carlos. "Carpentier o la doble adivinación." In his *La nueva novela hispanoamericana*, pp. 48–57. Mexico City: Cuadernos de Joaquín Mortiz, 1969.

García-Carranza, Araceli. "Bibliografía de una exposición." *Revista de la Biblioteca Nacional José Martí* (Havana), 3d series, 17, no. 1 (1975), 45–87. (Contains a partial bibliography and a list of the manuscripts donated by Carpentier to the library. The list is annotated and brief passages from manuscripts are quoted.)

García Castro, Ramón. "La pintura en Alejo Carpentier." *Tlaloc* (in press).

Gindine, Yvette, "The Magic of Black History: Images of Haiti." *Caribbean Quarterly* (Miami), 4, no. 4 (1974), 25–30.

Glissant, Edouard. "Alejo Carpentier et l'autre Amérique." *Critique* (Paris), no. 105 (1956), pp. 113–19.

González, Eduardo G. "*Los pasos perdidos*, el azar y la aventura." *RI*, 38 (1972), 585–614.

———. "*El acoso*: lectura, escritura e historia." In *El cuento hispanoamericano ante la crítica*, ed. Enrique Pupo-Walker, pp. 126–49. Madrid: Castalia, 1973.

González Echevarría, Roberto. " 'Semejante a la noche,' de Alejo Carpentier: historia/ficción." *MLN*, 87 (1972), 272–85. Also in *Asedios a Carpentier*. Santiago, Chile: Editorial Universitaria, 1972.

———. "With Borges in Macondo." *D*, 2, no. 1 (1972), 57–60.

———. "Isla a su vuelo fugitiva: Carpentier y el realismo mágico." *RI*, 40 (1974), 9–64.

———. "The Parting of the Waters." *D*, 4, no. 4 (1974), 8–17.

———. "Notas para una cronología de la obra narrativa de Alejo Carpentier, 1944–1954." In *Estudios de literatura hispanoamericana en honor a José J. Arrom*, ed. Andrew P. Debicki and Enrique Pupo-Walker, pp. 201–14. North Carolina Studies in the Romance Languages and Literatures Symposia, no. 2. Chapel Hill: University of North Carolina Department of Romance Languages, 1974.

———. "Apetitos de Góngora y Lezama." *RI*, 41 (1975), 479–91.

Lastra, Pedro. "Notas sobre la narrativa de Alejo Carpentier." *Anales de la Universidad de Chile*, no. 125 (1962), pp. 94–101.

Leal, Luis. "El realismo mágico en la literatura hispanoamericana." *CA*, 25, no. 4 (1967), 230–35.

Leante, César. "Confesiones sencillas de un escritor barroco." *Cuba*, 3, no. 24 (1964), 30–33. (Interview.)

———. "Mundo y ambiente en *El siglo de las luces*." *Cuba* (Havana), 3, no. 24 (1964), 22–29.

———. "Un reto a la novela moderna: *El siglo de las luces*." *Revolución* (Havana), April 8, 1965, p. 3.

León, María Teresa. "*La música en Cuba*, por Alejo Carpentier." *Revista Cubana* (Havana), no. 27 (1947), pp. 216–17.

Lévi-Strauss, Claude. "Introduction à l'oeuvre de Marcel Mauss." In Marcel Mauss, *Sociologie et anthropologie*, 4th ed., pp. ix–lii. Paris: Presses Universitaires de France, 1968.

Levine, Suzanne Jill. "Lo real maravilloso: de Carpentier a García Márquez." *Eco* (Bogotá), no. 120 (April 1970), pp. 565–76.

Liscano, Juan [signed Lorenzo Tiempo]. "Alejo Carpentier: un americano que regresa a América." *PLEN*, September 16, 1945, p. 2. (Interview.)

———. "El cuento de Alejo Carpentier." *EN*, August 29, 1946, p. 4.

———. "Alejo Carpentier, intérprete de mitos necesarios." In his *Caminos de la prosa (comentarios)*, pp. 75–91. Caracas: Ediciones El Pensamiento Vivo, 1953.

Loveluck, Juan. "Los pasos perdidos, Jasón y el nuevo vellocino." In his *Diez conferencias*, pp. 286–305. Concepción, Chile: Universidad de Concepción, 1963.

Magnarelli, Sharon. "El camino de Santiago' de Alejo Carpentier y la picaresca." *RI*, 40 (1974), 65–86.

Manuel, Frank E. and Fritzie P. "Sketch for a Natural History of Paradise." *Daedalus*, Winter 1972, "Myth, Symbol and Culture," pp. 83–128.

Marinello, Juan. "Una novela cubana." In his *Literatura hispanoameri-cana: hombres-meditaciones*, pp. 167–78. Mexico City: Ediciones de la Universidad de México, 1937.

——. "Sobre el asunto en la novela: a propósito de tres novelas recientes." In his *Meditación americana (cinco ensayos)*, pp. 55–77. Buenos Aires: Procyón, 1959.

——. "Un homenaje excepcional." *Bohemia* (Havana), August 7, 1964, pp. 94–95.

——. "Negrismo y mulatismo." In *Orbita de Juan Marinello*, ed. Angel Augier, pp. 67–81. Havana: UNEAC, Colección Orbita, 1968.

Márquez Rodríguez, Alexis. "Dos dilucidaciones en torno a Alejo Carpentier." *CLA*, no. 87 (1974), pp. 35–47.

Mauss, Marcel. "Esquisse d'une théorie générale de la magie." In his *Sociologie et anthropologie*, 4th ed., pp. 2–141. Paris: Presses Universitaires de France, 1968.

Meneses, Guillermo. "Alejo Carpentier regresó de la selva." *EN*, September 12, 1948, p. 4.

Menton, Seymour. "Asturias, Carpentier y Yáñez: paralelismos y divergencias." *RI*, 35 (1969), 31–52.

Morel, Jean-Pierre. "Breton and Freud." *D*, 2, no. 2 (1972), 18–26.

Müller-Bergh, Klaus. "Entrevista con Alejo Carpentier." *CA*, 28, no. 4 (1969), 141–44.

——. "Corrientes vanguardistas y surrealismo en la obra de Alejo Carpentier." *Revista Hispánica Moderna*, 35 (1969), 323–40. Also in *Asedios a Carpentier*, pp. 13–38. Santiago, Chile: Editorial Universitaria, 1972.

——. " 'Oficio de tinieblas,' un cuento escasamente conocido." In *Asedios a Carpentier*, pp. 53–62. Santiago, Chile: Editorial Universitaria, 1972.

Ortega, Julio. "El libro en la calle." *Mundo Nuevo*, no. 23 (May 1968), pp. 84–86. (Interview with Manuel Scorza.)

——. "Sobre *El siglo de las luces*." In *Asedios a Carpentier*, pp. 191–206. Santiago, Chile: Editorial Universitaria, 1972.

Ospovat, Lev. "El hombre y la historia en la obra de Alejo Carpentier." *CLA*, no. 87 (1974), pp. 9–20.

P., R. "La conférence de Alejo Carpentier." *Haïti-Journal* (Port-au-Prince), December 21, 1943, p. 4.

Paz, Octavio. "A Literature of Foundations." In *The Tri-Quarterly Anthology of Contemporary Latin American Literature*, ed. José Donoso and William A. Henkin, pp. 2–8. New York: Dutton, 1969.

Pérez, Niurka. "Los estudiantes universitarios contra el bonchismo." *Universidad de la Habana*, nos. 196–197 (1972), pp. 210–52.

Pineda, Rafael. "Del apocalipsis al génesis." *PLEN*, February 25, 1954, p. 6.

——. "Alejo Carpentier en la ciudad de las maquetas." *Imagen* (Caracas), March 14, 1972, pp. 2–3.

Portuondo, José Antonio. "La realidad americana y la literatura." In his *El heroísmo intelectual*, pp. 125–36. Mexico City: Tezontle, 1955.

——. "Mella y los intelectuales." In his *Crítica de la época y otros ensayos*, pp. 84–115. Santa Clara, Cuba: Universidad Central de Las Villas, 1965.

——. "Una novela revolucionaria." *CLA*, no. 71 (1972), pp. 105–6.

Quesada, Luis. "Desarrollo evolutivo del elemento negro en tres de las primeras narraciones de Alejo Carpentier." In *Literatura de la emancipación hispanoamericana y otros ensayos: Memoria del XV Congresco del Instituto de Literatura Iberoamericana*, pp. 217–23. Lima: Universidad Nacional Mayor de San Marcos, 1972.

Ripoll, Carlos. "La Revista de Avance (1927–1930), vocero de vanguardismo y pórtico de revolución." *RI*, 30 (1964), 261–82.

Roa, Miguel F. "Alejo Carpentier: el recurso a Descartes." *Cuba Internacional*, no. 59 (July 1974), pp. 46–51. (Interview.)

Rodríguez Monegal, Emir. "Las fuentes de la narración." *Mundo Nuevo*, no. 25 (July 1968), pp. 41–58. (Interview with Guillermo Cabrera Infante.)

——. "La nueva novela latinoamericana." In *Actas del Tercer Congreso Internacional de Hispanistas*, pp. 47–63. Mexico City: El Colegio de México, 1970.

——. "Alejo Carpentier: lo real y lo maravilloso en *El reino de este mundo*." *RI*, 37 (1971), 619–49. Also in *Asedios a Carpentier*. Santiago, Chile: Editorial Universitaria, 1972.

——. "Borges and la nouvelle critique." *D*, 2, no. 2 (1972), 27–40.

——. "Realismo mágico vs. literatura fantástica: un diálogo de sordos." In *Otros mundos otros fuegos: fantasía y realismo mágico en Iberoamérica. Memoria del XVI Congreso Internacional de Literatura Iberoamericana*, ed. Donald A. Yates, pp. 25–37. Pittsburgh: A Publication of the Latin American Studies Center of Michigan State University, 1975.

Roh, Franz. "Realismo mágico: problemas de la pintura europea más reciente." *RO*, no. 48 (June 1927), pp. 274–301.

Sambrano Urdanela, Oscar. "La novela de Alejo Carpentier." *PLEN*, May 23, 1957, p. 3.

Sánchez, Modesto G. "El fondo histórico de *El acoso*: 'Epoca Heróica y Epoca del Botín.'" *RI*, 41 (1975), 397–422.

Santana, Joaquín G. "Muertes, resurrecciones, triunfos y agonías." *Bohemia* (Havana), March 26, 1971, pp. 5–9. (Interview with Carpentier.)

Santander T., Carlos. "Lo maravilloso en la obra de Alejo Carpentier." *Atenea* (Revista de la Universidad de Concepción, Chile), no. 409 (1965), pp. 99–126.

Sarduy, Severo. "El barroco y el neobarroco." In *América Latina en su literatura,* ed. César Fernández Moreno, pp. 167–84. Mexico City: Siglo Veintiuno Editores—UNESCO, 1972.

Scheler, M. "El porvenir del hombre." *RO,* no. 50 (August 1927), pp. 129–59.

Schomburgk, Roberto Hermann. "Desde el Roraima hasta la piedra Cucui." *Cultura Venezolana,* no. 44 (December 1922), pp. 235–64.

Silva Cáceres, Raúl. "Una novela de Carpentier." *Mundo Nuevo,* no. 17 (November 1967), pp. 33–37.

Singleton, Charles S. "The Poet's Number at the Center." *MLN,* 80 (1965), 1–10.

Sommers, Joseph. "*Ecue-Yamba-O*: semillas del arte narrativo de Alejo Carpentier." In *Estudios de literatura hispanoamericana en honor a José J. Arrom,* ed. Andrew P. Debicki and Enrique Pupo-Walker, pp. 227–38. North Carolina Studies in the Romance Languages and Literatures Symposia, no. 2. Chapel Hill: University of North Carolina Department of Romance Languages, 1974.

Starobinski, Jean. "Freud, Breton, Myers." *L'Arc,* 34 (1968), 87–96.

———. "Le style de l'autobiographie." *Poétique,* 3 (1970), 257–65.

Sucre, Guillermo. "*Guerra del tiempo,* de Alejo Carpentier." *PLEN,* July 24, 1958, p. 8.

Valbuena Briones, Angel. "Una cala en el realismo mágico." *CA,* 28, no. 5 (1969), 233–41.

Valéry, P. "Notas sobre la grandeza y decadencia de Europa." *RO,* no. 46 (April 1927), pp. 1–14.

Vance, Eugene. "Augustine's *Confessions* and the Grammar of Selfhood." *Genre,* 6 (1973), 1–28.

Vela, Francisco. "León Frobenius en Madrid." *RO,* no. 9 (March 1924), pp. 390–94.

Volek, Emil. "*Los pasos perdidos.*" *Universidad de la Habana,* no. 189 (1967), pp. 25–37.

———. "Análisis e interpretación de *El reino de este mundo* y su lugar en la obra de Alejo Carpentier." *Unión* (Havana), 6, no. 1 (1969), 98–118.

———. "Algunas reflexiones sobre *El siglo de las luces* y el arte narrativo de Alejo Carpentier." *CLA,* no. 74 (1972), pp. 42–54.

Weber, Frances Wyers. "*El acoso:* Alejo Carpentier's War on Time." *PMLA*, 78 (1963), 440–48.

Wellek, René. "The Concept of Baroque in Literary Scholarship." In *Concepts of Criticism*, ed. Stephen G. Nichols, Jr., pp. 69–114. New Haven: Yale University Press, 1963.

Yalman, Nur. "Magic." In *International Encyclopedia of the Social Sciences*, IX, 521–28. New York: Macmillan and The Free Press, 1968.

Zabludovsky, Jacobo. "Habla Alejo Carpentier." *Siempre!* (Mexico City), July 25, 1973, pp. 44–45. (Interview.)

Index

Abrams, M. H., 21n, 160n
Africanist movement, 32, 42
Afro-Cuban movement, 15, 34, 42, 43, 46-48, 52, 60, 63, 68, 94, 96, 98, 118; and Fernando Ortiz, 44-51; and Oswald Spengler, 55
Afro-Cuban religion, 32, 47, 61, 85, 92, 195
Alegría, Ciro, 64, 258
Alegría, Fernando, 70, 80n, 125
Alemán, Mateo, 81
Allegory, 22, 80, 255
Allgemeine geist, Allgemeine Individuum, 160
Amberes, Juan de, 105
Anderson Imbert, Enrique, 202n
André, Marius, 39
Apollinaire, Guillaume, 38
Apuleius, Lucius, 120, 205n
Architecture, 145n, 191, 192-197, 205, 247, 252, 257-258
Ariosto, Ludovico, 267
Aristotle, 119, 120
Armas, Augusto de, 37, 94
Armstrong, Louis, in *Concierto barroco*, 269
Arrate, José Martín Félix de, 27n, 102
Asturias, Miguel Angel, 64, 112, 118, 128, 261
Augustine, Saint, 164, 187, 206n
Avant-garde, 40, 42, 213
Azorín (José Martínez Ruiz), 114

Babel, Isaak, 53
Bacardí, Emilio, 102
Balboa, Silvestre de, 267
Ballagas, Emilio, 36, 50, 51, 62n
Balthus, 40
Barnet, Miguel, 48n
Barnstone, Willis, 50n

Baroque, 19n, 22, 152, 166, 186, 223, 224
Barreda-Tomás, Pedro M., 75, 80, 98n
Barthes, Roland, 23
Batista, Fulgencio, 189n, 211, 214, 216n
Bazin, René, 59
Beaumarchais, Pierre Augustin Caron de, 271
Beethoven, Ludwig van, 36n, 181, 199, 202, 204, 209
Bello, Andrés, 21, 100
Benveniste, Emile, 165n, 199
Bergson, Henri, 117
Bifur, 76n
Bildungsreise, 160, 164
Blake, William, 29, 160, 223
Bonaparte, Joseph, 250
Bonaparte, Napoleon, 212, 229
Bonaparte, Pauline, 147, 153, 205
Bordeaux, Henry, 59
Borges, Jorge Luis, 26, 29, 111, 112, 114, 118-123, 126, 129, 136, 144, 146, 213, 239
Boyer, Jean Pierre, 140, 142
Breille, Corneille, 131
Breton, André, 57, 58, 59, 60, 68, 109, 121n, 122, 159
Bueno, Salvador, 48n, 163n
Byzantine romance, 25

Cabrera Infante, Guillermo, 23
Calderón de la Barca, Pedro, 22, 147, 149, 265
Campanella, Tomaso, 220
Camus, Albert, 38
"Canción," 62
Caribbean history, 25, 44, 227, 242; Bouckman's revolt, 131; Indian

Alejo Carpentier:
The Pilgrim at Home

Designed by R. E. Rosenbaum.
Composed by York Composition Company, Inc.,
in 10 point Linotype Electra, 3 points leaded,
with display lines in monotype Deepdene.
Printed letterpress from type by York Composition Company
on Warren's Number 66 text, 50 pound basis.
Bound by John H. Dekker & Sons, Inc.
in Joanna book cloth
and stamped in All Purpose foil.

Library of Congress Cataloging in Publication Data
(For cataloging purposes only)

González Echevarría, Roberto.
  Alejo Carpentier, the pilgrim at home.

  Bibliography: p.
  Includes index.
  1. Carpentier, Alejo, 1904–   Criticism and interpretation.   I.
Title.
PQ7389.C263Z69   863   76-28013
ISBN 0-8014-1029-0

R0140642135

R0140642135 HUM   860.
                     9
      16.50   C22G

GONZALEZ ECHEVARRIA, ROBE
      ALEJO CARPENTIER
THE PILGRIM AT HOME

R0140642135 HUM   860.
                     9
                    C22G

HOUSTON PUBLIC LIBRARY

CENTRAL LIBRARY
500 MCKINNEY